China's Urbanization and Socioeconomic Impact

Zongli Tang
Editor

China's Urbanization and Socioeconomic Impact

Springer

Editor
Zongli Tang
College of Public Policy and Justice
Auburn University at Montgomery
Montgomery, AL
USA

ISBN 978-981-10-4830-2 ISBN 978-981-10-4831-9 (eBook)
DOI 10.1007/978-981-10-4831-9

Library of Congress Control Number: 2017939913

Printed on acid-free paper

This Springer imprint is published by Springer Nature
The registered company is Springer Nature Singapore Pte Ltd.
The registered company address is: 152 Beach Road, #21-01/04 Gateway East, Singapore 189721, Singapore

Preface

Whether driven by market forces or by the government, urbanization has become an irresistible trend in China. It is reported that more than 274 million peasants are now working and living in cities and towns and the size is growing daily. China's urbanization has attracted scholars in various fields, including humanities, social sciences, and natural sciences in China and throughout the world. It is our responsibility to report this event and analyze the process and influence. This book, created by American and Chinese researchers, is the most recent effort to make contributions to this field.

China's urbanization is a process of multi-dimensional development. This book examines it from a cross-disciplinary viewpoint, covering diverse topics and involving a variety of subjects, including economics, demography, city planning, environmental sociology and politics, cultural studies, anthropology, and history. With four parts, this book is unique not only it provides up-to-date information, reports, and analyses based on most recent events, but it also places special emphasis on issues that have been ignored by prior studies.

Part I, containing three chapters, interprets China's urbanization from macro- and strategic perspectives. Authors in this part explore new directions for urbanization in the future, its interactions with industrialization, and the impact on policy reforms. In Chap. 1, Dr. Gu discusses issues found in the recent development of urbanization, illustrating solutions to these issues as well as strategies that, according to him, should be carried out in the 13th Five-Year National Development Period (2016–2020). First, urbanization in this period should shift from land-centered trajectory to people-oriented in order to overcome problems such as disparities between urban and rural residential registrations or *hukou* systems. Second, it should shift from inefficient development to efficient one, making best use of capitals, labors, land, and other production factors. Third, it should shift from resources-consuming urbanization to green-orientation pattern, getting rid of such issues as big-city disease, urban sprawl, ghost towns, and so on. Fourth, China can take full advantage of the radiation and leading role of core cities, moving away from urbanization based on an unreasonable scale and structure and toward the efficient integration of urban agglomerations and coordinated development. Fifth, it should shift from state-led development to market-driven one. The market should play a critical role in allocating resources, while the government plays a role in planning, system designing, public service, environmental protection, regulation, and social management. Sixth, it should shift from extensive and scattered cities and towns to intensive urban agglomerations. In this period, urbanization should give impetus to technological innovations and coordinate with rural development and industrialization. As the Deputy Chairman of the Committee of Financial and Economic Affairs, National People's Congress, and a well-known Chinese scholar in urban studies, Dr. Gu's opinions carry a great deal of authority.

While urbanization is influenced by many factors, a key structural determinant is industrialization. In Chap. 2, Dr. Zhang examines how industrial development affects urbanization. Does China's industrialization bring about urbanization? Is China under- or over-urbanized? How does China manage urban development so that the virtuous circle between urbanization and industrialization could realize? This chapter offers explanations to these questions, revealing that China's rapid industrialization is the key driver for urbanization. Being at the right speed, China has avoided over-urbanization problems that appeared in many developing countries and has also successfully promoted economic growth through agglomeration and consumption effects.

Rapid urbanization stimulates demand for residential dwellings and accordingly raises housing prices. In 2008, it was ¥3800/m^2 on average for commodity houses and jumped to ¥4681/m^2 in 2009, increasing by 23.2% in just one year. This trend continued in 2010–2011. Quickly, rising prices would exert an adverse effect on urbanization. Therefore, the government intends to introduce real estate tax as a tool to put the housing price under control and improve local fiscal revenue at the same time. In Chap. 3, Dr. Cui, a Professor at Dongbei University of Finance and Economics, analyzes the current situation with real estate market and issues with the local taxing system. She explores possible solutions to these issues and also directions for the taxing system reform in order to achieve the goals set by the government.

Part II in dealing with urban impact on regional development contains two chapters. During urbanization, regional differences have been widened. Authors in Chap. 4 develop a composite index to measure urban development level in five northwestern urban agglomerations during the period of 2005–2014. They analyze spatial gaps and dynamic evolution features in these agglomerations. Revealed by the research, regional differences in urbanization (between areas and within areas) are rather significant and also increasing. Urban development in northwestern regions is largely influenced by the size of population, geographic characteristics, and other socioeconomic factors. The authors conclude that the local governments' strategies and policies play a crucial role in shaping regional urban patterns.

Western China is a region that has not only the lowest level of economic and urban development, but also the most intensive coverage of ethnic minorities, accounting for 72% of China's total minority population. What causes the low urbanization level in this region? Is it special for minority areas as compared with others? What policies and strategies should the government adopt to promote urban development in minority areas? Dr. Si in Chap. 5 intends to answer the above questions by looking at the overall trend and selected autonomous regions in Gansu and Ningxia. The author discovers that the low urban development level in these minority areas is mainly resulted from their low level in industrialization. The governments at the central, regional, and local levels need to take a series of measures to accelerate industrial development in these areas.

There are four chapters in Part III, involving development in cities and the impact on women and environment. The unprecedented infrastructure development in China has created great opportunities for urban land development and construction activities. During the period of the 12th Five-Year Plan (2011–2015), China invested seven trillion Yuan ($1.03 trillion) in urban public infrastructure. Chapter 6 provides empirical evidence on how different levels of infrastructure provision influence the process of urbanization. By using a cross-sectional dataset from 650 Chinese cities, the authors examine effects of infrastructure development on urban expansion rates and urban land prices. Their research indicates that both intra- and inter-city infrastructure developments exert a great impact on urban expansion, land prices, and subsequently housing prices. This chapter also discusses the challenges and critical issues associated with the current infrastructure development in China.

China's policies during the post-socialist era have engendered demographic and socioeconomic changes that intersect with gender and class to both enable and restrict women's social mobility, autonomy, and independence. In Chap. 7, Dr. Gaetano evaluates the impact of these changes on the social mobility of women in cities, drawing upon relevant literature and her ethnographic studies of rural migrant women workers in Beijing and educated career women in Shanghai. She illuminates the material and discursive constraints that obstruct these women's achievement of personal goals under conditions of gender and class inequality as China urbanizes.

The rapid urbanization is not without downsides. The average 10 percent annual GDP growth in China for the last decade is taking a toll on its environment. Environmental pollution not only poses serious challenges to public health but also slows down economic development to some extent. In Chap. 8, Dr. Shao examines Chinese perceptions of environmental risk from 1995 to 2015, providing a glimpse into the evolution process by descriptive statistics based on WVS and PEW survey data. The author analyzes geographic distributions of people's environmental views and socio-demographic factors in affecting their perceptions. According to this research, the Chinese people display high concerns to environmental issues. They regard environmental protection more important than economic development, which sends a crucial signal to Chinese political leaders.

Many policymakers and scholars point to urbanization as major culprits in China's ecological decline. However, urbanization can also be powerful engines for sustainable development. Dr. Harrington in Chap. 9 attempts to answer the following questions: First, what factors are driving Chinese urbanization and industrial strategy? Second, what does the concept of sustainable development mean in the Chinese context? Third, what measures are being taken at the national level to encourage sustainable development? Fourth, what challenges do cities face in promoting sustainable development? Finally, what are the prospects for further deepening sustainable development as an integral part of China's overall revitalization strategy?

Part IV, consisting of the last three chapters, discusses impacts on rural clans, rural clan cultures, and villages brought by urbanization. In an attempt to explore changes in clan traditional culture during the process of urbanization, Dr. Tang conducted two surveys separately in 2009 and 2014 in Anhui rural areas. His research reveals a declining clan influence and identity among villagers, especially those well-educated youths. Meanwhile, a majority of the respondents in his surveys expressed traditional viewpoints regarding to ancestor worship, *xiao* (or filial piety), loyalty, clan rituals, and clan genealogy, reflecting historical continuity of culture. Indeed, urbanization has weakened traditional influence, but the impact is limited in scope and intensity. Migrant workers are still in their rural roots. The current urban development does not completely separate them physically and mentally from their native clan communities due to new technology in communication and transportation. Traditional culture remains not only in their memory but also in their daily life. Urban effects move slowly on them. Cultural changes bear strong Chinese characteristics.

The autocratic monarchy system in ancient China was established on the basis of patriarchal clans. Chapter 11 examines the clan society in the Qin and Han Dynasties when cities expanded and business flourished. During that time, the clan system experienced three major changes as it developed from the ancient pattern to the feudal. At that time, the noble descent influence began to weaken. The further development of cities and business made the local clan societies stable, however, under certain conditions. In the Han Dynasty, Confucianism achieved ideological supremacy. The rituals of ancestor worship became more regulated and rigorous, which gave more power to local clan societies. The great unity in the Qin and Han Dynasties promoted the formation of the cultural melting pot. A new clan culture as well as a unified clan society was born.

With rapid urbanization, settlement patterns are changing dramatically. While there has appeared a large body of research on changes in cities, we know relatively little about the countryside. Now, the traditional settlement in rural villages is being demolished. Villagers are resettled into apartments and urban communities at an astonishing scale and speed. In Chap. 12, Dr. Huang analyzes the dynamics and impact on rural Jiangsu. She argues that local government's thirst for more construction land and the land-based revenue system are the roots for urbanized settlement in rural areas. It is further driven by the central government's policy for developing new rural areas. While villagers may benefit from the improved housing conditions, they suffer serious social and economic consequences. This forced urbanization is especially detrimental to the elderly and the poor, overshadowing the government campaign for a modern countryside and a harmonious society.

This book is made feasible through the support and encouragement of my colleagues and friends. First of all, I wish to express my sincere gratitude and appreciation to the contributors to this book. Without them, this book could hardly have been completed properly. My gratitude also goes to Dr. Eric Yang, Prof. Eric Sterling, Prof. Yuexin Lan, Dr. Hua Xu, and Ms. Sarah Li for their help from the beginning. It has been made easily legible by the editing of Matthew Shoemaker and Caitlin Celka. A number of friends were helpful specifically with this book. This book has been partially supported by a research grant from Confucius Institute of Auburn University at Montgomery.

Montgomery, AL, USA Zongli Tang

Contents

Part I
New Urbanization, Industrialization, and Impact on Policies

Chapter 1
Transformation and Healthy Development of Urbanization in China's 13th Five-Year National Development Period (2016–2020)

Shengzu Gu

Abstract China has experienced rapid urbanization for more than three decades and has pulled more than 500 million people out of poverty. However, as the social and economic situation changes, traditional modes of urbanization will no longer be appropriate to the needs of further development. A series of problems have emerged, such as incomplete migration (or semi-urbanization), inefficient use of land, shortage of capital and labor, increasing use of resources, pollution, and so on. New directions and transformations in urbanization are required. First, urban development should shift from a land-centered trajectory to a people-oriented one in order to overcome problems such as disparities between urban and rural residential registrations or *hukou* systems. Second, urban development should shift from inefficient development methods to efficient ones, making the best use of capital, labor, land, and other production factors. Third, urban development should shift from resources-consuming to green-orientation, getting rid of such issues as big-city diseases, urban sprawl, ghost towns, and so on. Fourth, China can take full advantage of the radiation and leading role of core cities, move away from urbanization based on an unreasonable scale and structure, and go towards the efficient integration of urban agglomerations and coordinated development. Fifth, urban development should shift from a state-led trajectory to a market-driven one. The market should play the critical role in allocating resources while the government plays a role in planning, system designing, public service, environmental protection, regulation, and social management. Sixth, urban development should shift from an extensive and scattered trajectory to smart and intensive urban clusters.

Keywords Urbanization · New direction · Transformation

S. Gu (✉)
The Central Committee of China's Democratic National Construction Association/Wuhan University, Beijing/Wuhan, China
e-mail: gusz7190@vip.sina.com

Z. Tang (ed.), *China's Urbanization and Socioeconomic Impact*,
DOI 10.1007/978-981-10-4831-9_1

Urbanization is a path to modernization, a vehicle of industrialization, a platform of marketization, a stage of internationalization, and the most powerful latent force driving China's future economic growth. The statistics from the *2015 China New-type Urbanization Report* show that the permanent urban population in China increased by 600 million, from 170 million in 1978 to 770 million in 2015, and that the urbanization rate rose by three times, from 18 to 56%. Though the urbanization rate in China is growing rapidly, the urban development faces many challenges. Therefore, measures must be taken to accelerate the transformation of urbanization processes in order to tackle the current problems of unbalanced, uncoordinated and unsustainable development.

How should the transformation be carried out? In the 13th five-year national development period, we must integrate the new development ideas of "innovation, coordination, green development, opening-up and sharing" into the new-type urbanization; hence the transformation of new-type urbanization will be carried out via the following six methods: (1) transforming urbanization based on land expansion into people-oriented urbanization; (2) turning urbanization based on inefficient use of labor, land, and capital into efficient and high quality urbanization; (3) moving from high energy consumption, high emissions and high pollution to green urbanization based on sustainable development in population, resources, and the environment; (4) shifting from an unreasonable scale, structure and uncoordinated development among small, medium-sized and large cities to urbanization based on efficient integration of urban agglomeration and coordinated development; (5) transforming government-dominated urbanization into market-driven and government-guided urbanization; and (6) moving from the lack of coordination between urbanization and industrialization, informatization and agricultural modernization and disconnection between industries and urbanization to a synchronized and integrated model of development.

1.1 Based on the People-Oriented Principle, Urbanization Focusing on Land Expansion Will Be Transformed into a People-Centered Development. This Will Change the Mentality that Migrant Workers Have of Being "an Urban Visitor" and Allow More Than 200 Million Migrant Workers to Better Integrate into Urban Life

China has enjoyed rapid land urbanization for a long period of time. In contrast to this, the urbanization of its rural population has lagged far behind. In accordance with statistics over the past three decades, China has seen an urban land increase of 5.6 times; however, the registered urban population has only increased by 2.6 times while permanent residents have more than tripled (see Fig. 1.1). Urbanization of the rural migrant population has progressed slowly, forming a state of

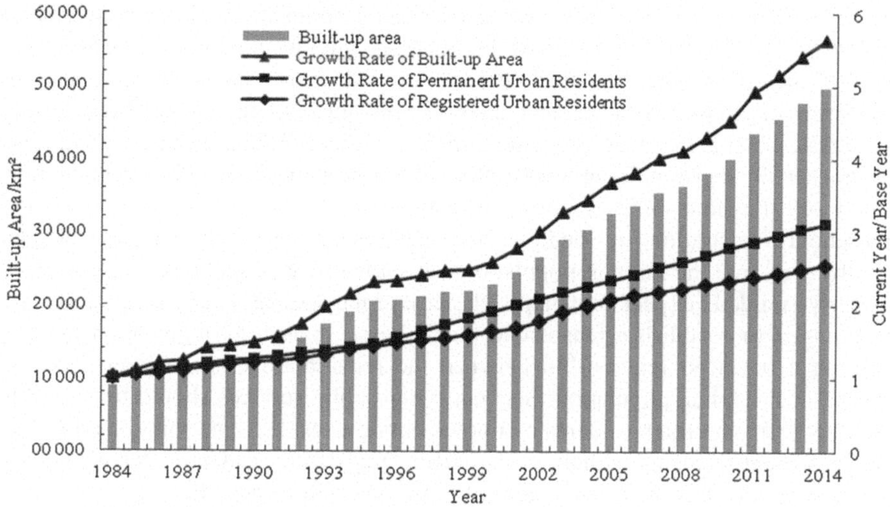

Fig. 1.1 Comparison of speed between population urbanization and land urbanization. *Data sources* China Statistical Year Book and China Population and Employment Statistics Year Book over the past years. *Note* 1984 is the base year (suppose the base number is 1); the number in each year from 1985 to 2014 is the rate to 1 in that year

"semi-urbanization." As basic urban public services are provided subject to registered residency, migrant workers can enjoy only a few of the basic public services from the cities in which they live. As a result, it is hard for them to transform from peasants to urban residents and enjoy real city life. In accordance with the *China Statistical Year Book* of 2015 and the *2014 National Survey on Migrant Workers*, China's insured migrant workers' pension, medical care, unemployment and maternity accounted for only 17, 18, 11 and 8% of the total migrant workers respectively, while the insurance in the above aspects covered 68, 62, 34 and 34% of registered urban population respectively. This demonstrates a large gap between the migrant workers and the registered urban population. The rural migrant population can hardly find stable jobs in cities as they are generally less educated and lack professional skills. In 2015, only 36% of migrant workers signed labor contracts with their employers, a nearly 2% drop compared with the figure of the previous year (NBS 2016). In addition, migrant workers seldom regard themselves as townspeople. Deeply rooted peasant ideas, a strong "visitor" mentality and the psychology of "being marginalized" are the most formidable obstacles that prevent them from merging into city life.

"People" are the subject and the core of urbanization. The new-type urbanization, with people as the core, can only be realized when migrant workers fully become urban residents. Based on the multiple demands of the rural migrant population, their transformation into urban residents can be achieved through two channels. First, a policy of differentiated household registration and a points-based system can be implemented so that the qualified migrant population can be registered as urban residents (Gu et al. 2014a, b, c). Measures should also be taken to transform city-based villages and shantytowns into urban areas where former peasants can settle down as permanent urban residents. While lifting all restrictions for household registration in small cities, the government should also encourage migration of whole families into nearby towns and cities. The policy hindering household registration in medium and large-sized cities should be loosened step-by-step, and the migrant population can settle down in said cities as a result of properly guided expectation and choices. Metropolises and megacities are encouraged to establish a reasonable points-based household registration system, forming a balanced relationship between the registration of newcomers and the control of the urban population. Second, basic public services should be available for all permanent urban residents by implementing a residence permit system so that the permanent residents without urban *hukou* (registered residency) can also enjoy public services; thus the urbanization of those who fail to meet the requirements or do not want to be registered in cities can be achieved in an orderly way.

The residence permit system is a new lawful channel in addition to the household registration policy. As an innovation for the population management system, it carries the rights and welfare of the floating population in China. To realize full access to basic urban public services for all urban residents, more financial support should be given to the urbanization of the rural migrant population, and a dynamic adjustment mechanism should be established in order to increase the expense ratio of basic public services in GDP. What is essential is that the criterion for transfer payment distribution must be shifted from being determined by *hukou* (registered residency) to being decided by permanent residence status in order to gradually bridge the gap of public services between cities of different scales and between different types of population living in the same city. In addition, the service systems for migrant workers' employment and entrepreneurship should be improved to better stabilize urban employment. Industrial foundations in small and medium-sized cities are to be strengthened to create more jobs for migrant workers. Efforts should be made to encourage widespread entrepreneurship and innovation, improve business support system for migrant workers, simplify administrative procedures and exploit the multiplication effect accrued from innovation and entrepreneurship.

1.2 Through Striving to Attain Efficiency, We Can Turn the Urbanization Based on Inefficient Use of Labor, Land, and Capital into High Quality Urbanization. This Will Change the Current Model of Urbanization Which Overly Relies on "Land Resources" and "Cheap Labor"

Over the years, China has owed its rapid urbanization largely to increased investment, cheap labor and land resources. Yet, inefficient use of these growth factors in the process of urbanization has become increasingly prominent, resulting in the need to improve urbanization quality. First, in order to attract investment, local governments, by using administrative means, deliberately distorted or brought down industrial land prices for a long period of time, leading to widespread waste and inefficient use of land. According to the data of Communiqué on Land and Resources of China (2011–2015), land prices in 105 major monitored cities across China are too low. The price for industrial land in 2015 was 760 yuan (about $120 USD) per square meter, only 11% of the commercial land price (see Fig. 1.2). On the one hand, the low price of industrial land prompted blind land expansion by many enterprises; hence a small scale of investment, unreasonably low return and long-term idle and inefficient use of industrial land was inevitable. On the other hand, the low price of industrial land controlled by the government raised the prices of residential and commercial land, inflating the real estate and housing markets.

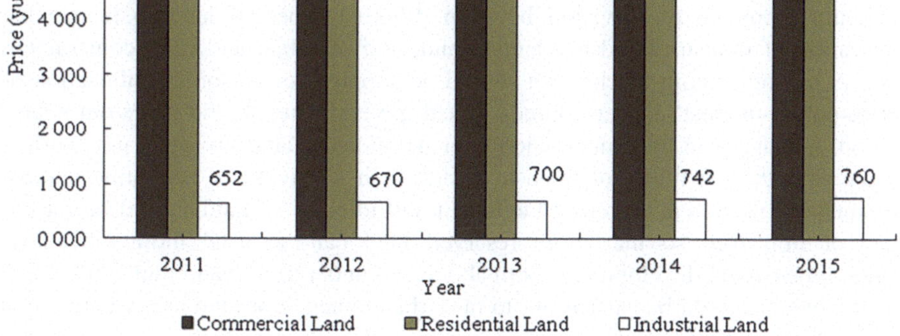

Fig. 1.2 Land price of 105 major cities in China. *Data source* The Communiqué of Land and Resources of China (2011–2015) by National Bureau of Statistics

Second, in the process of urbanization, investment has been mainly made in the fields of real estate and infrastructure, and over-investment and repeated investment have become commonplace, leading to inefficient use of capital. In accordance with the data published in the *Statistical Communiqué of the National Economy and Social Development*, the investment in real estate development and infrastructure in 2015 accounted for 35% of the total amount of investment in fixed assets, and investment in real estate alone took up more than 15% of total investment over the past 20 years. Meanwhile, driven by the aspiration for short-term GDP growth, local governments engaged in a campaign of tearing down old buildings for large-scale property development, causing a serious problem of repeated investment. Ignoring the actual situation of urban development and people's real demands, some local governments invested haphazardly in urban infrastructure, which was another example of over-investment.

Third, the kind of urbanization driven by and depending on cheap labor is unsustainable. On the one hand, China's "demographic dividend" is based on huge amounts of cheap labor and will gradually disappear. Statistics from the *2015 Observations of Migrant Workers* show that the growth rate of migrant worker population in China was declining and that the growth rate of the total migrant population dropped by 0.5, 1.5, 0.5 and 0.6% in 2012, 2013, 2014, and 2015 respectively. In addition, China's labor cost was constantly rising. In 2015, the average monthly income of migrant workers was 3072 yuan, a 50% increase from five years ago. China' labor cost is not competitive any more compared with those in India, the Philippines, Vietnam, and other developing countries in Asia. On the other hand, China does not have a system to improve the quality and skills of rural migrant laborers. Most of them have low productivity and are employed in labor intensive industries. In 2015, 55% of migrant workers were employed in the second industry, among which 31% engaged in the field of manufacturing and 21% in construction.

China has to transform its urban development processes away from inefficient use of land, capital and labor to an urbanization driven by effective utilization of these resources. A series of land system reforms should be carried out for more efficient use of urban increment and reserved land. Efforts should be made to gradually eliminate the division between different types of land to realize the integration of industrial and residential land, and of urban and rural construction land. A market-pricing mechanism should be adopted for reasonable allocation of "none-public-interest" land resources. Local governments should carry out examination, management and supervision over incremental land projects, and conduct debate over the feasibility of them to ensure their survival and economic returns. A management system targeting inefficient and idle use of land should be formulated or improved so that more reserved land can be used more efficiently. Three-dimensional developments both above and underground and multi-functional developments should be carried out to raise the efficiency of land use, whether it is used land or reserved land.

The reform of fiscal and taxation systems should be deepened to establish a local finance mechanism in line with respective administrative power. The current situation in which local government relies solely on land for local revenue must be changed so as to relieve their dependence on "land finance." Actions should be taken to accumulate the human capital the rural migrant population as a way to improve labor productivity. Systemic obstacles impeding labor migration from rural areas to cities or from city to city should be removed to allow free flow of labor. Through vocational training and company education, human labor capital of can be raised to meet the requirement of increasingly updated industrial development, employment and reemployment can be promoted and labor productivity and income can be improved. Urban capital must be used more efficiently, and haphazard investment by local governments must be prevented. More importance should be attached to the advancement of urban IT facilities and drainage systems, etc., to avoid over-investment. Exchange and cooperation in urban investment between cities, regions and countries should be strengthened, and shared service of urban resources should be enhanced to avoid repeated investment.

1.3 By Adhering to the Principle of Green Development, High Energy Consumption, High Emissions and High Pollution Will Give Way to Green Urbanization Based on Sustainable Development in Population, Resources and the Environment. Harmonious Coexistence Between Humans and Nature Will also Be Promoted, and Sustainable Urbanization Will Be Achieved by Improving Urban Management

The model of unsustainable economic growth, featuring inefficient resource utilization and unreasonable energy structure, and accompanied by serious pollution affecting many cities, seriously restrains adding green development to the process of urbanization. Recently, China has become one of the countries that suffers serious ecological overshoot, of which air pollution, deteriorated water quality and water shortage are the most apparent problems. Data from the *2015 Report on the Environmental State of China* shows that air quality in 78% of the 338 cities at or above the prefecture level failed to meet standards. Since 2013, PM2.5 readings in 74 monitored cities across the country have been much higher than the international standard, not even up to the national standard of level 2. Among the three major regions, the Beijing-Tianjin-Hebei region suffers from the most serious air pollution. In 2015, only 9% of China's underground water was of excellent/good quality, per capita water resource in China was only 28% of the world average, and nearly two thirds of Chinese cities were affected by water shortage (MEP 2016). In addition, China's urban planning, construction and management are still quite poor, and it is hard to put environmental regulations into practice. Many cities suffer from "urban maladies", including deteriorated environmental pollution, traffic

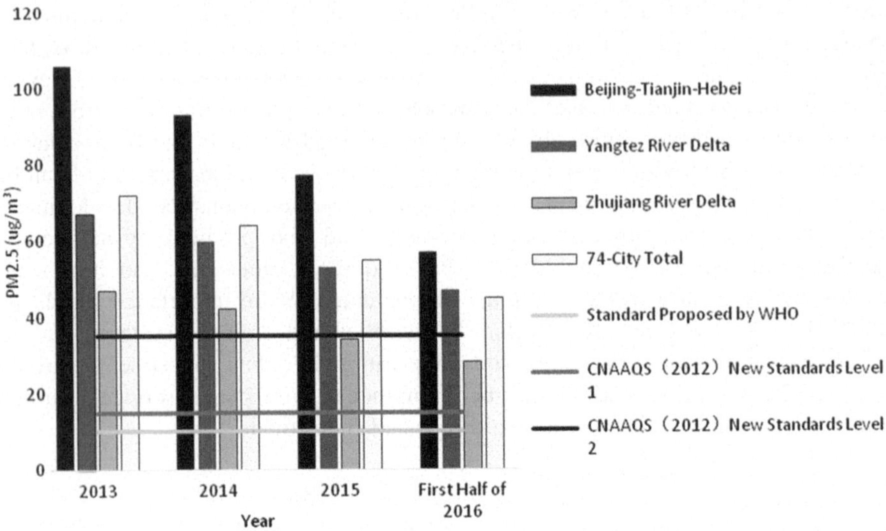

Fig. 1.3 Monitoring results of PM2.5 among 74 pilot cities and three regions (2013–2016). *Data source* A series of Reports on the Environmental State of China

congestion, poor sewage and garbage treatment, poor drainage systems and sanitary conditions and slow emergency responses (Gu et al. 2014a, b, c; Fig. 1.3).

There is an urgent need for China's urbanization to move in the direction of sustainable development in population, resources and the environment. The 13th Five-Year Plan notes that China will adhere to green prosperity of the country and green welfare to the people. The idea of green development must be spread to all aspects of urbanization. The structures of the industrial and energy sectors must be adjusted and optimized, and the current model of economic growth must be able to push China's urbanization in the direction of green development. Measures must be taken to improve the structure of the energy sector, upgrade efficient use of energy through technological innovation and reduce the exploitation and consumption costs of clean energy in order to develop a resource-conserving and environment-friendly production model. Meanwhile, the structure of the industrial sector needs to be adjusted and optimized in order to nurture, introduce and develop energy-efficient and environment-friendly industries, as well as the green service industry. Efforts should focus on the commercialization of green industries for economic, social, and ecological benefits. During the process of transforming urbanization into green development, it is essential to integrate capital, talents and markets and other factors so as to improve green technology and realize a transformation from factor-driven development to innovation-driven urbanization. We will thus explore an intensive, intelligent, green and low-carbon path to new-type urbanization.

The idea of ecological civilization should be merged as a principle into the process of urbanization and urban management and services are to be improved, creating an environment suitable for residential and business purposes. It is fundamentally important to develop urban designs according to local conditions and reasonably decide city scale, development margins and intensity and protective space. The government should amend or formulate laws and regulations concerning environmental protection and establish a stringent environmental protection system. We should work to better protect the environment. Action plans for pollution prevention and control and pollutant emission standards need to be formulated, and measures must be taken to improve environmental facilities for issues such as sewage treatment and garbage disposal. Green consumption and a low-carbon lifestyle should be encouraged, and environmental protection regulations and plans should be well implemented. Authorities must intensify the supervision and control of environmental protection and publicize environmental information. Tax preference and financial subsidies should be given to the enterprises who do well in energy saving and emission reduction; a "double punishment" and "daily penalty" system can be implemented to curb polluting enterprises with high energy consumption. Meanwhile, concerning carbon emission rights, water rights and pollutant emission rights, a system for the use and trade of such rights should be developed so that resource and energy consumption and environmental loss can be taken as a part of business costs. A coordination system should be set up in polluted areas to jointly control environmental pollution. Governments should speed up the establishment of the ecological compensation system to realize coordination and fair play in regional development.

1.4 By Using Urban Agglomerations as Platforms, China Can Take Full Advantage of the Radiation and Leading Role of Core Cities and Can Move Away from Urbanization Based on an Unreasonable Scale and Structure, and on the Uncoordinated Development Between Small, Medium, and Large-Sized Cities Towards Urbanization Based on the Efficient Integration of Urban Agglomerations and Coordinated Development

China is faced with an unbalanced scale and structure in urban development. First of all, the number of cities in China does not match the number of the urban population. Along with the progress of urbanization, the urban population is growing while the number of cities is shrinking. When the urbanization rate in the US increased from 20 to 70%, its number of cities increased from 300 to more than 2700, and when the urbanization rate in Japan rose from 30 to 70%, the number of cities jumped from more than 160 to more than 650. However, in China, the number of cities dropped from 668 to 656 when the urbanization rate increased from 31% to nearly 55% (RGAMR 2013). Second, the numbers of small, medium and large-sized cities in China fails to form a pyramid shape (with the number of large cities at the top), which is generally regarded as a reasonable and balanced structure.

The number and population of large cities account for an increasingly larger portion, while the number of small and medium-sized cities and their populations are continually shrinking, especially in the cities with 200 thousand or less people. Calculated in accordance with non-agricultural urban population, 7 cities were added to the group of largest cities of 4 million or more people from 1998 to 2014, and the population increased by 2.5 times. However, the number of small cities of less than 500 thousand people decreased by nearly 100, especially the number of cities below 200 thousand people, which dropped by 133, and the population in these cities suffered a 28% decline (see Table 1.1). It is not hard to see that urbanization in China overly depends on metropolises and megacities instead of urban circles. The scale of small and medium-sized cities is still too small, and the industrial and population agglomeration effect is far from satisfactory. In addition, there are many limitations for the development of small and medium-sized cities, and it is hard for large towns to be granted municipal status. In 2014, there were 238 largest townships in China each with a population of over 100,000 in its built-up area, and another 885 towns each with a population of 50,000 (NCDR 2016). All of these towns were large enough both in population and economic scale to be established as cities. However, they could not be granted municipal status because of the township management system and the administrative restrictions; therefore, their growth vitality and potentials cannot be fully released.

During the 13th Five-year national development period, we should strive to build better urban agglomerations and more small and medium-sized cities, working towards the goal of coordinated development among small, medium and large-sized cities. We need to accelerate urban agglomeration construction, establish and strengthen urban development coordination mechanisms, define functional orientations of urban agglomerations and advance the formation of reasonable industrial division so as to realize inter-connectivity between infrastructures and shared public services and accelerate a shift from “industrial isomorphism, disorderly competition and local protection” to the integration of urban agglomerations. Steps should be taken to optimize urban agglomerations in the east to strengthen their spatial spillover effect and their leading role through orderly industrial transfer to inland cities, thus realizing mutual benefit between different regions. The advantages of abundant resources and good locations will be combined to foster urban agglomerations and circles in the central and eastern regions and to create more growth poles supporting regional development.

With urban agglomerations as platforms, we shall extend the radiation effect of central cities and the social effect of small and medium-sized cities in providing jobs in order to push forward coordinated development between small, medium and large-sized cities and economic integration within urban agglomerations. Yet, the development margin of central urban areas should be well planned, and the population and the land use scale of large cities should be properly controlled.

Table 1.1 Changes in city size and proportion, 1998–2014

City size	1998			2014			Changes, 1998–2014			
(in 10,000)	Count	Count %	Pop. %	Count	Count %	Pop. %	Count	Count %	Pop. %	Pop. Growth %
400+	3	0.45	9.39	10	1.52	19.96	7	1.07	10.57	252.28
200–400	10	1.51	12.78	17	2.59	13.46	7	1.08	0.68	74.54
100–200	24	3.62	14.26	42	6.4	16.88	18	2.78	2.62	96.15
50–100	47	7.09	14.42	103	15.7	19.37	56	8.61	4.95	122.64
20–50	206	31.07	28.86	244	37.2	21.51	38	6.13	−7.35	23.51
<20	373	56.26	20.29	240	36.59	8.81	−133	−19.67	−11.48	−28
Total	663	100	100	656	100	100	−7	0	0	65.72

Source China's Population and Employment Statistics Year Book, 1999/2015
Note Urban population is calculated in accordance with the non-agricultural population

The development of small and medium-sized cities and the towns with special industries should be accelerated to increase their attractiveness and push forward local urbanization. Location advantages, resources, industrial foundation, trade, infrastructures, culture, and science and technologies must be relied on to attract professional talents, capital, and other production factors, and to build industrial clusters with local characteristics. We will take industrial and labor force transfer as an opportunity for the central and western regions to absorb the industrial transfer from the coastal areas (Gu et al. 2014a, b, c) and accelerate industrial transformation. Authorities should upgrade large towns into small cities, especially the promising ones in urban agglomerations. Efforts should be made to strengthen the construction of infrastructure and public services in order to improve urban functions. Active measures should be taken to develop small and medium-sized cities out of urban agglomerations, especially those in the central and western regions, and foster population aggregation and industrial agglomeration, creating conditions for the floating population to be locally urbanized.

1.5 By Adhering to the Market-Oriented Principle, Government-Dominated Urbanization Can Be Transformed into Market-Oriented and Government-Guided Urbanization; the Laws of Economic Growth and Urbanization Must Be Respected and Followed, and the Roles of a "Hands Off" Market and "Hands On" Government Should Be Fully Utilized

In the past, urbanization was mainly dominated by the government, which had too much control over the process of urban development. On the one hand, the government utilized this power and even replaced enterprises as market suppliers and families as consumers in order to allocate resources. This excessive and improper intervention from the government distorted the rational allocation of resources. Take the capital factor as an example, some local governments became major investors in urbanization and undertook almost all the projects regarding infrastructure, public utilities and public service supply, taking up a large amount of space for private capital. Administrative divisions caused not only unbalanced demand and supply of resources between cities at different levels, but also the over dependence of many cities on resources from the administrative channel, further weakening the role of the market. On the other hand, the government did too little in the areas of environmental protection, the top-level design of urbanization, social management and market supervision.

In the new-type urbanization, the relationship between the government and the market has to be reshaped, and the border of government and market functions has to be redefined to develop a healthy system of market-oriented and government-guided urbanization can be well established. Governments of all levels should respect economic and urban development laws, and allow free flow of resources between regions, industries, and departments relying on market mechanisms in order to realize an effective and dynamically balanced allocation of resources. Urbanization is the aggregation of market players in a certain space when sharing external economic benefits as well as the process of market players' free choices for space (Li 2013). Therefore, fully utilizing the decisive role of the market in resource allocation will help raise the urbanization rate. Government conduct should be regulated and restrained to prevent it from interfering in the running of the market. With the advancement of a fair competition mechanism and removal of investment obstacles, governments should "let it go" or "retreat" step-by-step from competition in general fields so that various dominant or recessive thresholds can be removed and private capital can be fully utilized in more areas including infrastructure and public unities.

At the same time, the cooperation mechanism between the government and private businesses must be improved, and the incentive and pricing mechanism of Public-Private Partnership (PPP) projects in the new-type urbanization should be established so that limited financial capitals can leverage more private investment in urban development, forming a synchronized operation between government investment and private capital. We need to accelerate the shift from a management-oriented government to service-oriented government as a way to enable the government to play a better role in the areas of planning, system design, public service, environmental protection, market supervision and social management, thus creating a sound legal and policy environment for urbanization and fully utilizing the concepts of a "hands off" market and a "hands on" government. The government has to be the plan-maker to avoid mindless actions in urbanization, the system supplier to deliver urbanization "dividends" through system innovation, the public service provider to supplement what the market cannot do, the environment protector to push forward the transformation of urbanization and the market supervisor to regulate market performance, as well as the society manager to mobilize all forces to participate in urbanization.

1.6 By Adhering to the Principle of Coordination, China Can Move from a Lack of Coordination Between Urbanization and Industrialization, Informatization and Agricultural Modernization to a State of Synchronized and Integrated Development; Coordination Between Urbanization and Commercialization Should Be Emphasized to Boost In-depth Integration of Different Sectors

Industrial development is the foundation of urbanization. The level of industrial development decides the quality of urbanization. Yet, urbanization in some areas of China is disengaged from industrial development and is not synchronized with industrialization, informatization and agricultural modernization. In the process of urbanization driven by the government, the supporting role of industries was neglected, resulting in a weak industrial foundation in cities. Therefore, many newly urbanized peasants who had no land any more could not be employed in cities, and some of them had nothing to do other than becoming urban vagrants because there was no way to find jobs. Urbanization in some areas was even mutated into real estate development, and huge tracts of land were used for the so-called "town-building movement." On the one hand, the local ecological environment was destroyed and cultivated land wasted, which was detrimental to agricultural modernization; on the other hand, many of the said newly-built towns became "empty towns" or "ghost towns" due to the lack of basic living facilities and industrial support (Gu et al. 2013), leading to a weak capability to offer jobs. As a result, these new residential areas could not attract residents to live there and were therefore unsustainable, further intensifying the pressure on real estate destocking.

In the process of the new-type urbanization, what we must do is to speed up synchronized development dominated by industrialization with informatization as our means, urbanization as the key and agricultural modernization as the foundation. We must insist on the integrated development between urbanization and industries and properly carry out industrial planning and layout so as to realize the goal of building modern industrial systems. Coordination between urbanization and industrialization must be strengthened. On the basis of improved infrastructure and public services, efforts shall be made to develop the real economy by taking advantage of upgraded industries, regional industrial transfers, and local resources and special industries. We must prevent urbanization from evolving into "real estate development," and strive to boost the de-bubbling of the real estate industry in megacities and destocking in small and medium-sized cities. Meanwhile, we should also prevent "empty cities," creating a sound industrial and service environment to promote industrial agglomeration. In the process, emphasis shall be laid on the development of industrial parks, which will create conditions for industrial agglomeration to drive population agglomeration. The coordination between urbanization and agricultural modernization should be promoted for the purpose of industry, nurturing agriculture and cities driving the country.

We shall take the opportunity to enact rural land reform on "separable rights" (meaning that ownership, contract right and management right may belong to different people) to allow more flexibility of land operation. By doing so, land operation right can naturally flow to leading agricultural enterprises, specialized farmer co-operatives and farming experts so as to improve the farmland utilization rate, raise farming productivity and promote intensive cultivation and agricultural modernization. As a result, more rural labor can be liberated from rural land and transferred into cities, providing a large population for urbanization. The coordination between urbanization and informatization shall also be enhanced to further harvest the benefits through improving the quality of urbanization by building smart cities. A smart city is the in-depth combination of urbanization, industrialization and informatization, and the important direction of China's urbanization in the future. We shall make full use of the new generation of information technologies including the Internet of Things, cloud computing and big data to realize smart urban planning, construction, management and services. Thus we may upgrade the quality of urbanization by building smart cities and enjoy the benefits thereof.

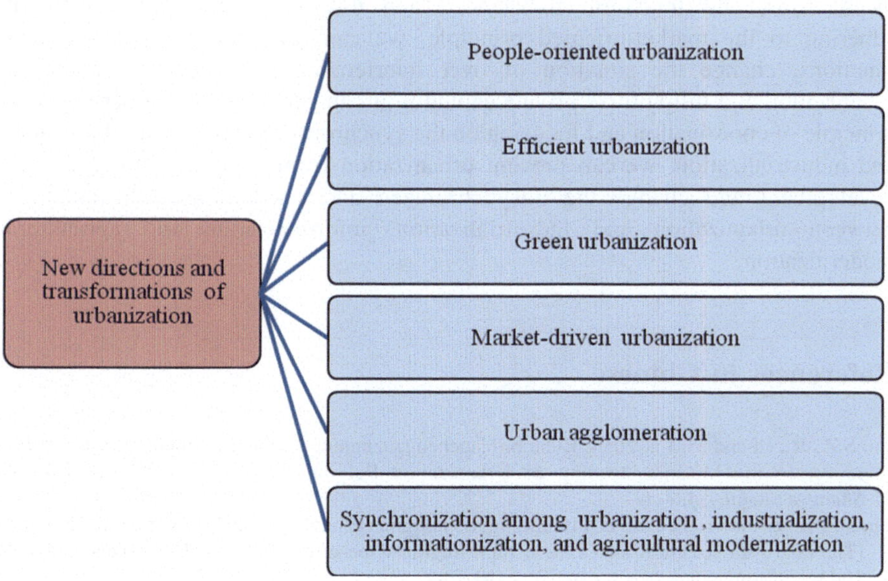

Fig. 1.4 Six transformations of urbanization in China during the 13th Five-Year Plan

1.7 Conclusion

In the 13th Five-year national development period, China will strive to speed up the transformation of urbanization in six directions for the goal of healthy urbanization (see Fig. 1.4): (1) Based on the people-oriented principle, a differentiated household registration policy will be implemented and combined with a residence permit system known as "double channel" urbanization, a transfer payment system will be connected with permanent residents, and a healthy employment and service system will be established for migrant workers so as to realize the transformation from "land-centered" development to "people-oriented" urbanization. (2) Through striving to attain efficiency and quality, we can improve the efficiency of labor, land and capital utilization. This will change the current model of urbanization which overly relies on "land resources" and "cheap labor" and raise the quality of urbanization. (3) By adhering to the principle of green development, the structure of the industrial and energy sectors can be adjusted and optimized, overall urban management will be improved and a change in high energy consumption, high emissions and high pollution will be seen. (4) By using urban agglomerations as platforms, we can build better urban agglomerations and more small and medium-sized cities, establish and improve urban development and coordination mechanisms, and transform unbalanced and disorderly urbanization. (5) By adhering to the market-oriented principle, we can fully transform government functions, change the situation of over interference from the government in urbanization and fully utilize private capital in urbanization. (6) By adhering to the principle of coordination and focusing on the synchronization between urbanization and industrialization, we can prevent urbanization from evolving into real estate development and change the unsynchronized and uncoordinated development between urbanization and industrialization, informatization and agricultural modernization.

References in Chinese

Gu, S.Z., R., Li and M. Lu. 2013. Ruhe bimianchengzhenghua bei fangdichanhua de wuqu [How to Avoid the Misunderstanding of Urbanization Relying on Real Estate Development]. *Shangye shidai*, 14, 4–6.

Gu, S.Z, R., Li and Y.B., Cao. 2014a. Zhongguo nongmingong shimihua de erwei lujinjing xuanze [The dual-path selection for Chinese rural migrants' becoming citizens: In the perspective of *Hukou* reform]. *Zhonggio renkou* 2: 2–10.

Gu, S.Z., C., Zheng, and L. Fan. 2014b. Chengzhenghua yu gongyehua gaosu fazhanxi de daqi wuran zhili [Air pollution control in the context of rapid urbanization and industrialization]. *Lilun xuekan* 6: 42–45.

Gu, S.Z., C., Zheng and Y.B. Cao. 2014c. Dali fazhan zhongxiao chengshi tuijin junheng chengzhenghua de zhanlu sikao [Strategic thinking on developing small and medium-sized cities to balance urbanization]. *Renkou yanjiu*, 4: 19–26.

Li, P.F. 2013. Xinxing chengzhenghua de jiben moshi juti lujing yu tuijin duice [The basic patterns, specific paths and promotion countermeasures of new-type urbanization]. *Jianghai xuekan* 1: 87–94.

MEP (Ministry of Ministry of Environmental Protection). 2016. *2015 Nian quanguo chengshi kongqi zhiliang zhuangkuang* [The quality of urban air in China in 2015]. http://www.mep.gov.cn/gkml/hbb/qt/201602/t20160204_329886.htm#.

NBS (National Bureau of Statistics). 2016. *2015 Nian nongmingong jiance diaocha baogao* [Report on monitoring of rural migrants in 2015]. http://www.stats.gov.cn/tjsj/zxfb/201604/t20160428_1349713.html.

NCDR (National Committee of Development & Reform). 2016. Guojia xinxing chengzhenghua baogao [Report of new-type urbanization in 2015]. Beijing: Zhongguo jihua chubanshe.

Chapter 2
Urbanization and Industrial Development in China

Kevin H. Zhang

Abstract Over the period 1978–2016, more than 550 million migrants moved to China's cities, resulting in a large rise of urbanization from 18 to 57%. While urbanization is influenced by many factors, this study focuses on industrialization, a key structural determinant of urban development. How does industrial development affect China's urbanization? Does China's industrialization lead to its urbanization? Is China under- or over-urbanized? How does China manage urban development so that the virtuous circle between urbanization and industrialization could realize? This chapter offers explanations to the questions as follows: China's rapid industrialization is the key driver of its urbanization; China's urban development is at the right speed, avoiding many problems of over-urbanization in developing countries; and China successfully guided urbanization to promote economic growth through agglomeration and consumption effects.

Keywords Urbanization · Urban development · Industrialization · Industrial development

2.1 Introduction

China's rapid urbanization and high economic growth for 38 years (1978–2016) have been unprecedented in human history. In 1978, less than one-fifth (17.9%) of China's 975 million people lived in cities. But over the past 38 years, more than half a billion (558 million) people moved from rural areas to urban areas, seeking work in manufacturing and services as China industrialized its economy through developing special economic zones and export-oriented industries. This urban transformation, 57% of Chinese people in cities in 2016, has been mostly successful. Real per capita income increased by about 20 times in 1978–2016, lifting half a billion people out of poverty (World Bank 2017).

K.H. Zhang (✉)
Illinois State University, Normal, USA
e-mail: khzhang@ilstu.edu

Z. Tang (ed.), *China's Urbanization and Socioeconomic Impact*,
DOI 10.1007/978-981-10-4831-9_2

Urbanization in China seems to be directly associated with industrial development. Industry, especially manufactures, has been viewed as an engine of economic growth for all economies. Unlike dependence on services in growth in India and on natural resources in Brazil and Russia, China's economic miracle is largely a manufacturing success. China's rapid industrialization since 1978 has increased incomes, raised living standards, and made China the world's largest manufacturer and exporter.[1] As workers shifted to urban employment with higher productivity and with labor productivity rising across sectors through large investments, real output per worker increased by a factor of 12 (WB and DRCC 2014). With an annual average growth rate of over 9% for three decades, China became the world's second largest economy in 2010, and more than half of Chinese was urbanized as rural people moved to cities.

While there are many studies on China's urban development, several issues of the urbanization-industrialization link have been remained on debate (Gollin et al. 2016; WB and DRCC 2014; Zhang 2002). Does China's industrialization lead to its urbanization? Is China under- or over-urbanized? How does China guide urbanization to enhance its economic growth? Based on a solid theoretical framework and comprehensive international evidences, this chapter intends to offer explanations to the questions. The main conclusions can be summarized as follows. First, while international experiences suggest that urbanization could go with or without industrialization, China follows the standard approach of urbanization led by industrialization. In the last decades starting 1978, China's rapid urbanization is largely caused by its successful industrialization. Second, the fact that China's urbanization is lower than that of the world average at different income level is not a symbol of under-urbanization in China but over-urbanization in many developing countries. China managed well the speed of urbanization in order to avoid some of the common ills of urbanization that occurred in other developing countries, such as urban poverty, unemployment, and squalor. Third, China seems to have successfully guided urbanization to promote economic growth through agglomeration effects and consumption effects. This is vital for China's growth model transformation in the sense that China has to shift its exported-oriented to more domestic-consumption oriented economy, especially facing the anti-globalization challenge from the new president of United State in 2017.

[1]Industrial development is desirable not only as a source of higher productivity growth and per capita income, but also to achieve greater diversity of the economic structure, which reduces a country's vulnerability to poverty and external shocks. Industry, especially manufacture, has long been considered a sector that plays a key role in economic growth for developing countries (UNIDO 2002, 2013; Zhang 2010).

2.2 Theoretical Framework of Urbanization-Industrialization Nexus

Three views on the urbanization-industrialization link may be identified from the literature (Alvarez-Cuadrado and Poschke 2011; Brückner 2012; Davis and Henderson 2003; Fay and Opal 2000; Glaeser 2013; Glaeser and Gottlieb 2009; Gollin et al. 2016; Hamer and Linn 1987; Lucas 2004; Michaels et al. 2012; Williamson 1988): urbanization led by industrialization; urbanization without industrialization; and a virtuous circle between industrialization and urbanization.

Urbanization Led by Industrialization Theoretical studies suggest several channels through which industrialization causes urbanization: industrialization leads to economic transformation of agriculture to industry and services; industry, especially manufactures, hires more rural people with higher wages; industry creates more jobs in services for rural people; and industrialization leads to rural-urban migration due to better life in cities than villages. In sum, industrialization results in the process of urbanization, in which urban population increases and rural population falls as industry and services expand.[2]

Urbanization is a natural and inevitable consequence of industrialization, because industrialization entails a massive shift of labor and other inputs from rural agricultural sectors to urban industrial sectors (Hamer and Linn 1987). The fall in agriculture's share of the labor force and the rise in industry's and services' shares during industrialization involve two phenomena: demand shifts and supply shifts. On the demand side, the share of income spent on food falls, and the shares spent on industrial products and services rise, as income increases. This process raises returns to labor and other inputs in industry and services relative to those in agriculture so that labor and other inputs are induced to move from rural agriculture to urban industry and services. On the supply side, the costs and prices of industrial products may fall relative to those of agricultural products, due to faster technical progress and larger benefits from capital accumulation, scale economies, and highly educated labor force in industry than in agriculture. Along with industrialization, cost reductions in industry are likely to cause large inflows of labor in that sector and thus increase urbanization (Williamson 1988).[3]

---

[2]Standard theories of development economics view urbanization and industrialization as essentially synonymous, reflecting a stylized development process in which the structural transformation from agriculture into manufacturing and services involves a shift of labor out of rural areas and into urban ones (Alvarez-Cuadrado and Poschke 2011; Brückner 2012; Michaels et al. 2012; Williamson 1988).

[3]Industrialization caused urbanization because it offered more jobs and attracted people to the city. The urbanization process typically begins when factories are established within a region and creating a demand for factory labor. Other businesses such as building manufacturers, retailers and service providers then follow the factories in order to meet the product demands of the workers. This creates even more jobs and demands for housing, thus establishing an urban area. As industrialization creates economic growth, the demand for the improved education and public works agencies that are characteristic of urban areas increases. This demand occurs because

The view of the urbanization led by industrialization emphasizes the role of sectoral labor productivity in driving structural change; i.e. the decline in agriculture, the rise and fall of manufacturing, and the rise of services. The "labor push" approach shows how a rise in agricultural productivity reduces the "food problem" and releases labor for the modern sector. The "labor pull" approach describes how a rise in non-agricultural productivity attracts underemployed labor from agriculture into the modern sector (Zhang 2002; Alvarez-Cuadrado and Poschke 2011).[4]

Urbanization without Industrialization A large endowment of natural resources in a country may lead to a strong income effect, shifting labor into urban areas, but as the relative productivity of the industrial sector has not increased this will result in urbanization without industrialization (Gollin et al. 2016). Urbanization thus is driven by the income effect of natural resource endowments: resource rents are disproportionately spent on urban goods and services, and the mix of workers is heavily skewed towards non-tradable services. This particular pattern of urbanization creates so called "consumption cities", as their emergence is explained by the consumption of a resource rent in the form of urban goods and services. These cities consist mainly of workers in non-tradable services, while the industrial goods are mainly imported from abroad. Consumption cities involve a larger fraction of workers in non-tradable services such as trade and transportation, personal and government services (Glaeser et al. 2001; Duranton 2008; Glaeser 2013). Cities driven by industrialization have more workers in industrial sectors such as manufacturing and tradable services.

Feedback of Urbanization to Industrialization/Economic Development There is a virtuous circle between industrialization/economic development and urbanization, since they usually go hand-in-hand (Davis and Henderson 2003; Xie and Zhang 2004; Zhang 2002; Henderson 2003, 2010). High correlation of between the percent urbanized in a country and GDP per capita suggests a close interaction between them. Industrialization involves the transformation from an agricultural based economy to an industrial-service based economy. Production of manufacturing and services is much more efficient when concentrated in dense business-industrial districts in cities. As the process of growing share of national population living within urban settlements, urbanization has been a key force in economic development. Close spatial proximity, or high density, enhances economic growth through information spillovers amongst producers, more efficiently functioning labor markets, and savings in the transport costs.

(Footnote 3 continued)

businesses looking for new technology to increase productivity require an educated workforce, and pleasant living conditions attract skilled workers to the area.

[4]Urban areas under industrialization offer better opportunities for housing and education, and city living allows people to benefit from diversity and marketplace competition. Cities offer access to wealth and services that many rural areas lack. Rural inhabitants typically move to cities to exploit economic opportunities and improve their social mobility. The lack of specialist services in rural areas further stimulates urbanization.

There are varieties of channels through which urbanization can enhance economic growth (Glaeser et al. 1992; Glaeser and Gottlieb 2009). First, cities play a vital role in labor productivity by offering opportunities for education, employment and health services. Second, urbanization implies agglomeration of people and firms, which reduces production costs. Urbanization permits external scale and scope economies, reduces transactions costs, and allows specialization among firms leading to low costs of production. Third, urbanization is a key factor in entrepreneurship. Fourth, there are spillover effects or positive externalities of urban development on rural areas.

It is worth mentioning the positive feedback of urbanization to economic growth through agglomeration (Glaseser and Gottlieb 2009). As an important growth driver, urban areas offer positive agglomeration effects, including larger, more efficient labor markets, lower transaction costs, and easier knowledge spillovers. Agglomeration effects can also occur in smaller cities with sufficient specialization and transport linkages to larger urban areas. In the absence of sound public policy, however, those agglomeration effects may be easily outweighed by congestion costs —pollution, traffic congestion, and higher costs of living.

2.3 Worldwide Experience and International Perspective of Chins

Industrialization first sparked urban growth in United Kingdom in the late 18th century and throughout the 19th century in Europe and North America. Historically, pre-industrial societies were not urbanized. Urbanization rates of 15% (as opposed to 5%) characterized societies that were relatively developed for their time (UN 2011). The successful European and North American countries achieved high levels of urbanization (more than 50%) only in the course of industrialization. As these countries further developed, they saw a higher urbanization level (over 80%) due to marked expansions in services, in particular skill-intensive services.

Table 2.1 presents urbanization in China and the world in 1960–2015. In general, many countries, including China, conform to the standard view of urbanization led by industrialization through structural transformation, as suggested by the middle of the table in which urbanization is positively relation to income level by countries. Developing countries have urbanized dramatically over since 1960. Their urbanization process shares many similarities with developed countries in the past: urbanization is tightly correlated with income. This is confirmed by the positive relationship between urbanization and income per capita in 1960–2015 for country groups by income (Song and Zhang 2002; Zhang 2002, 2010).

Viewed from a global perspective, China's rapid urbanization is largely a case of norm rather than exception (UNIDO 2013; Song and Zhang 2002; Zhang 2002; Zhang and Song 2003). In line with global trends, although legging behind initially but catching up lately, China's urbanization in 38 years (1978–2016) increased by

Table 2.1 China's urbanization relative to the world: 1960–2015

Region/Country	1960	1970	1980	1990	2000	2010	2015
China	16.2	17.4	19.4	26.4	35.9	49.2	55.6
World	33.6	36.5	39.3	42.9	46.5	51.5	53.9
By income level							
Low income	11.8	15.6	19.1	22.6	25.4	28.7	30.7
Lower middle income	19.7	22.5	26.2	29.9	32.9	36.8	39.0
Upper middle income	28.3	32.2	36.4	43.2	50.3	59.7	64.1
High income	63.8	68.9	72.0	74.5	76.8	79.9	81.1
By developing regions							
East Asia and Pacific	16.9	18.8	21.3	28.2	36.7	47.7	52.9
Latin America and Caribbean	48.4	56.3	63.7	69.9	74.9	78.2	79.6
Middle East and North Africa	35.0	42.7	49.6	54.9	58.6	62.5	64.2
Sub-Saharan Africa	14.6	18.0	22.2	27.0	30.8	35.2	37.7

Notes Not including high-income economies for East Asia & Pacific and Latin America & Caribbean
Sources World Bank (2016)

39% points (from 18 to 57%), with annual growth of 1.02% point. Although the rate is not extraordinary in light of the experience of the newly industrialized economies, the scale indeed is overwhelming. In the past three decades, urban residents in China soared by more than 550 million, 1.67 times of U.S. entire population (330 million). Now 775 million Chinese—i.e., roughly the total population of Europe—live in cities.

China has avoided some of the common ills of urbanization that occurred in other developing countries, such as urban poverty, unemployment, and squalor (UN 2011; WB and DRCC 2014). China's growth had been driven by investment rather than productivity, and investment has become less effective in generating growth at the national as well as the city level. Urbanization has relied excessively on land conversion and land financing, which is causing inefficient urban sprawl and, on occasion, ghost towns and wasteful real estate development. Barriers to migration have kept China's urbanization rate too low, thus underutilizing people's potential and exacerbating urban-rural income inequality. Unequal access to public services between citizens with urban household registration (*hukou* in Chinese) and those without, although diminishing, remains and is a barrier to mobility. At the same time, the large influx of migrants puts pressures on urban services, and urban citizens perceive an erosion of service quality. Rural-urban land conversion has been inequitable in the distribution of its gains, has added to wealth inequalities, and has fed social unrest among farmers whose land has been expropriated. Despite progress in environmental standards and policies, the cost of pollution to the nation's health is rising as China's population is increasingly concentrated in cities. And land-intensive urbanization has reduced the availability of farmland, is competing for scarce water resources, and is adding to pollution that affects the quality of farm produce and food production capacity.

The bottom part of Table 2.1 shows global regional pattern of urbanization in the developing world. Latin America & Caribbean and the Middle-East & North Africa are relatively more urbanized than Sub-Saharan Africa and Asia, with urbanization rates about 80 and 60% in 2015 respectively. In both Africa and Asia, the urbanization rate was only 10–15% in 1960, which is characteristic of preindustrial societies. It is now around 40%, as high as in developed countries after the Industrial Revolution. Asia and Latin America & Caribbean region are examples of the standard story of urbanization with industrialization. The successful Asian and Latin American economies typically went through industrialization, with urbanization following along as their economic activity shifted away from agricultural activities.[5]

While many developing countries have followed the typical pattern of urbanization with industrialization, a different pattern appears in a small group of countries that rely on resource exports. Urbanization in these countries has increased rapidly as well, but not been associated with industrialization. In these countries, urbanization is driven instead by the income effect of resource endowments. These countries include Kuwait, Gabon, Saudi Arabia, Libya, Algeria, Angola and Nigeria. They are as urbanized as East Asian economies like South Korea, Malaysia, and China, but their cities have never really achieved significant industrialization (Gollin et al. 2016). The relatively more urbanized countries export oil (e.g., Angola, Gabon and Nigeria), gold and/or diamonds (e.g., Botswana and South Africa), copper (e.g., Zambia) or cocoa (e.g., Ghana and Ivory Coast). Most of them export oil and are less industrialized than their Asian counterparts for the same income level.

2.4 Virtuous Circle Between Urbanization and Industrialization in China

China's urbanization since 1978 has been accompanied with its outstanding industrial performance (Zhang 2015a, b). Manufacturing jobs in China increased dramatically from 70 million in 1978 to 225 million in 2011, averaging a yearly growth rate of 3.6%; and that of the service sector from 49 to 273 million, averaging a yearly growth rate of 5.3%. Consequently, China became the world's manufacturing center, producing 85% of all TVs, 70% of all air-cons, 50% of all refrigerators, and 40% of all washing machines in the world. Such rapid industrial transformation has sustained high growth rates of the Chinese economy in the past three decades, and lifted 500 million people out of poverty. Per capita income in China in 1978 was a mere US$155, but has since increased to US$8280 in 2015, as

[5]A few exceptions are Brunei, Mongolia and Venezuela which were also heavily dependent on natural resource production post-1960. Some countries are both industrialized and resource-exporters, such as Chile, Indonesia, Malaysia, and Peru.

Table 2.2 China's position in the top 15 economies: 2015

Rank	Country	GDP (billions $)	PPP GDP (billions $)	Urbanization (%)	GDP per capita ($)	PPP GDP per capita ($)
1	USA	17,968	17,968	82	55,904	55,904
2	China	11,385	19,510	56	8280	14,190
3	Japan	4116	4842	93	32,481	38,211
4	Germany	3371	3842	75	41,267	47,033
5	UK	2865	2660	83	44,118	40,958
6	France	2423	2647	80	37,728	41,221
7	India	2183	8027	33	1688	6209
8	Italy	1819	2174	69	29,847	35,665
9	Brazil	1800	3208	86	8802	15,690
10	Canada	1573	1628	82	43,935	45,489
11	Korea	1393	1849	82	27,513	36,528
12	Australia	1241	1137	89	51,642	47,310
13	Russia	1236	3474	74	8447	23,744
14	Spain	1221	1636	80	26,327	35,270
15	Mexico	1161	2220	79	9592	18,335

Note According to International Comparison Program of World Bank (2015), China passed the US to become the world's number one economy in purchasing power parity (PPP) GDP in 2014
Sources World Development Indicators (World Bank 2015)

indicated by Table 2.2. History shows that no nation has been able to become high-income countries (i.e., when per capita income reaches US$12,000) without successful urbanization (e.g., average urbanization of advanced economies is 76%), and China seems to be well on its way.

The overall trend of China's industrial performance since 1978 may be illustrated with Fig. 2.1. In 35 years (1978–2013), China's GDP grew 26 times over, but industry is a sector with fastest growth and the largest contribution (about 42 times of that in 1978). By 2014, China became the second largest economy in the world in current exchange rate, and number one in purchasing power parity value (World Bank 2016), as reported in Table 2.2. As the most populous country, however, China' GDP per capita lags far behind the US and other developed economies.

The position of China's industrial competitiveness (IC) is revealed in Table 2.3, which reports top 15 of the world IC ranking in 1992–2012.[6] Among the most

[6]Based on the method developed by UNIDO (2013), a country's industrial competitiveness (IC) may be assessed with three indicators: industrial capacity, industrial intensity, and industrial quality. Industrial capacity, defined as the ability to produce and export manufactures, includes four indexes: manufacturing value added per capita, manufactured exports per capita, manufacturing value added share in world, and manufactured exports share in world. Industrial intensity denotes shares of manufacturing value added in GDP and manufactured export in total exports.

industrially competitive nations in the world, we find high income industrialized countries, as well as China ranked fifth in 2012. The top three positions are occupied by Japan, Germany, and the US, which have held top positions in the ranking since 1990. As the only developing country in the top 15 economies, China is obviously outstanding in industrial performance, especially the unbelievable rise in position. While some small East Asian economies (South Korea, Taiwan and Singapore) moved up their ranks by 2–13 positions, China gained 27 in merely 22 years, from the 32th in 1990 to the 5th in 2012, contrasting falls in many Western European economies.

Figure 2.2 displays the overall trend of China's urbanization in 1949–2015, in which Chinese urban development underwent dramatic transformations as a consequence of two major systemic changes.[7] During the first three decades (1949–1978), sustained low levels of urbanization and a brief episode of anti-urbanism accompanied centralized planning and city-based industrialization. Since 1978, Chinese urbanization has witnessed major economic and spatial shifts away from the socialist patterns (see Fig. 2.3). Among the many facets of urban transformation since 1978 are a more heterogeneous urban population, rural–urban migration, spatial reorganization through urban land-use change, new housing development, globalization, suburbanization, polycentric restructuring of urban form, and changes in the spatial/administrative systems of cities (Song and Zhang 2002; Zhang and Song 2003). The Chinese trajectory of urban development is seen as more different from than similar to the experiences of other economies (Gollin et al. 2016; WB and DRCC 2014).

It was not until the economic reform of 1978 that China's urbanization started to take off and, since then, the two processes have fed off each other (Xie and Zhang 2004; Zhang 2002, 2010, 2015a). With the introduction of market mechanisms in the 1978 reform, growth factors such as labor, land, capital and technologies (including vernacular techniques) could be mobilized for increased economic accumulation. The pace of China's urbanization has been much faster in 1979–2015 than 1949–1978. According to China's first Census in 1953, there were only

(Footnote 6 continued)

Industrial quality defined as technological deepening and upgrading in industries, includes medium- and high-tech manufacturing value added share in total and medium- and high-tech manufactured Exports share in total.

[7]China's statistics regarding urban population sometimes can be misleading because of the various criteria used to calculate urban population. In the 1953 census, urban essentially referred to settlements with populations of more than 2500, in which more than 50% of the labor force were involved in nonagricultural pursuits. The 1964 census raised the cut-off to 3000 and the requirement for nonagricultural labor to 70%. The 1982 census used the 3000/70% minimum but introduced criteria of 2500–3000 and 85% as well. In addition, in calculating urban population, the 1982 census made a radical change by including the agricultural population residing within the city boundaries. This explains the dramatic jump in urban population from the 138.7 million reported for year-end 1981 to the 206.6 million counted by the 1982 census. In 1984 the urban guidelines were further loosened, allowing for lower minimum population totals and nonagricultural percentages. The criteria varied among provincial-level units.

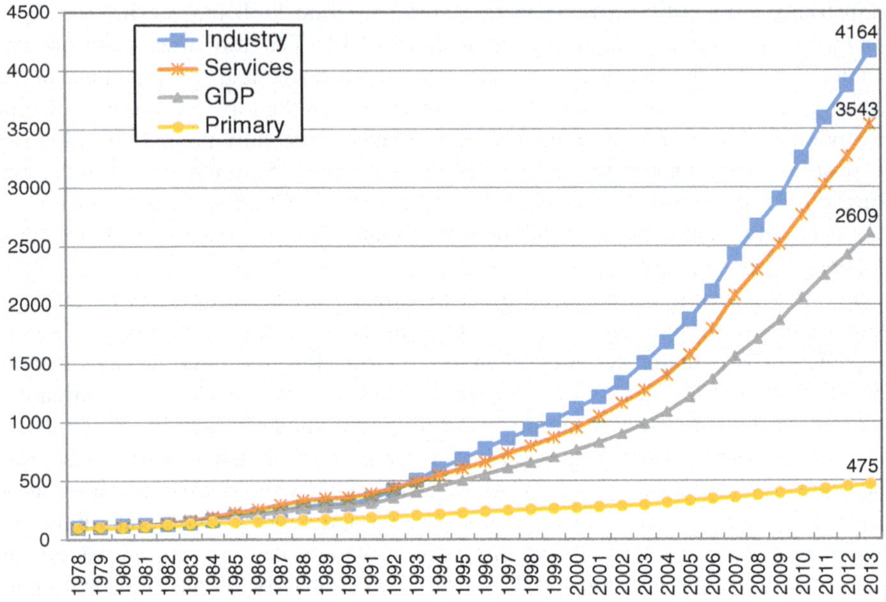

Source: *China Statistical Yearbook 2014* (NBSC 2014).

Fig. 2.1 Growth of industry as China's GDP component in 1978–2013 (1978 = 100). *Source* China Statistical Yearbook 2014 (NBSC 2014)

Table 2.3 Rank of Top 15 economies of industrial competitiveness: 1990–2012

Economy	2012	2010	2005	2000	1995	1990	Changes in 1990–2012
Germany	1	1	1	2	2	1	0
Japan	2	2	2	1	1	2	0
USA	3	3	3	3	3	3	0
Korea	4	4	6	12	13	17	+13
China	5	7	19	22	27	32	+27
Switzerland	6	5	9	9	7	7	+1
Singapore	7	6	10	10	11	12	+5
Netherlands	8	8	11	13	10	9	+1
Belgium	9	12	5	8	8	8	−1
Ireland	10	11	12	11	17	19	+9
Taiwan	11	13	13	14	12	13	+2
France	12	10	7	6	6	6	−6
Italy	13	9	4	4	4	4	−9
UK	14	14	8	5	5	5	−9
Austria	15	16	16	17	15	11	+4

Source United Nations Industrial Development Organization Database (UNIDO 2015)

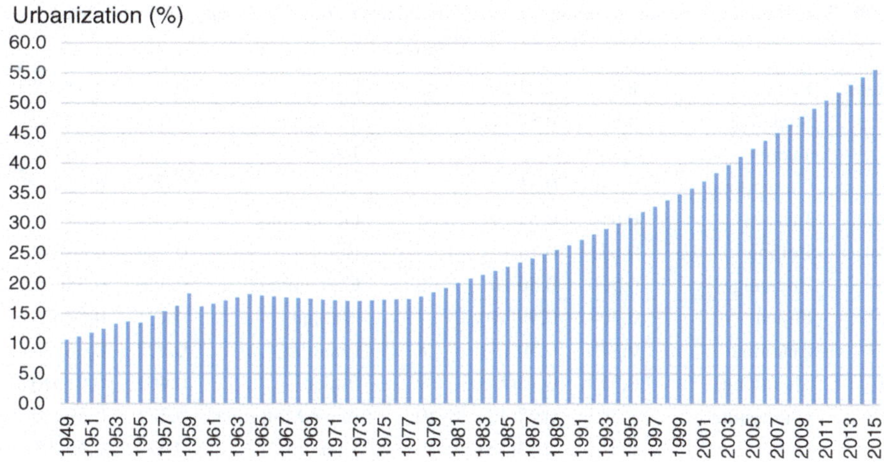

Source: *China Statistical Yearbook 2016* (NBSC 2016).

Fig. 2.2 China's urbanization: 1949–2015. *Source* China Statistical Yearbook 2016 (NBSC 2016)

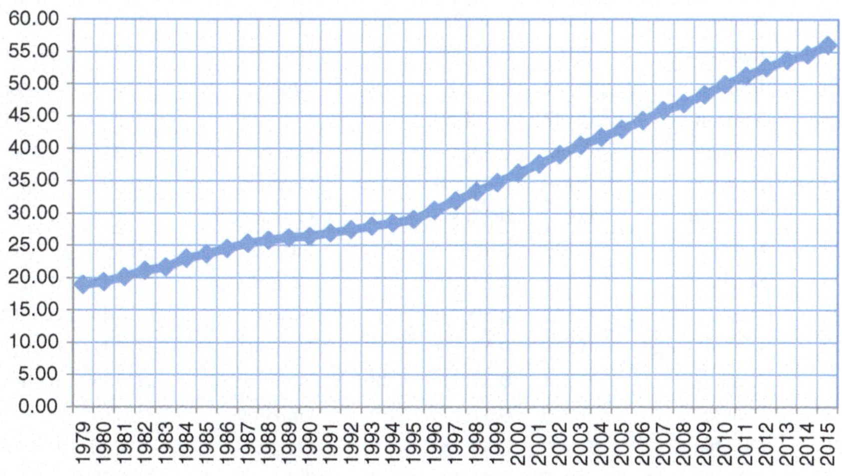

Source: *China Statistical Yearbook 2016* (NBSC 2016).

Fig. 2.3 China's urbanization level (in percentage): 1979–2015. *Source* China Statistical Yearbook 2016 (NBSC 2016)

77.3 million urban residents, accounting for 13.3% of the total population (NBSC 2016). In three decades (1949–1978), the urbanization rate rose only 4.6% points (13.2–17.8%), with an average annual increase of 3.8 million urban people. Most of this modest increase in urban population occurred in the 1950s, when China had rapid industrial development. The period of 38 years (1978–2016) thus saw an

Table 2.4 Industrial competitiveness (*IC*) and urbanization (*U*) by region: 2005 and 2013

2005				2013			
Rank	Region	IC	U (Rank)	Rank	Region	IC	U (Rank)
1	Shanghai	0.942	0.89 (1)	1	Shanghai	0.955	0.90 (1)
2	Tianjin	0.800	0.75 (3)	2	Jiangsu	0.854	0.66 (6)
3	Guangdong	0.680	0.61 (4)	3	Tianjin	0.697	0.82 (3)
4	Jiangsu	0.658	0.51 (9)	4	Guangdong	0.667	0.68 (4)
5	Beijing	0.641	0.84 (2)	5	Beijing	0.569	0.86 (2)
6	Zhejiang	0.500	0.56 (6)	6	Chongqing	0.446	0.58(10)
7	Fujian	0.408	0.49(10)	7	Zhejiang	0.431	0.64 (7)
8	Liaoning	0.379	0.59 (5)	8	Liaoning	0.422	0.66 (5)
9	Shandong	0.313	0.45(14)	9	Fujian	0.401	0.61 (8)
10	Chongqing	0.263	0.45(12)	10	Inner Mongolia	0.381	0.59 (9)
11	Hubei	0.212	0.43(15)	11	Jilin	0.379	0.54(13)
12	Inner Mongolia	0.200	0.47(11)	12	Sichuan	0.367	0.45(24)
13	Hebei	0.195	0.38(19)	13	Hubei	0.339	0.55(12)
14	Ningxia	0.189	0.42(16)	14	Shandong	0.330	0.54(14)
15	Sichuan	0.185	0.33(26)	15	Hebei	0.282	0.48(21)
16	Hunan	0.183	0.37(22)	16	Shaanxi	0.265	0.51(18)
17	Anhui	0.169	0.36(24)	17	Hunan	0.244	0.48(22)
18	Jiangxi	0.163	0.37(23)	18	Jiangxi	0.233	0.49(19)
19	Jilin	0.156	0.53 (8)	19	Anhui	0.232	0.48(23)
20	Yunnan	0.148	0.30(29)	20	Ningxia	0.220	0.52(17)
21	Guangxi	0.146	0.33(25)	21	Henan	0.211	0.44(27)
22	Henan	0.140	0.31(27)	22	Guangxi	0.200	0.45(25)
23	Guizhou	0.137	0.27(30)	23	Hainan	0.196	0.53(15)
24	Hainan	0.133	0.45(13)	24	Shanxi	0.192	0.53(16)
25	Shaanxi	0.128	0.37(20)	25	Heilongjiang	0.185	0.57(11)
26	Gansu	0.123	0.30(28)	26	Gansu	0.144	0.40(29)
27	Heilongjiang	0.119	0.53 (7)	27	Yunnan	0.141	0.40(28)
28	Xinjiang	0.048	0.37(21)	28	Xinjiang	0.138	0.44(26)
29	Shanxi	0.000	0.42(17)	29	Guizhou	0.112	0.38(30)
30	Qinghai	0.000	0.39(18)	30	Qinghai	0.000	0.48(20)
31	Tibet	0.000	0.21(31)	31	Tibet	0.000	0.24(31)
	China	0.408	0.4299		China	0.454	0.5373

Sources Author's calculations based on the data from China Industrial Economy and Statistical Yearbook 2006 and 2014 (NBSC 2006–2014) and China Statistical Yearbook 2006–2014 (NBSC 2006–2014)

increase of 97% points (from 18 to 57%). The urban population increased from 185 million to more than 750 million, an average annual increase of 15 million, nearly four times of the rate of the pre-reform era.

China has successfully guided urban development to promote economic growth so that urbanization can support high growth and rapid transformation of the economy (WB and DRCC 2014). Rapid urbanization allowed people—among them some 260 million migrants—to move from agriculture to more productive activities. In the process, 500 million people were lifted out of poverty, and China managed unprecedented growth that averaged more than 9% a year for three consecutive decades. China's cities, with abundant labor, cheap land, good infrastructure, and competition among local governments to attract industry and investment, have created an environment that has been highly conducive to growth. Growing cities that have become increasingly connected with each other and with the rest of the world have added to productivity growth through agglomeration effects, and China's mega cities now have income levels comparable to some developed countries (Zhang and Song 2003; WB and DRCC 2014). As suggested in Table 2.4, there is an obvious virtual circle between industrialization and urbanization at China's regional level.

The concentration of economic activity in large cities is the most dynamic in the Chinese economy. Cities with a population of 2.5 million or more generate 95% of China's urban exports, and the GDP of top five cities (Beijing, Guangzhou, Shanghai, Shenzhen, and Tianjin) amounted to $1 trillion in 2010—comparable in size to Korea's economy (WB and DRCC 2014). Incomes in these cities have climbed swiftly as well: between 2000 and 2010, per capita GDP rose from 35,000 yuan (Chinese currency) to 82,000 yuan in Shenzhen and from 32,000 to 66,000 yuan in Shanghai. Agglomeration effects became more important for China as the economy shifted increasingly to services. In China's richer cities, services will become more important as a share of GDP. Agglomeration effects play an even more important role in services than in industry. Close proximity also stimulates the growth of other specialized services such as legal, software, data processing, advertising, and management consulting firms. Urban density allows frequent face-to-face contact among employees, entrepreneurs, and financiers—contact that in turn promotes innovation and productivity.

2.5 Concluding Remarks

China's urbanization over the period of 1978–2016 has been unprecedented in scale: more than 550 million migrants have moved to cities from rural areas due to rapid industrialization, supporting the country's rapid economic growth and development progress. Despite the enormity of this transition, China has avoided some of the ills often associated with urbanization, particularly large-scale urban poverty and unemployment. While there are many studies on China's urban development, several issues of the urbanization-industrialization link have been remained on debate. Does China's industrialization lead to its urbanization? Is China under- or over-urbanized? How does China guide urbanization to enhance its economic growth?

Based on a solid theoretical framework and comprehensive international evidences, this chapter intends to offer explanations to the questions. The main conclusions can be summarized as follows. (a) While international experiences suggest that urbanization could go with or without industrialization, China follows the standard approach of urbanization led by industrialization. (b) In the last decades starting 1978, China's rapid urbanization is largely caused by its successful industrialization. (c) The fact that China's urbanization is lower than that of the world average at different income level is not a symbol of under-urbanization in China but over-urbanization in many developing countries. (d) China managed well the speed of urbanization in order to avoid some of the common ills of urbanization that occurred in other developing countries, such as urban poverty, unemployment, and squalor. (e) China seems to have successfully guided urbanization to promote economic growth through agglomeration effects and consumption effects. This is vital for China's growth model transformation in the sense that Chin has to shift its exported-oriented to more domestic-consumption oriented economy, especially facing the anti-globalization challenge from the new president of United State in 2017.

References

Alvarez-Cuadrado, F., and M. Poschke. 2011. Structural change out of agriculture: Labor push versus labor pull. *American Economic Journal: Macroeconomics* 3 (3): 127–158.

Brückner, M. 2012. Economic growth, size of the agricultural sector, and urbanization in Africa. *Journal of Urban Economics* 71 (1): 26–36.

Davis, J.C., and J.V. Henderson. 2003. Evidence on the political economy of the urbanization process. *Journal of Urban Economics* 53 (1): 98–125.

Duranton, G. 2008. Viewpoint: From cities to productivity and growth in developing countries. *Canadian Journal of Economics* 41 (3): 689–736.

Fay, M., and C. Opal. 2000. Urbanization without growth: A not-so-uncommon phenomenon. World Bank Policy Research Working Paper Series No. 2412.

Glaeser, E., J. Kolko, and A. Saiz. 2001. Consumer city. *Journal of Economic Geography* 1 (1): 27–50.

Glaeser, E.L. 2013. A world of cities: The causes and consequences of urbanization in poorer countries. National Bureau of Economic Research (NBER) Working Papers 19745.

Glaeser, E.L., and J.D. Gottlieb. 2009. Wealth of cities: Agglomeration economies and spatial equilibrium in the United States. *Journal of Economic Literature* 47 (4): 983–1028.

Glaeser, E.L., H.D. Kallal, J.A. Scheinkman, and A. Shleifer. 1992. Growth in cities. *Journal of Political Economy* 100 (6): 1126–1152.

Gollin, D., R. Jedwab, and D. Vollrath. 2016. Urbanization with and without industrialization. *Journal of Economic Growth* 21 (1): 35–70.

Hamer, A.M., and J.F. Linn. 1987. Urbanization in the developing world: patterns, issues, and policy. In *Handbook of regional and urban economics*, vol. II, ed. E.S. Mills. Amsterdam: Elsevier-North Holland.

Henderson, J.V. 2003. The urbanization process and economic growth: The so-what question. *Journal of Economic Growth* 8 (1): 47–71.

Henderson, J.V. 2010. Cities and development. *Journal of Regional Science* 50 (1): 515–540.

Lucas, R.E. 2004. Life earnings and rural-urban migration. *Journal of Political Economy* 112 (1): 29–59.
Michaels, G., F. Rauch, and S.J. Redding. 2012. Urbanization and structural transformation. *The Quarterly Journal of Economics* 127 (2): 535–586.
National Bureau of Statistical of China (NBSC). 2014. *China statistical yearbook 2004–2012*. Beijing, China: China Statistics Press.
National Bureau of Statistical of China (NBSC). 2016. *China industrial economy and statistical yearbook 2004-2012*. Beijing, China: China Statistics Press.
National Bureau of Statistical of China (NBSC). 2006–2014. *China industrial economy and statistical yearbook 2004–2012*. Beijing, China: China Statistics Press.
National Bureau of Statistical of China (NBSC). 2006–2014. *China statistical yearbook 2004–2012*. Beijing, China: China Statistics Press.
Song, S., and K.H. Zhang. 2002. Urbanization and city-size distribution in China. *Urban Studies* 39 (12): 2317–2327.
United Nations (UN). 2011. *World urbanization prospects: The 2011 revision*. New York: United Nations, Department of Economic and Social Affairs.
United Nations Industrial Development Organization (UNIDO). 2002. *Industrial development report 2002/2003*. New York: United Nations.
UNIDO. 2013. *Industrial competitiveness of nation: Looking back, forging ahead*. Vienna: United Nations.
UNIDO. 2015. *UNIDO database*. New York: United Nations.
Williamson, J.G. 1988. Migration and urbanization. In *Handbook of development economics*, vol. I, ed. H. Chenery, and T.N. Srinivasan. Amsterdam: Elsevier-North Holland.
World Bank. 2016. *World bank development indicator 2016*. Washington DC: World Bank.
World Bank. 2017. *WDI Database*. Washington DC: World Bank.
World Bank and Development Research Center of China (WB and DRCC). 2014. *Urban China: Toward efficient, inclusive, and sustainable urbanization*. Washington DC: World Bank.
Xie, J., and K.H. Zhang. 2004. Urban population in the reform era. In *Urban transformation in China*, eds. Chen, A., G.G. Liu, and Zhang, K.H. New York: Ashgate, 83–96.
Zhang, K.H. 2002. What explains China's rising urbanization in the reform era? *Urban Studies* 39: 2301–2315.
Zhang, K.H., and S. Song. 2003. Rural-urban migration and urbanization in China: Evidence from time-series and cross-section analysis. *China Economic Review* 13 (4): 386–400.
Zhang, K.H. 2010. How does globalization affect industrial competitiveness? *Contemporary Economic Policy* 28 (4): 502–510.
Zhang, K.H. 2015a. Macro- and micro-drivers of manufacturing performance of China. *The Chinese Economy* 48 (6): 399–412.
Zhang, K. H. (2015b). China's manufacturing performance and industrial competitiveness: International comparison and policy reflection. In *China's domestic transformation in a global context*, eds. Song, L., R. Garmaut, Fang, C., and L. Johnston, Canberra, Australia: Australian National University Press, 297–314.

Chapter 3
Urban Real Estate Tax Reforms in China

Huiyu Cui

Abstract As a result of urban development and an imperfect fiscal revenue system of local government, a real estate tax reform has been initiated. It is also accompanied by a rapid increase in real estate prices and adjustment of imbalanced wealth distribution. This paper analyzes the current situation in China and other typical foreign countries in terms of the real estate tax system, the real estate tax burden level and relating real estate charges. It then comes up with urgent problems to be resolved in order to carry forward real estate tax reform according to the overall situation and trend of China's real estate practice.

Keywords Real-estate tax · Taxation system · International comparison

Real estate tax reform started with the formation and development of the property tax. "Reforming urban construction tax and fee, levying property tax when it is proper, and offsetting relative charges at the same time" was put forward at the Third Plenary Session of the Sixteenth Chinese Communist Party (CPC) Central Committee in 2003. It was the first time a property tax was brought up. In October 2005, a property tax was officially included in the "11th Five-year Plan". The ministry of finance and the state administration of taxation have successively approved Beijing, Jiangsu, Shenzhen, Chongqing, Liaoning and Ningxia as pilots to levy real estate tax since 2003. In 2007, Henan (Puyang and Jiaozuo), Anhui (Wuhu and Maanshan), Fujian (Longhai and Shaxian) and Dalian were added to the pilots. In 2010, reforming real estate tax was proposed in "the 12th Five-year Plan," and property tax started to gradually fade away. On January 28, 2011, Chongqing and Shanghai began to reform real estate tax as pilot areas. However, a real estate

This article only discusses the urban real estate tax reform, not including the rural collective real estate.

H. Cui (✉)
Dongbei University of Finance & Economics, Dalian, China
e-mail: huiyucui@sina.com

Z. Tang (ed.), *China's Urbanization and Socioeconomic Impact*,
DOI 10.1007/978-981-10-4831-9_3

tax has still not been implemented country-wide. What key obstacles China's real estate tax reform faces are of great value and should be considered and discussed.

3.1 Background of the Real Estate Tax Reform in China

3.1.1 Urbanization and Prosperity of Real Estate Market

Urbanization is marked by constant gathering of populations in towns. It is an inevitable stage for any country during industrialization. Urbanization serves as an important engine for China's developing economy as it not only increases effective investment but also stimulates consumption. The urbanization rate of China has been continuously increasing since the end of last century. According to the research report "China in 2030" published by World Bank and Development Research Center of the State Council (DRC), the urbanization rate of China is expected to reach 70% in 2030, 20% higher than that of 2010. The acceleration of urbanization will consequently expand demand for urban commercial residential buildings. Accordingly, it will raise housing prices. In 2008, the price of commodity housing was ¥3800/m^2 on average in China. However, it jumped to ¥4681/m^2 one year later, increased by 23.2% in only one year, a trend maintained in 2010 and 2011. To some extent, urbanization brings up housing prices. But housing prices will have an adverse effect on urbanization when it goes beyond a certain extent. The process of urbanization is hampered due to the excessive-priced houses with high growth rate (Table 3.1).

3.1.2 Further Enlargement of Income Distribution Disparity

In recent years, Chinese residents' income has increased rapidly. Meanwhile, the disparity between residents' income also increased rapidly, influencing the stability and development of economic society. Take Anhui province for example, its ratio of rural–urban residents' income in 2000 was 1:2.74 and this ratio increased to 1:2.99 in 2010. The ratio of low income households to high income households in town in 2000 was 5:1 and 6.35:1 in 2010. The ratio of high industry revenue to low industry revenue in 2000 was 2.1:1 and turned to 9.9:1 in 2010. The main reason why residents' income distribution disparity grows so rapidly is because of the fallaciously designed property rights system. And it is also relevant to the rapid increase of housing prices. With housing prices increasing so rapidly, on the one hand, property income from investing real estate is doubled. But on the other hand, there is no effective tax to adjust property income. This leads to the Matthew Effect, where the poor become poorer while the rich become richer, which increases residents' income distribution disparity. Imposing a real estate tax is beneficial for adjusting residents' property income and eventually narrowing the income gap.

Table 3.1 Data sheets for urbanization and real estate industry

Year	Urbanization rate (%)	Average selling price of commodity housing (¥/m^2)	Real estate investment (100 million)	Land purchased by real estate developers (10,000 m^2)
1998	33.35	2063	3614	10,109
1999	34.78	2053	4103	11,959
2000	36.22	2112	4984	16,905
2001	37.66	2170	6344	23,409
2002	39.09	2250	7791	31,357
2003	40.53	2359	10,154	35,696
2004	41.76	2778	13,158	39,785
2005	42.00	3168	15,909	38,254
2006	44.34	3367	19,423	36,574
2007	45.89	3864	25,289	40,246
2008	46.99	3800	31,203	39,353
2009	48.34	4681	36,241	31,909
2010	49.95	5032	48,259	39,953
2011	51.27	5357	61,797	44,327
2012	52.57	5791	71,804	35,667
2013	53.7	6237	86,013	38,814

Source *China Statistical Yearbook* from 1999 to 2014 and *China Real Estate Statistical Yearbook* from 1999 to 2014

3.1.3 Defective Local Government Tax System

The financial capacity of multilevel governments has been moving upward since the reform of tax distribution systems in 1994. Although revenue of local governments exceeded that of the central government in 2011 for the first time, local governments still lack a stable and continuous tax system with the change from business tax to value-added tax and the expansion of consumption tax. Local government, especially government at the county level, has to function depending on the transfer payments from higher level government. Most of their fiscal expenditures relying on transfer payments will, in turn, lower local governments' financing positivity. Take Anhui province for example, its fiscal revenue was ¥263.28 billion and local fiscal revenue was ¥146.34 billion in 2011. Local fiscal revenue was only about half of this province's fiscal revenue. The report of the 18th National Congress of the Communist Party has proposed to speed up reforming the fiscal and taxation system and the building of a local tax system. To achieve this objective, the tax sharing system should be improved to make a clear division and thorough arrangement between central and local taxation rights. With the acceleration of industrialization and urbanization, scale of real estate in city and county level has been increasing greatly. Imposing real estate tax might become a stable source for local fiscal revenue in the long run, which is beneficial for the formation of local tax system.

3.2 Current Situation of Real Estate Tax in China

3.2.1 The Constitution of China's Current Real Estate Tax System

A real estate tax is the taxing of real estate objects. It is a property tax collected from the owner or the actual user of the real estate based on the properties' market value, residual value or rental income, etc. It has the following features: difficulty of hiding tax base, difficulty of transferring tax bearing, stability of tax income and second allocation to the taxpayer's income.

The first time that China imposed real estate tax was in 1986, but it only collected tax from commercial housing in urban, industrial or mining areas. The tax rate was 1.2% of the housing residual value or 12% of the housing rental income. But today, it just represents one tax category among the real estate tax system, which contains a dozen of tax categories (Fig. 3.1).

From the process of tax collection, enterprises that get land from local government must pay a deed tax, urban land use tax and farm land occupation tax in the real estate procurement process. During the process of a real estate transaction, the seller will pay six related taxes, including business tax, city construction and maintenance tax, education surcharge, income tax, land appreciation tax and stamp tax. The purchaser will pay two taxes, deed tax and stamp tax. In the real estate tenure process, two taxes are set up for owner-occupied behavior of the housing, those are real estate tax and urban and rural land use tax; for real estate leaseholder behavior, it involves business tax, city construction and maintenance tax, educational surcharge, stamp tax, income tax, house property tax and urban and rural land use tax. All these above constitute a relatively complete real estate tax system (Table 3.2).

From the categories of tax, real estate tax can be classified into several types, such as real estate property tax, real estate commodity tax, real estate income tax

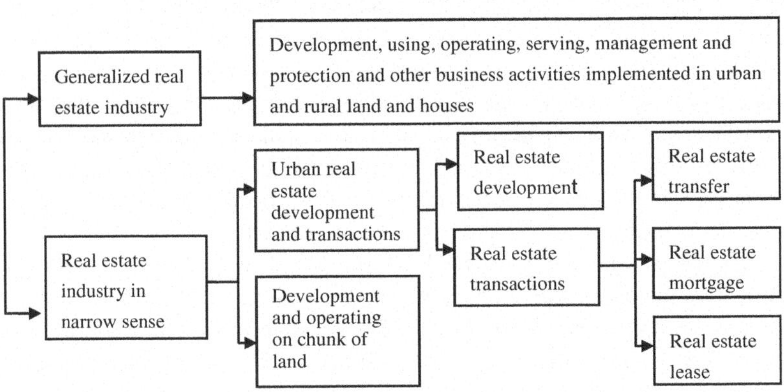

Fig. 3.1 The scope of real estate industry

Table 3.2 The distribution of real estate tax in collection process

Land procurement process	The deed tax, the urban land use tax and the farm land occupation tax
Real estate transaction process	The sellers: business tax, city construction and maintenance tax, education surcharge, enterprise income tax (personal income tax), land appreciation tax, stamp tax
	The purchaser: deed tax and stamp tax
Real estate tenure process	Real estate tax and the urban land use tax
Real estate lease process	Business tax city construction and maintenance tax, education surcharge, enterprise income tax (personal income tax), real estate tax and urban land use tax

Source Related tax laws of the PRC

and other taxes. The real estate property tax contains a property tax, urban and rural land use tax and farm land occupation tax. Real estate commodity tax incorporates a business tax, city construction and maintenance tax and education surcharge. Real estate income tax involves a land appreciation tax, business income tax and individual income tax. Other taxes include deed taxes and stamp taxes (Li 2011) (Table 3.3).

From the correlation between real estate and tax categories, there are five distinctive tax categories directly related to real estate: house property tax, urban land use tax, farm land occupation tax, deed tax and land appreciation tax. Among them, the deed tax itself is relatively independent from the others and it creates a system of its own.

3.2.2 *The Scale of Real Estate Taxes in China*

The article uses house property tax, urban land use tax and land appreciation tax to illustrate the scale of real estate related taxes in China.

Table 3.4 and Fig. 3.2 show that although the ratio of real estate related taxes in local tax system has been rising in the past few years, the proportion is comparatively small, and it only reached 12.24% in 2013.

3.2.3 *The Non-tax Revenue Related to Real Estate*

Land rents and land charges are very important factors in real estate tax research. Land rent represents government's ownership of the land; it is a financial compensation the government collects in the form of land transfer fees or rental, and the purpose is to exploit the countries' land resources. At the same time, as the public

Table 3.3 Related information of real estate tax of China

Classifications	Tax categories	Year of publication	The publish department	The legal norm	The file No.
Real estate property tax	Real estate tax	Sep 15. 1986	The State Council	Interim Regulations of the PRC on Real Estate Tax	The State Council Decree [1986] No. 90
	Urban land use tax	Dec 31. 2006	The State Council	Interim Regulation of the PRC on Urban Land Use Tax	The State Council Decree [2006] No. 483
	Farm land occupation tax	Dec 1. 2007	The State Council	Interim Regulation of the PRC on Farm Land Occupation Tax	The State Council Decree No. 5ll
Real estate commodity tax	Business tax	Nov 10. 2008	The State Council	Interim Regulation of the PRC on Business Tax	The State Council Decree No. 540
	City construction and maintenance tax	Feb 8. 1985	The State Council	Interim Regulation of the PRC on City Construction and Maintenance Tax	The State Council Decree [1985] No. 19
	Education surcharge	Apr 28. 1986	The State Council	Interim Regulation of Education Surcharge Collection	The State Council Decree [1986] No. 50
Real estate income tax	Land appreciation tax	Dec 13. 1993	The State Council	Interim Regulation of the PRC on Land Appreciation Tax	The State Council Decree [1993] No. 138
	Enterprise income tax	Mar 16. 2007	The National People's Congress	The Law of the People's Republic of China on Enterprise Income Tax	Presidential Decree No. 63
	Personal income tax	Dec 29. 2007	The National People's Congress	The Law of the People's Republic of China on Personal Income Tax	Presidential Decree No. 85
Other taxes	Deed tax	Jul 7. 1997	The State Council	Interim Regulation of the PRC on Deed Tax	The State Council Decree No. 224
	Stamp tax	Aug 6.1988	The State Council	Interim Regulation of the PRC on Stamp Tax	The State Council Decree No. ll

Table 3.4 The scale of related taxes of real estate tax in China

Year	Real estate tax	Urban land use tax	Land appreciation	Total	The total local tax revenue	Proportion of local tax revenue (%)
1999	183.36	59.06	6.81	249.23	4934.93	5.05
2000	209.38	64.76	8.39	282.53	5688.86	4.97
2001	228.42	66.15	10.33	304.9	6962.76	4.38
2002	282.38	76.83	20.51	379.72	7406.16	5.13
2003	323.86	91.57	37.28	452.71	8413.27	5.38
2004	366.32	106.23	75.04	547.59	9999.59	5.48
2005	435.96	137.34	140.31	713.61	12,726.73	5.61
2006	514.85	176.81	231.47	923.13	15,233.58	6.06
2007	575.46	385.48	403.1	1364.04	19,252.12	7.09
2008	680.34	816.9	537.43	2034.67	23,255.11	8.75
2009	803.66	920.98	719.56	2444.2	26,157.44	9.34
2010	894.07	1004.01	1278.29	3176.37	32,701.49	9.71
2011	1102.39	1222.26	2062.61	4387.26	41,106.74	10.67
2012	1372.49	1541.71	2719.06	5633.26	47,319.08	11.90
2013	1581.50	1718.77	3293.91	6594.18	53,890.88	12.24

Units: 100 million/%
Source China Statistical Yearbook from 2000 to 2014

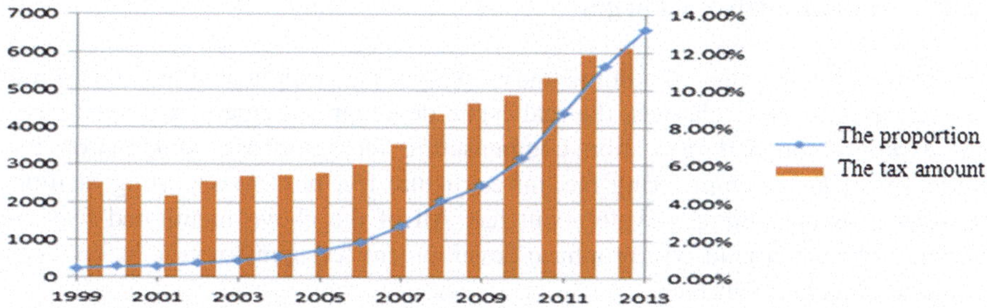

Fig. 3.2 The scale of relate taxes of real estate tax

administrator, government collects real estate related charges to make up for the cost of the quasi-public goods and services.

3.2.3.1 Land Transfer Fees

The main form of land rent is land transfer fees. Land transfer fees have been increasing in the past few years and have become a major source of raising construction funds for local governments.

In 2001, the income from land transfer fees in China was ¥780.3 billion, accounting for 13.3% of local fiscal revenue. But in 2013, this number rose to

Table 3.5 The level of land transfer fees in China

Year	Land transfer fees (100 million yuan)	Accounting for local fiscal revenue (%)
2001	7803	13.30
2002	8515	16.97
2003	9849	20.86
2004	5894	49.56
2005	5505	36.45
2006	7677	41.94
2007	12,764	54.15
2008	9737	33.98
2009	15,910	48.79
2010	28,197	69.43
2011	31,140	59.26
2012	26,652	43.64
2013	39,073	56.62

nearly ¥4000 billion, and it constituted more than half of local governments' fiscal revenue. And in some local governments the ratio even reached 60–70%, becoming the genuine "Land Finance." (Table 3.5).

3.2.3.2 Administrative Charges

The items and procedures of administrative charges are complicated in China. From the categories of these charges, the real estate development enterprises must pay a land expropriation and relocation compensation fee, prophase construction fee, building installation engineering fee, infrastructure fee, public supporting facilities fee as well as an indirect development fee. All of the above mentioned fees are distributed between land cost,prophase development fees,construction safety costs and direct development fees.

For example, land cost mainly comes from two aspects: the land acquisition fee and land development cost. The land acquisition fee includes land transfer fee, purchase fee, property registration fee, development compensation fee, infrastructure supporting fee, etc. Land development cost includes a relocation compensation fee, relocation demolition fee, infrastructure construction fee, land expropriation fee, relocation consultation fee and sunshine occlusion compensation fee, etc. During the early stage of development, the real estate administrative charges include a feasibility study fee, designation fee, application fee, survey fee, bidding management fee and a construction drawing examination fee, etc. Regarding construction safety cost, the real estate administrative charges include prophase engineering, geotechnical engineering, fundamental engineering, civil engineering for sale, conventional electrical engineering for sale, supporting facilities, special electromechanical engineering, outdoor construction and indoor intensive decoration, etc. In terms of direct development costs, the real estate administrative charges contain an engineering supervision fee, engineering insurance fee, engineering water and electricity fee, bidding agency fee, cost consultation fee and a construction disturbance fee (Figs. 3.3, 3.4, 3.5 and 3.6).

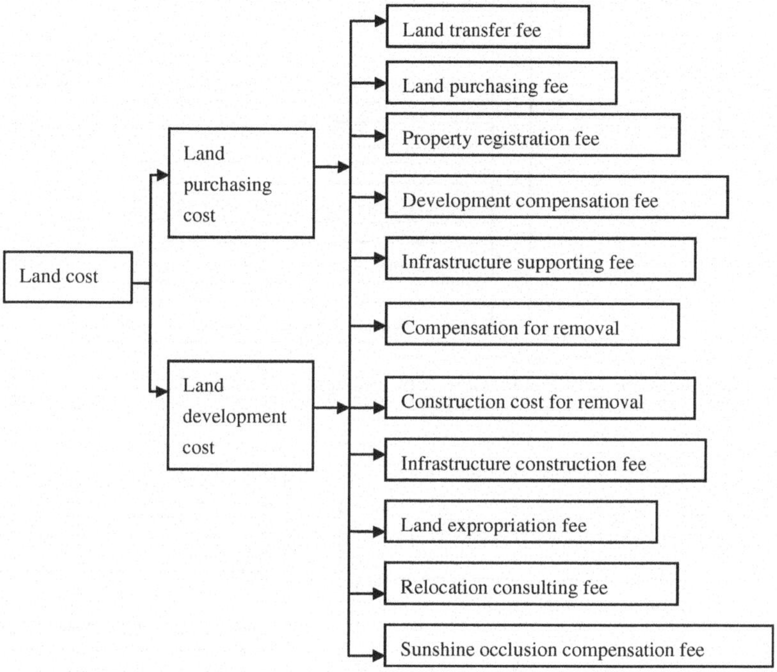

Fig. 3.3 The process of real estate charge: Land cost

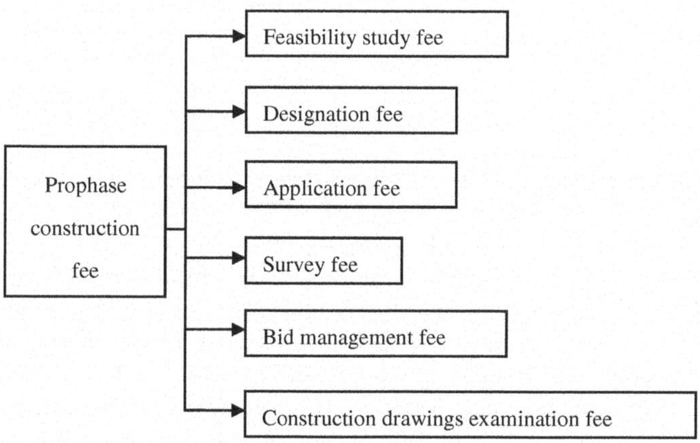

Fig. 3.4 The process of real estate charge: Prophase construction fee

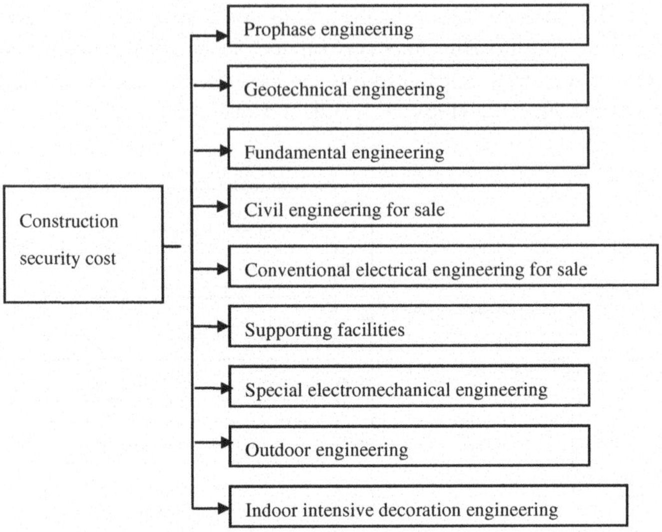

Fig. 3.5 The process of real estate charge: Construction security cost

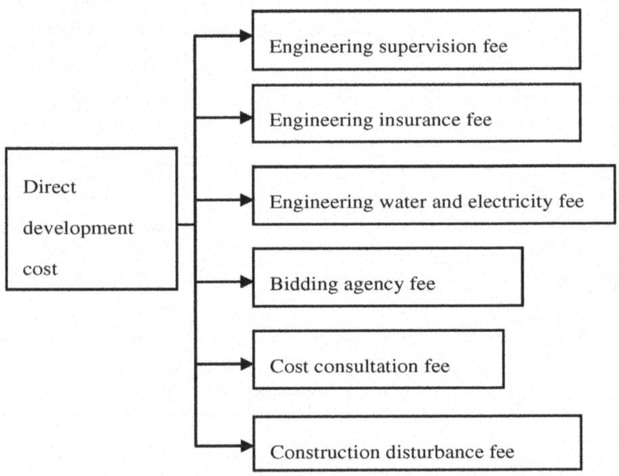

Fig. 3.6 The process of real estate charge: Direct development cost

For example, in Beijing, there are more than 100 types of taxes and fees in the entire development and sales process, 12 of which belong to real taxes; others are all in form of fees. With regards to charging items, since they are determined by local government and departments, it varies greatly from region to region, leading to inconsistency in charging titles, types and criteria. This has caused overlap charging in most cases. From the charging ratios, real estate charges account for 30–50% of housing price (including the land price), which is 35% of sales revenue, and 75% of operation fees and expenses. It is obvious that the non-standard real estate charging system has significant negative effects on housing price, resulting in bigger proportion of fees in housing price (Table 3.6).

Table 3.6 Real estate charging items and standards

Charging items	Charging standards
public utility construction fee	100 ¥/m^2 green land
Running water construction fee	12 ¥/m^2
Sewage treatment fee	10 ¥/m^2
Heating plant construction fee	30 ¥/m^2
Gas construction fee	29 ¥/m^2
Green construction fee	8 ¥/m^2
Park construction fee	40 ¥/m^2 green land
Green compensation fee	240 ¥/m^2 green land
Street lamp maintenance fee	8 ¥/m^2
Sanitation facilities fee	1 ¥/m^2
Power consumption fee	40 ¥/m^2

3.2.4 The Composition of Housing Price

From the composition of housing prices, the overall tax level is relatively low in China. Generally, the current housing price consists of the following: (1) Land development fees. Land development fees include land acquisition compensation, relocation allowance, land transaction fees, “seven-provided and one leveled” fees and exploration and design fees, etc., which makes up 20–25% of the housing price. (2) Installation costs. Installation costs include the installation of the building, the attached work and outdoor projects. This accounts for 30–50% of the housing price. (3) Public utility. Public utility accounts for 15–25% of the housing price. (4) Related taxes and fees. Those include environmental fees, city construction and maintenance fees, etc., which compose 10–15% of the housing price. (5) The profit of real estate enterprises. The profit usually accounts for 25–30% of the housing price (Fig. 3.7).

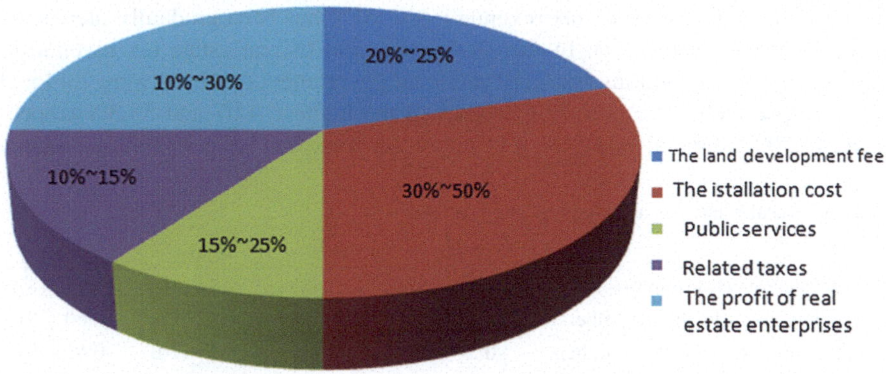

Fig. 3.7 Composition of the housing price

3.3 Experience of Foreign Real Estate Tax System

Currently, developed countries and regions have relatively mature systems of levying real estate taxes, which plays an important role in regulating their economies, ensuring healthy development of the real estate market and meeting the basic housing needs of residents. Some differences exist in taxation modes, tax levying and the design of real estate tax elements among countries with different levels of economic development and real estate market conditions. Nevertheless, there are still many common features from a general point of view.

3.3.1 The Purpose of Levying Real Estate Tax

The purpose of levying a real estate tax is to narrow the gap between the rich and the poor, adjust social conflicts, enhance social justice and curb the waste of land resources rather than curbing the rising house prices (Wang 2013). In addition, real estate tax revenue is mostly used to provide public services and ensure social welfare. In America, 70% of real estate tax revenue is used to improve regional teaching, public security and living environments (Ren 2015). In some states, the proportion of real estate tax put into the school district even reaches 65%. As school districts have no other rights to impose tax, their spending is mainly dependent on property tax revenue. In Britain, real estate tax revenue is used to support education and local infrastructure construction.

3.3.2 Real Estate Tax Is One of the Main Sources of Local Government Fiscal Revenue

The proportion of real estate tax revenue in the GDP has been gradually increasing since 1970s (see Table 3.7). In the 1990s, the ratio of real estate tax revenue in OECD countries accounting for GDP and local government revenues were 1.44 and 17.9% respectively. The ratio in Canada was the highest, 4.07 and 53.3% respectively. In 2007, the real estate tax revenue of America was $376.95 billion in total,

Table 3.7 Real estate tax and its proportion in GDP

	1970s	1980s	1990s	2000s
OECD countries (%) (numbers)	1.24 (16)	1.31 (18)	1.44 (16)	2.12 (18)
Developing countries (%) (numbers)	0.42 (20)	0.36 (27)	0.42 (23)	0.60 (29)
Countries in transition (%) (numbers)	0.34 (1)	0.59 (4)	0.54 (20)	0.68 (18)
Total countries (%) (numbers)	0.77 (37)	0.59 (49)	0.75 (59)	1.04 (25)

Source The number in 2000 is calculated by the average of the number in 2001 and the number in 2002

Table 3.8 Revenues of multilevel governments in America and the proportion of the real estate tax (2007)

	Total	Country	City	Town	Special district	School district
Local fiscal revenue	8404.3	2189.8	2865.5	337.7	916.4	2094.9
Local tax revenue	5258.2	1307.1	1765	267.9	228.8	1689.4
Property tax	3769.5	902.8	851.6	242.3	151.9	1620.9
Property tax in local fiscal revenue (%)	44.90	41.20	29.70	71.80	16.60	77.40
Property tax in local tax revenue (%)	71.70	69.10	48.20	90.40	66.40	95.90

Units: 100 million dollars
Source http://www.census.gov/govs/estimate/historical-data-2007.html

accounting for 44.9% of local fiscal revenue and 71.7% of tax revenue (Liu 2011a, b). The level has been maintained in the long run (Table 3.8).

On the other hand, the proportion of total tax revenue in China, including the current real estate tax, urban land use tax and land appreciation tax, accounts for merely 10% of local government revenue in recent years. Although Shanghai and Chongqing carried out reform of the real estate tax in 2011, the real estate tax revenue increment in both cities is not remarkable. According to the data of 2013, only 8.45% of local tax revenue came from these three taxes in Shanghai, and 14.05% in Chongqing, which is only slightly higher.

3.3.3 *Tax Collection*

In terms of tax collection, real estate tax involves the acquisition, holding and transfer of real estate. It basically covers all aspects of the real estate industry and the whole process of real estate transaction. In the process of real estate transaction, a capital gains tax, business tax, registration tax and stamp tax are imposed in Japan. Additionally, there are also succession tax and gift tax in real estate acquisition (Guo et al. 2005). In the United States, corresponding taxes are also designed in acquisition, holding and transfer of real estate (Table 3.9).

3.3.4 *Taxation System Design*

In terms of taxation system design, tax is imposed on all kinds of housing property based on the evaluation of real estate market value or rent. According to different values and purposes of real estate, a differential tax rate is implemented to make the tax reflect market fluctuation and the function of income adjustment. Real estate tax reduction or withdrawal is applied to public interest organizations and poverty groups. In United States, the nature of real estate fees is service oriented, thus there

Table 3.9 Property taxes in typical countries

Countries	Procurement process	Transaction process	Tenure process
America	Inheritance tax and gift tax	Income tax Real estate income tax	General property
England	Real estate property tax inheritance tax and gift tax	Income tax Capital gains tax	Business buildings tax
Japan	Real estate Procurement tax Registration license fees Stamp tax	Inheritance tax and gift tax Income tax	Fixed assets tax city planning tax Special land tenure taxes

are only a few types of fees (Bai 2009). Administrative fees are generally divided into a stipulated fee and special assessment fee. The stipulated fee is equal to the housing property registration fee in China whose principle is cost charging. The special assessment fee is equal to the supporting facility fee in China whose principle is special compensation. Land tax is mostly applied to foreign real estate. During any stage of social reproduction, the taxes and fees have only a few types with small amount, accounting for 1–2% of real estate value generally. Even so, many western countries put it into the local government budget and determine the direction and scope of usage. The stipulated fee not included in the local government budget is also assigned specific purposes.

3.3.5 Tax Supporting Facilities

Many countries possess a computer evaluation system (CAMA) combined with a geographic information system to evaluate real estate or establish property registration system regularly (Liu 2011a, b). Most countries have developed a standardized, rigorous, feasible real estate tax law system, ensuring that there are laws to abide by in levying real estate tax.

3.4 Prospects of Propelling the Reform of Urban Real Estate Tax in China

3.4.1 Clarify the Goal of Real Estate Tax Imposition

Under the background of the economic expansion and overheated real estate investment, the Shanghai and Chongqing real estate tax pilot was carried out. As such, the tax imposition target is set to regulate the real estate market, curb the blind investment and speculation and slow down the soar of housing prices. This causes public misunderstanding of the real estate tax as an effective method to push down housing prices. Real estate tax is even considered to be "the last straw of house price" in some regions. This is a distortion overemphasizing the policy function of the real estate tax and overlooks its capability of organizing fiscal revenue, adjusting social wealth distribution and enhancing society stabilization. It additionally confuses the role and function of government and market in the allocation and controlling of real estate resources.

There are three negative impacts of this distortion: (1) Obliterating the basic functions of the real estate tax, such as organizing fiscal revenue and income redistribution. (2) Provoking a backlash of the vested interests and increasing the difficulty of imposing a real estate tax nationally. (3) Weakening far-reaching policy measures into short-term policy tools.

3.4.2 *Clarify the Ownership of Real Estate Tax Rights*

Real estate tax belongs to local taxes in foreign countries, but there is no clear law to clarify real estate taxes as a local tax in China. Due to the public ownership of land and local government's lack of tax legislation power, tax-related legislative issues have become a serious problem. Overall arrangements are needed to clarify which level of government the real estate income belongs to. If regional differences are not taken into account, and the central government unifies real estate tax standards throughout the country, it will certainly cause "guillotine cutting problem," which not only makes it difficult to implement the economic and social adjustment function of the real estate tax, but also further exacerbates the regional economic gap, eventually leading to social instability. But if the real estate levying power is totally delegated to local government, problems can also occur in terms of chaotic tax levying and rent seeking, breeding corruption and jeopardizing social security. If the use of real estate tax revenues directly belongs to the central government, it will eliminate the enthusiasm of local government. On the contrary, local government has the potential to abuse tax rights and breed corruption. Thus, it is vital to seriously consider the ownership of real estate tax rights.

3.4.3 *The Problems in Designing Real Estate Tax System*

There are three major elements in this perspective.

The first is how to determine the tax base. Further development of real estate tax reform will make individual housing taxable. However, a huge negative influence on daily life of residents can occur if the reform does not consider the financial ability of tax payers and include all real estates into the incidence of taxation. In the Shanghai and Chongqing real estate tax pilots, the taxed object is only the incremental housing and the housing stock is excluded. This practice, on the one hand, leads to narrowing the scope of the real estate tax, weakening the effectiveness of the tax in practice. It is increasingly difficult for the real estate tax to become the major tax of local government taxes and is harder to generate adequate fiscal revenue for indemnificatory housing construction. On the other hand, contrary to the legal principle of fairness, this practice makes tax different by artificially dividing incremental housing and housing stock. It is very likely to cause chaos in real estate market by exempting housing stock holders (especially investment speculators) from real estate taxes.

Secondly, the determination of tax rates is important. In the Shanghai and Chongqing real estate tax pilots, tax rates are set at different levels with housing prices as the standard, and tax rates are lower than the current real estate tax rates. But it is still likely to cause tax evasion and increase collection and administrative costs. In addition, both two pilot cities follow a taxation system based on progressive rates, and the effectiveness of its function to regulate income distribution is still uncertain. Clearly, this tax rate has limited capability to rein real estate investment speculation when housing prices are still going up. Not to mention adjusting income distribution and alleviating gap between the rich and the poor. However, if tax rates are set too high, it will not only increase the burden of real estate owners, but also negatively affect the development of real estate and related industries.

Lastly, the taxation base is also a vital part in the tax system. In the Shanghai and Chongqing pilots, levying tax is based on a certain percentage of the housing market value. Under this policy, many tenants living in prime locations with high-market-value houses have to pay higher taxes when their income remains relatively low. It can be seen that this standard is unfair as a taxation base. Furthermore, it is to be discussed whether to include land price when calculating real estate values. Further discussion is needed on how to set the threshold and cater to the demand of residents for improvement if the area of house property is used as taxation base. If the number of house properties is used as taxation base, then the principle of calculation has to be determined, such as using the family or individual as calculation unit.

3.4.4 Greater Tax Bearing Due to Increasing Real Estate Tax

At present, China has many types of taxes and fees regarding real estate. For instance, there are more than 60 types of taxes imposed on the transfer process of real estate. Further propelling real estate tax reform will surely increase the tax burden of real estate owners. It is highlighted especially in the existing housing stock where urban land use tax has already been imposed when buyers purchase houses. Thus imposing real estate tax will cause duplicate taxation, resulting in unfair taxes.

Judging from the current situation, personal residences have taken on great infrastructure and public services related taxes in the real estate transaction phase.

These numerous taxes on the transfer of real estate still need a valid cleanup before further reform. If not, to impose a real estate tax in such a case, which greatly increases the tax burden of real estate holders, will inevitably arouse dissatisfaction from all sectors of society and hinder national real estate tax reform.

3.4.5 Problems of Real Estate Tax Collection and Administration

One principle of taxation is simplicity: effective tax is easy to measure and impose. Therefore the collection and administration of real estate tax can be a major problem in further practicing of real estate tax.

Many aspects should be taken into consideration and one is the acquisition of real estate information (Feng 2011). Real estate information integrity is a key factor of whether the real estate tax can be collected. Although The Interim Regulations of Real Estate Registration have been put into effect since March 2015, further advancing real estate registration and building a platform to integrate information are still formidable tasks. Second of all, problems still exist in real estate evaluation. From international experience and effects of real estate tax, taking the periodically estimated value of real estate as a tax base is the direction of reform in China, but there are no effective real estate assessment techniques at the moment. Lastly, the huge workload of real estate tax collection and difficulties in administration also pose problems. China has only a limited number of tax authorities and inspectors, and there is a shortage of capable personnel with the ability of tax collection and administration.

References in Chinese

Bai, Y.F. 2009. Meiguo wuyeshui de shuishouyiuhui jizhi jiqi jingyanjiejian [American relief mechanism of property tax and its inspirations]. *Chongqing shehui kexue* 7: 117–121.

Feng, H.B. 2011. Duochongmubiao zhiyuexia zhongguo de fangchanshui gaige [Property tax reform in China: Multiple policy objectives and constraints]. *Caimao jingji* 16: 24–30.

Guo, W.H., T.Y. Cao, et al. 2005. *Guowai budongchan shuishouzhidu yanjiu [Foreign research on the real estate tax system]*. Beijing: Zhongguo dadi chubanshe.

Li, J. 2011. *Zhongguo fangchanshui tixi yanjiu [Research on the reform of China's real estate tax system]*. Dongbeicaijingdaxue boshilunwen.

Liu, H.Y. 2011a. Fangchanshui gaigede guojijingyan yu qishi [The international experience and implication of the reform of real estate tax]. *Gaige* 2: 84–88.

Liu, R. 2011b. Fangchanshui shuizhi de guojibijiao yu qishi [Real estate tax's international comparison and inspiration]. *Gaige* 3: 145–148.

Ren, Q. 2015. Fangchanshui: meiguoshijian ji jiejian [Real estate taxes: United States practice and reference]. *Caizheng yanjiu* 1: 53–57.

Wang, C.L. 2013. Guojijingyan:fangchanshui meiyou yonglai tiaofangjia de [International experience: Real estate tax is not used to adjust prices] [N]. *Zhongguo jingjidaobao* 2013: 9–26.

Part II
Urbanization and Impact on Regional Development

Chapter 4
Regional Differences in Urbanization: A Case Study of Urban Agglomerations in Northwestern China

Lili Wei, Peng Wang and Jing Zhang

Abstract Since China's economic reform and the open-door policy launched almost 40 years ago, urbanization in China has made remarkable achievements, but at the same time, huge regional differences have emerged. In this chapter, we identify three regions (eastern, central and western areas) in China based on four indicators of urbanization (regional development, urban-rural links, urban spatial distributions and urban function partitions). Then we conduct a case study of the northwestern urban agglomerations as a typical case of urbanization in the Western region. Using the entropy method, we develop a composite index of urbanization based on four subsystems (population, economy, society and land), which measures urbanization levels of five northwestern urban agglomerations during 2005–2014. Using clustering analysis and standard deviation, we analyze the spatial gaps in urban agglomerations and their dynamic evolution. The findings are as follows: (a) There are significant and persistent regional differences in urbanization (both between areas and within areas); (b) Urbanization in northwestern regions is largely influenced by population and land as well as economic and social factors; and (c) Government regional development strategies and urban policies play a critical role in shaping the patterns of regional urbanization in China.

Keywords Urbanization · Regional differences · Urban agglomerations · Comprehensive urban development

L. Wei (✉) · P. Wang · J. Zhang
School of Economics, Lanzhou University, Lanzhou, China
e-mail: weill@lzu.edu.cn

P. Wang
e-mail: wangpeng2014@lzu.edu.cn

J. Zhang
e-mail: jingzhang15@lzu.edu.cn

Z. Tang (ed.), *China's Urbanization and Socioeconomic Impact*,
DOI 10.1007/978-981-10-4831-9_4

4.1 Introduction

Since China launched its reform and open-door policy nearly 40 years ago, the rapid development of China's urbanization has been widely concerning. During 1978–2014, China's urbanization rate increased from 17.92 to 54.77%. The annual growth of the rate is 1.05%, which has reached 1.36% (Fig. 4.1) especially since 1996.

This rapid urbanization within a short period of time is astonishing compared to the rest of the world. For example, urbanization in the UK started from the Industrial Revolution around 1760, and it took the U.K. about 90 years to become the first country in the world that had more than 50% of its people living in urban areas (in 1851). And it took the US 80 years (1860–1940) to increase its urbanization rate from 19.8 to 56.5%. However, it took China only 35 years to make this huge leap.

China's urbanization has made remarkable achievements in urban development, but at the same time, the rapid urbanization process has also brought problems. For example, the land urbanization is quicker than population urbanization, the "urban diseases" are serious, the urban system is not rational, and the regional difference is huge. Because China adopts an unbalanced development strategy and China's Eastern region has good regional advantages, urbanization developed firstly in the eastern coastal area. The regional difference in urbanization is huge and persistent, with the urbanization level in the Eastern region the highest, followed by the Central and then Western region (Fig. 4.2). For instance, in 2014, the urbanization rate in Tibet was the lowest (25.75%), 63.85% lower than that in Shanghai, which is the highest (89.6%). These large regional differences in China's urbanization have been the subject of wide concern by scholars in China and from all over the world, who have conducted many studies on this issue.

The famous American sinologist G. William Skinner is among the first who have shown concern about the problem of regional differences in China's urbanization. In addition to the preferential policy biased toward eastern coastal region, Skinner et al. (2000) argues that the reasons for the persistent regional difference in China's

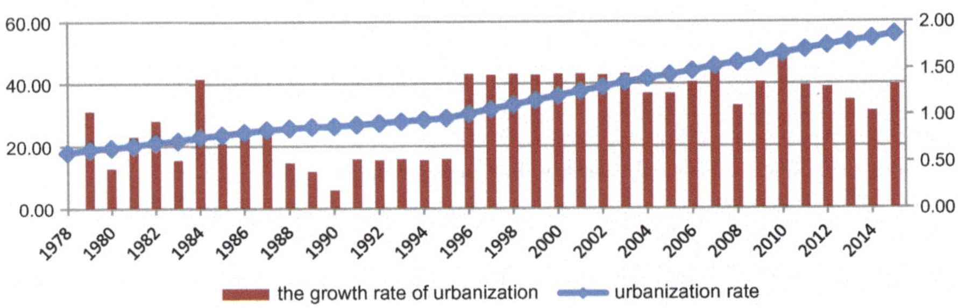

Fig. 4.1 China's urbanization rate development trend and growth rate (1978–2015). Data source: *China Statistical Yearbook 2015*

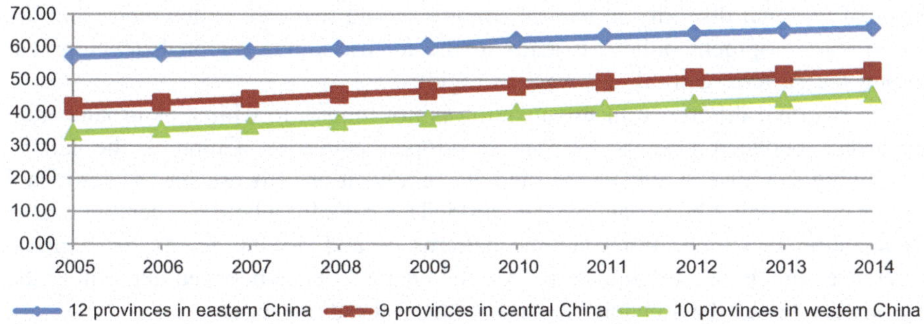

Fig. 4.2 The difference of three regions' urbanization level (2005–2014). Data source: Through the statistics of the relevant data from *China Statistic Yearbook*. *Note* The urbanization rate of each region is derived from the proportion of the total permanent population in cities and towns of the provinces in the region, accounting for the total population of the whole region

urbanization include five closely related factors: population density, regional labor distribution, technological development level and its application in transportation and other fields, regional commercialization level, and foreign trade level. All of these factors function interactively and jointly, leading to the continuous expanding of the regional difference in China's urbanization. Marton (2000) divided the Chinese mainland into eastern, central and western areas based on the economic development level, which makes it convenient for the study of the current economic development differences in the regions and is also significant for the research on the regional difference in China's urbanization development level. Fan (1999) argues that using economic factors as the main driving forces to promote urban development in China may not be applicable given the socialist Chinese economy; instead, institutional factors may be more critical to China's urban development. Therefore, government policies to promote urbanization have great impacts on the regional differences in urbanization in China.

Cao and Liu (2011) believe that governmental policies, such as economic reform and opening up, are one of the main sources for the regional unbalance in regional development and urbanization of China. During the early years of reform and opening up, the nation made the coastal areas its strategic key point in regional development and enacted a series of preferential policies for the eastern area. So the eastern coastal area and southern provinces became the key regions of the nation's urbanization while the urbanization in the central and western areas lagged behind, leading to the remarkable regional differences in urbanization. As China further deepened its reform and opening up beyond the Eastern region, large scale development strategies such as "Western Development," "Transforming and Vitalizing the Northeast of China," and "Rise of the Central China" have been carried out one by one, offering preferential policies to the Central and Western regions. Thus the Central and Western region have become the priority regions for development, as the Eastern region did decades ago. Guan et al. (2016) argue that there is apparent spatial agglomeration in China's urbanization, which is mainly a result of regional disparity in natural conditions and resource endowment, and the nation's development policy. It leads to the inharmonious regional development among the eastern, central and western regions.

The regional difference in urbanization is not unique to China, as urbanization levelsvary between regions even in developed countries. China is the largest developing country in the world, and its urbanization process has a significant impact on not only China but also the world. This calls for a better understanding of urbanization in China. What are the patterns of and driving forces for regional differences in China's urbanization? Are the characteristics between and within the regions the same? This chapter aims to address these questions.

4.2 Features and Regional Types of China's Urbanization

China's urbanization shows significant regional differences, and the urbanization level in eastern coastal provinces is apparently higher than that in inland provinces in central and western China. The national average level of urbanization was 54.77% in 2014. Among 31 provinces (municipality directly under the central government) in China, only 13 provinces have higher levels of urbanization than the nation's average. They are Beijing, Tianjin, Inner Mongolia, Liaoning, Heilongjiang, Shanghai, Jiangsu, Zhejiang, Fujian, Shandong, Hubei, Guangdong and Chongqing, 9 of which are in the eastern coastal area. In contrast, among the 12 regions/municipalities in Western China, Chongqing is the only one with an urbanization level higher than national average (Fig. 4.3).

In addition, there are large differences in an urbanization levels within regions. Although China's urbanization level has reached 56.1% in 2015, the urban system is not optimal. Besides, some big cities are over-urbanized, and the polarization effect is obvious within those regions and the urbanization level in most of those

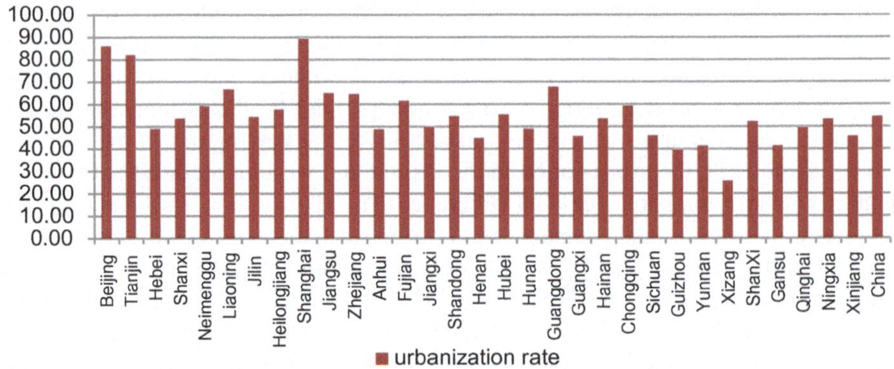

Fig. 4.3 The urbanization rate of China's 31 provinces and municipalities directly under the central government in 2014. Data source: *China Statistical Yearbook* 2014

areas is still not high. Taking the northwestern area as an example, as shown in Fig. 4.4, only 7 cities of 17 cities in the area reached the nation's average level of urbanization in 2014. The city of Jiayuguan (Gansu Province) has the highest urbanization level (83.6%) and the city of Dingxi (Gansu Province) has the lowest level (14%), with a difference of 69.6% points. This indicates the extremely large difference of urbanization development within the same region.

To scrutinize the regional differences in China's urban development, this chapter develops a comprehensive method to classify the regional types of the urbanization. Moreover, this chapter identifies three types of regions from the four perspectives: regional development, urban-rural links, urban spatial distributions, and urban function partition (Table 4.1).

The first type of urbanization region refers to the regions located in eastern China where the development level is both high in urban and rural areas and where cities and towns are located in the core and the ordinary urbanized areas. This region specifically includes 8 provinces: Beijing, Tianjin, Shanghai, Hebei, Jiangsu, Zhejiang, Fujian and Hainan. The second type of urbanization region refers to the areas located in central China where the urban-rural relationship is characterized with "strong urban and weak country" and to the areas between the key construction districts and special cities and towns. This region specifically includes 8 provinces: Shandong, Shanxi, Hebei, Henan, Chongqing, Shanxi, Jilin, and Heilongjiang. The third type of urbanization region refers to three kinds of areas: the area approximately located in northwest inland and under-development areas where both the urban and rural development are lagging behind, areas with the regional center as its support and special area such as minority regions. This region includes 16 provinces: Hubei, Hunan, Anhui, Jiangxi, Neimenggu, Sichuan, Ningxia, Xinjiang, Guangxi, Gansu, Qinghai, Yunnan, Guizhou, and Tibet.

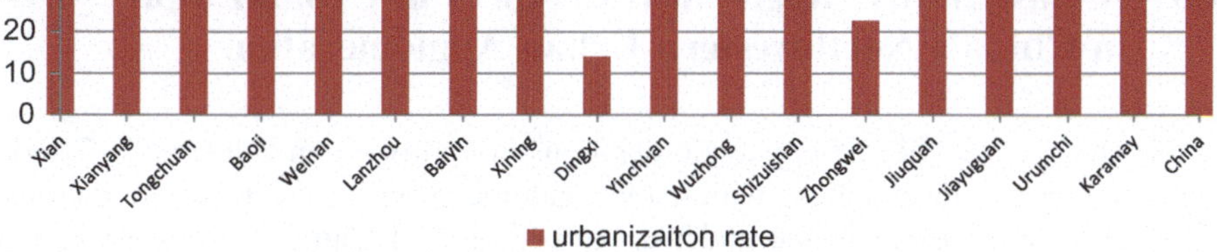

Fig. 4.4 The urbanization rate of 17 cities in the northwest region of China in 2014. Data source: *China Statistical Yearbook 2015*. *Notes* The *blue line* in the figure indicates China's urbanization rate in 2014 is 54.77%

Table 4.1 Division of regional types from the comprehensive perspectives

Type/Perspective	1st type of urbanization region	2nd type of urbanization region	3rd type of urbanization region
Regional development	Eastern region	Central region	Western region
Urban-rural relationship	Strong-strong region (Both the development level in urban and rural areas are high)	Strong-weak region (Unbalanced urban-rural development with strong urban area and weak country area)	Weak-weak area (Both the development level in urban and rural area are low)
Urban spatial distributions	Core region (Optimizing development district with apparent development priority)	Key region (Weaker than core area, but with comparatively large development potential)	Regional center (Provinces and cities of regional center except for the optimizing development districts and key rural areas)
Urban function partition	Ordinary region (Better resource and environment carrying capacity and better economic and population agglomeration conditions)	Featured region (Key agricultural regions, special agricultural, forest, pasturing, fishery regions, resource regions, tourism regions, etc.)	Special region (Old revolutionary base areas, minority regions, border areas, poor and marginal areas, ecologically secure and sensitive areas, etc.)

In fact, the regional imbalance of China's urbanization is manifested not only among the eastern, middle and western regions, but also among different provinces, even different cities and countries. The regional difference in China's urbanization not only refers to the quantity difference of the urbanization, but also the quality level of the urbanization. Therefore, China's urbanization must solve the problem of harmonious regional development by dealing with different type of regions according to their specific characteristics, especially when dealing with the regional difference problem in the third type of urbanization region.

4.3 A Case Study: Regional Differences in Urbanization in China's Northwestern Urban Agglomeration

In this chapter, we chose 5 city agglomerations in northwestern China and 17 node cities (prefecture-level cities) within the agglomeration as the research regions. These cities are located in the under-developed area of China's northwest inland area where the urban-rural development has lagged behind. These cities are regional centers of China's city planning system, with shared characteristics of vulnerable ecologies, high poverty rate and concentration of many ethnic groups. Thus the region is a typical third urbanization region and also is the vital supporting region for the new Silk Road Economic Belt strategy. Therefore, a careful study of the urbanization and differences within the region is of vital and practical significance for combating poverty, promoting regional development and facilitating the development of Silk Road Economic Belt.

4.3.1 Construction of the Composite Index System that Measures Urbanization Level

The level of urbanization is conventionally measured by the proportion of the urban population out of the total population. Yet, this method measures only the quantity not the quality of urbanization. Urbanization refers to not only the migration process of the population from rural areas to urban areas, but also the transformation of the industrial structure, lifestyle, production modes and other aspects (Yao et al. 2014). Therefore, this chapter constructs a composite index system to measure the urban development level according to the processes involved in urbanization. By choosing 20 indicators to construct the composite index system, this chapter measures the urban development level of northwestern city agglomerations based on four aspects of urbanization: population, economy, society and land (Table 4.2).

4.3.2 The Cross-sectional Analysis of the Regional Difference in the Comprehensive Urbanization Development of Northwestern Urban Agglomerations

4.3.2.1 The Regional Difference in the Urbanization Development Level of Urban Agglomeration

There are obvious regional differences in the comprehensive urbanization of the 5 urban agglomerations in Northwest China, and the V curve displays the "sunken" feature, showing that both ends of the curve are better than the middle (Fig. 4.5). According to Fig. 4.3, the urban agglomerations in Guanzhong and on the north slope of the Mountain Tianshan, located respectively in the eastern and western end of Northwest region, and the comprehensive urban development level of them are respectively 0.2645 and 0.3656. From the ends to the center of Northwest region, the comprehensive urban development of the urban agglomerations successively are JiuJiaYu (Jiuquan, Jiayuguan and Yumen) (0.1457), and LanBaiXi (Lanzhou, Baiyin, and Xining) (0.1339). But the index of the comprehensive urban development of the urban agglomeration on Yinchuan plain is 0.0903, which is the lowest (Table 4.3).

Table 4.2 The index system of urbanization level to comprehensively measure the Northwestern urban agglomerations

Objective level	Subsystem level	Index level
The index system of urbanization level to comprehensively measure the northwestern urban agglomerations	Urbanization of population U_1	Urban population proportion (%)
		Urban population scale (ten thousand)
		The proportion of employed people in the second and third industries (%)
		Employment people amount in the second and third industry (ten thousand)
		People density in municipal district (personnel/km^2)
	Urbanization of economy U_2	GDP per capita (yuan)
		General industrial production per capita (yuan)
		GDP density in the second and third industries (ten thousand yuan/km^2)
		Total amount of fixed assets (ten thousand yuan)
		Proportion of non-agricultural industry (%)
	Urbanization of society U_3	Retailing amount of social consumer goods per person (yuan)
		Amount of post and telecommunications per person (yuan)
		Average salary of the staff on post (yuan)
		Number of theaters
		Number of Doctors in ten thousand people
		Number of college students in ten thousand people
	Urbanization of land U_4	Constructed areas (km^2)
		Laying-road areas per person (m^2)
		Green land areas per person (m^2)
		The proportion of the city's construction land accounting to the municipal area (%)

Notes The index of population proportion (%) in cities and towns is counted based on the population of permanent residents and the population scale in cities and towns (ten thousand) is counted based on the permanent non-agricultural population

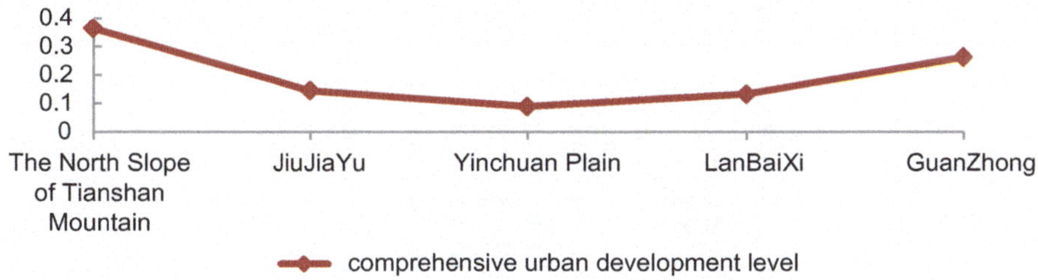

Fig. 4.5 The development trend of urbanization in the northwest of China in 2014

Analyzing the urbanization subsystem levels of each urban agglomeration, we can find that the contribution rate of the leading urbanization subsystems of the 5 urban agglomerations in Northwestern region show remarkable regional difference. According to the comprehensive score and contribution rate of the subsystems, the urbanization level of population and economy has the largest impact on the comprehensive urban development of the urban agglomerations. The contribution rate of urbanization of population in Guanzhong and LanBaiXi are respectively 38.52 and 41.32%;the contribution rate of urbanization of economy in JiuJiaYu city and on the north slope of Mountain Tianshan are respectively 47.84 and 41.00%; and the contribution of the urbanization of land on the Yinchuan plain is 37.34%.

4.3.2.2 The Regional Difference of the Urban Development Level Among the Node Cities of Each Urban Agglomeration

Analyzing the node cities of the urban agglomerations, we find that the regional differences in urban agglomerations of Northwestern China are remarkable, displaying the following two aspects:

On the one hand, the regional difference of the node cities' comprehensive urban development level is remarkable. According to the comprehensive score of 17 node cities' urbanization of urban agglomerations in Northwestern China, and by using a hierarchical clustering analytic method, we can find that the comprehensive urbanization of the 17 node cities can be classified from high to low into four groups. The city in the first group is only Xi'an. 7 cities are in the second group, including Lanzhou, Urumchi, Jiayuguan, Karamay, Xining, Yinchuan and Xianyang. The third group includes 3 cities and they are Baoji, Weinan and Shizuishan. And the fourth group includes Tongchuan, Jiuquan, Wuzhong, Baiyin, Dingxi and Zhongwei (Fig. 4.6 and Table 4.4).

On the other hand, the leading subsystem of the 17 node cities' urban development level is greatly different and the balanced development degree of each subsystem is generally not high. We can find from Table 4.4 that the urbanization of land has great impact on the comprehensive urban development level of 17 cities in Northwestern China. However, the development level of the subsystems in each city's urbanization is significantly different from each other. For instance,

Table 4.3 The comprehensive development level of the urbanization, the score of each subsystem and the contribution rate in the northwest of China, 2014

Urban agglomeration	Comprehensive development level	Urbanization of population U_1		Urbanization of economy U_2		Urbanization of society U_3		Urbanization of land U_4	
		Level	Contribution rate (%)	Level	Contribution rate (%)	Level	Contribution rate (%)	Level	contribution rate (%)
GuanZhong	0.2645	0.1019	38.52	0.0731	27.63	0.0572	21.62	0.0323	12.23
LanBaiXi	0.1339	0.0553	41.32	0.0116	8.67	0.0425	31.77	0.0244	18.24
Yinchuan Plain	0.0903	0.0189	20.92	0.0131	14.47	0.0246	27.26	0.0337	37.34
JiuJiaYu	0.1457	0.0189	12.96	0.0697	47.84	0.0321	22.05	0.0250	17.15
North slope of Tianshan Mountain	0.3656	0.0545	14.92	0.1499	41.00	0.1078	29.47	0.0534	14.61

Notes The comprehensive urbanization development and the development of each subsystem is measured by the entropy method, and the contribution rate is the proportion of the subsystem urbanization accounting for the comprehensive urban development of the city agglomeration

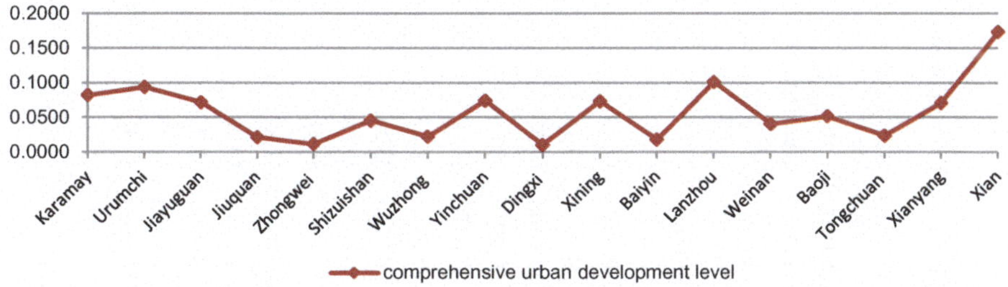

Fig. 4.6 The development level of the 17 node cities in the northwest of China in 2014

urbanization of population is the leading subsystem in cities like Weinan and Dingxi, urbanization of economy is the leading subsystem in cities like Baoji and Lanzhou, and urbanization of land is the leading subsystem in cities like Shizuishan and Wuzhong. And cities such as Xi'an, Urumchi, Yinchuan and Xianyang, ranking respectively as the 1st, 3rd, 5th, and 8th, developed relative harmony between subsystems of urbanization and have superior urbanization quality.

4.3.3 The Temporal Analysis of the Regional Difference of the Comprehensive Urbanization Development of Northwestern Urban Agglomerations

Using the entropy method, we measure the comprehensive development level of urbanization in Northwestern urban agglomerations and each node cities during 2005–2014 (Tables 4.5 and 4.6).

Analyzing from the evolution of regional differences of the comprehensive urbanization level, we can find that the general level of the 5 urban agglomerations in Northwestern China is rising while the regional gap is expanding. From 2005 to 2014, the comprehensive development of the 5 urban agglomerations in Northwestern China shows an increasing trend year by year though it fluctuates sometimes (Table 4.5). According to the standard deviation analysis of the comprehensive urban development of 5 urban agglomerations as shown in Table 4.5, the standard deviation in northwestern urban agglomerations increases from 0.0115 in 2005 to 0.0340 in 2014. This indicates that the regional gap of urbanization of Northwestern urban agglomerations is expanding.

Corresponding with the evolution features of the regional difference of the urbanization in Northwestern urban agglomerations, the urban development level of node cities shows an increasing trend generally and that of the Northwestern urban agglomerations is rising gradually. Different from the evolution features of the regional difference of the urbanization in Northwestern urban agglomerations, the regional difference between the node cities' urbanization level is even larger.

Table 4.4 The comprehensive development level of the urbanization, the score of each subsystem and the contribution rate of 17 cities in the northwest of China, 2014

City	Comprehensive development level	Order	Urbanization of population U_1		Urbanization of society U_3		Urbanization of society U_3		Urbanization of society U_4	
			Level	Contribution rate (%)	Level	Contribution rate (%)	Level	Contribution rate (%)	Level	Contribution rate (%)
Xi'an	0.1744	1	0.0487	27.94	0.0376	21.54	0.059	33.85	0.0291	16.67
Xianyang	0.0718	8	0.0274	38.17	0.0153	21.30	0.0118	16.43	0.0173	24.09
Tongchuan	0.0248	12	0.0058	23.52	0.0084	33.77	0.0064	25.71	0.0042	16.99
Baoji	0.0528	9	0.0134	25.32	0.0123	23.23	0.0213	40.31	0.0059	11.13
Weinan	0.0414	11	0.0185	44.54	0.0084	20.21	0.0067	16.07	0.0079	19.18
Lanzhou	0.1016	2	0.0245	24.07	0.0141	13.91	0.0432	42.52	0.0198	19.50
Baiyin	0.0188	15	0.0047	24.90	0.0051	27.32	0.0036	19.09	0.0054	28.69
Xining	0.0739	6	0.0231	31.24	0.0114	15.47	0.0216	29.23	0.0178	24.06
Dingxi	0.011	17	0.0059	53.06	0.0014	12.26	0.0036	32.15	0.0003	2.53
Yinchuan	0.075	5	0.0164	21.92	0.014	18.68	0.0269	35.86	0.0176	23.54
Wuzhong	0.0232	13	0.0055	23.54	0.0035	14.92	0.0066	28.66	0.0076	32.88
Shizuishan	0.0464	10	0.0046	9.91	0.0104	22.47	0.009	19.35	0.0224	48.26
Zhongwei	0.0126	16	0.0015	11.89	0.0028	22.02	0.0043	34.22	0.004	31.87
Jiuquan	0.0224	14	0.0032	14.36	0.0061	27.46	0.0085	37.89	0.0045	20.28
Jiayuguan	0.0725	7	0.0036	5.03	0.0344	47.41	0.0147	20.28	0.0198	27.28
Urumchi	0.0945	3	0.0152	16.10	0.0181	19.12	0.0311	32.86	0.0302	31.92
Karamay	0.083	4	0.0043	5.17	0.0403	48.54	0.0183	22.00	0.0202	24.28

Table 4.5 The comprehensive development level of urbanization in Northwest urban agglomerations in 2005–2014

Urban agglomerations	2005	2006	2007	2008	2009	2010	2011	2012	2013	2014
GuanZhong	0.0263	0.0234	0.0381	0.0529	0.0982	0.0965	0.1441	0.1292	0.1649	0.2264
LanBaiXi	0.0243	0.0221	0.0317	0.0485	0.0613	0.0847	0.2087	0.1329	0.1536	0.2323
Yinchuan Plain	0.0136	0.0250	0.0362	0.0473	0.0621	0.0665	0.2362	0.1424	0.1369	0.2337
JiuJiaYu	0.0103	0.0130	0.0321	0.0490	0.1354	0.0606	0.2762	0.1133	0.1419	0.1684
North Slope of Tianshan Mountain	0.0393	0.0700	0.0475	0.0466	0.0571	0.0748	0.1532	0.1320	0.2100	0.1694
Standard deviation	0.0115	0.0225	0.0064	0.0024	0.0337	0.0143	0.0557	0.0106	0.0292	0.0340

Notes The standard deviation reflects the dispersion degree of the data variation, and the bigger the standard deviation, the larger the data dispersion, and vice versa

Table 4.6 The comprehensive development level of urbanization in 17 cities of Northwest urban agglomerations, 2005–2014

City	2005	2006	2007	2008	2009	2010	2011	2012	2013	2014
Xi'an	0.0349	0.0250	0.0400	0.0660	0.1050	0.0925	0.1077	0.1329	0.1659	0.2300
Xianyang	0.0986	0.0177	0.0398	0.0569	0.0901	0.0905	0.1446	0.1193	0.1473	0.1953
Tongchuan	0.0207	0.0132	0.0149	0.0275	0.1962	0.0602	0.2420	0.1117	0.1697	0.1438
Baoji	0.0411	0.0329	0.0617	0.0711	0.0638	0.1087	0.1754	0.0942	0.1519	0.1993
Weinan	0.0299	0.0396	0.0470	0.0485	0.0717	0.0773	0.1483	0.1084	0.2961	0.1331
Lanzhou	0.0178	0.0287	0.0422	0.0500	0.0733	0.0767	0.1391	0.1281	0.1954	0.2487
Baiyin	0.0808	0.0232	0.0297	0.0345	0.0595	0.0569	0.1936	0.0782	0.2728	0.1709
Xining	0.0234	0.0340	0.0414	0.0625	0.0527	0.1075	0.1911	0.1685	0.1380	0.1808
Dingxi	0.0097	0.0096	0.0271	0.0353	0.0600	0.0544	0.1754	0.0997	0.2184	0.3102
Yinchuan	0.0317	0.0458	0.0404	0.0443	0.0707	0.0694	0.1799	0.1217	0.1490	0.2471
Wuzhong	0.0224	0.0188	0.0303	0.0386	0.0421	0.0559	0.2175	0.0995	0.2260	0.2490
Shizuishan	0.0122	0.0200	0.0348	0.0605	0.0706	0.0742	0.2543	0.2166	0.0924	0.1643
Zhongwei	0.0425	0.0306	0.0462	0.0444	0.0962	0.0478	0.2362	0.0692	0.1344	0.2525
Jiuquan	0.0177	0.0226	0.0321	0.0496	0.1517	0.0791	0.2312	0.0983	0.1273	0.1903
Jiayuguan	0.0155	0.0194	0.0387	0.0549	0.0657	0.0633	0.3250	0.1309	0.1386	0.1479
Urumchi	0.0580	0.0720	0.0635	0.0452	0.0653	0.0695	0.1249	0.1330	0.1854	0.1832
Karamay	0.0320	0.0623	0.0509	0.0455	0.0476	0.0641	0.2213	0.1184	0.1939	0.1639
Standard deviation	0.0243	0.0167	0.0120	0.0118	0.0392	0.0179	0.0549	0.0342	0.0531	0.0483

For example, in 2014, the standard deviation of the urban development level among node cities is 0.0483, compared to 0.0340 for Northwestern urban agglomerations.

Through the above measurement and analysis of the urbanization development levels in Northwestern urban agglomerations, the regional difference in urbanization in Northwestern urban agglomerations shows the following two features:

Firstly, there are two aspects of the regional difference in urbanization in Northwestern urban agglomerations. On the one hand, the general urbanization development level of Northwestern urban agglomerations shows a V curve with "sunken" features. Geographically speaking, the urban agglomerations in Guanzhong and on the north slope of the Tianshan Mountain are located respectively in the two ends of the five Northwestern urban agglomerations. And the urbanization level of the two urban agglomerations is remarkably higher than that of LanBaiXi, JiuJiaYu and Yinchuan plain. On the other hand, the node cities' urbanization development level within the Northwestern urban agglomerations shows a wave-like distribution. Taking the 17 node cities' urbanization development level of Northwestern urban agglomerations in 2014 as an example, the urban development level of the node cities in the Northwest varies greatly in terms of spatial difference.

Secondly, measuring the results of the comprehensive urbanization development levels of 5 urban agglomerations and 17 node cities of the Northwestern urban agglomerations from 2005 to 2014 tells us that the general level of the agglomerations shows a remarkably rising trend and the regional difference between the levels is expanding. We can also conclude that the development difference in urbanization of economy and land expands significantly. And the comprehensive urban development level of 17 node cities as well as the dynamic evolution features of the 4 subsystems shows an increasing trend in terms of regional difference.

4.4 Conclusions

Firstly, because of the imbalanced development strategies in China, the regional difference in China's urbanization is evident, showing both among different regions and within the regions. Since the 21th century, with the successive implementation of Western Development, Transformation and Vitalization of northeastern China and Rise of Central China, the police advantage in the eastern area has been gradually weakened. And the urbanization development difference between the eastern, middle and western regions shows a narrowing trend, while the urban development level within the regions shows a more diverging trend. Taking the Northwestern region as an example, the regional difference of the urbanization development level in the northwest of China expands.

Secondly, although the conventional measure for urbanization (the proportion of the urban population accounting for the total population) is widely used due to its convenience, this method measures only the quantity but not the quality of urbanization. In addition to the complex national conditions in China (territory, nature, administration, policy and other factors), this method alone cannot reflect China's urbanization development level objectively and truthfully. So when analyzing the regional disparity in China's urbanization, we should take population, economy, society and land into consideration to measure China's urbanization development level.

Thirdly, the driving force for the regional difference in China's urbanization is the regional development strategy and urbanization policy. During the early years of the reform and opening up, China put its strategic key point of the regional development into the eastern coastal region, and the eastern coastal and southern provinces became the key regions of the nation's urbanization. Along with the further deepening of the reform and opening up policy into the central and western China, the policies such as West Development, Transformation and Vitalization of Northeast of China and the Rise of Central China are carried out successively. These policies lead to rapid urbanization development in the central and western China. Besides, the population density and regional labor distribution conditions in urbanization of population, technological development level in urbanization of society, transportation facilities in urbanization of land as well as commercialization and foreign trade levels in urbanization of economy, are critical factors influencing the regional difference in China's urbanization.

To promote better and more harmonious urban development in China, we propose the following suggestions based on our research results.

Firstly, China's urban development strategy should put human beings at the center of urbanization. The *National New-Type Urbanization Plan (2014–2020)*, issued in March, 2014, points out that the new urbanization is people-oriented. During the urbanization process, the urbanization is not simply equivalent to the construction of city, but refers to a series of transformations from the "country" to "city," such as industrial structure, employment modes, inhabitant environments and social security. It also means the harmonious promotion of urbanization from the aspects of population, economy, society as well as land, in order to realize the comprehensive, harmonious and sustainable development of urbanization. The measurement of the urban development level needs to be more comprehensive and scientific, taking the transformation of the agricultural population to non-agricultural industry and of the agricultural migration's production and living style to urban ways into comprehensive consideration.

Secondly, the establishment of China's urbanization strategy should pay more attention to the development of the regions of the third type of urbanization. These regions have high poverty rate, ethnic groups, poor natural conditions and vulnerable ecological environments, but at the same time, they are endowed with certain regional advantages as well as new development opportunities brought by the new Silk Road Economic Belt strategy. Therefore, these regions are of great importance and deserve more attention in terms of their urbanization in China's urban development.

References in English

Fan, C.C. 1999. Migration in a socialist transitional economy: Heterogeneity, socioeconomic and spatial characteristics of migrants in China and Guangdong Province. *International Migration Review* 33 (4): 954.

Marton, A. 2000. *China's spatial economic development: Restless landscape in the lower Yangzi Delta*. London: Routledge.

Skinner, G.W., M. Henderson, and J. Yuan. 2000. China's fertility transition through regional space: Using GIS and census data for a spatial analysis of historical demography. *Social Science History* 24 (03): 613–652.

References in Chinese

Cao, G.Z., and T. Liu. 2011. Zhongguo chengzhenghua diqu gongxian de neiluhua yanbian yu jieshi—jiyu 1982–2008 nian shengqu shuju de fenxi [The evolution and interpretation of the contribution of urbanization in China—Analysis of provincial data based on 1982–2008]. *Dili xuebao* 12: 1631–1643.

Guan, X.L., H.K. Wei, S.H. Lu, and Y. Deng. 2016. Zhongguo chengzhenghua jincheng zhong de kongjian jiju, jili jiqi kexue wenti [Spatial agglomeration, mechanism and scientific problems during the urbanization process in China]. *Dili yanjiu* 2: 227–241.

Yao, S.M., P.Y. Zhang, C. Yu, G.Y. Li, and C.X. Wang. 2014. Zhongguo xinxing chengzhenghua lilun yu shijian wenti [The theory and practice of new-type urbanization in China]. *Dili yanjiu* 6: 641–647.

Chapter 5
Urbanization in Ethnic Minority Areas of Western China: Is It Special?

Lijuan Si

Abstract Western China is a region that has not only a low level of economic and urban development, but also an extremely high level of ethnic minorities (72% of China's total). What causes the low urbanization in Western China? Is it special just for the minority resident area? What policies and strategies should the government adopts to promote urban development in this area? This chapter attempts to answer these questions by examining the overall trend of urbanization in Western China and a few cases in Linxia and Gansu. Like other regions, the main driving force for urbanization in these areas is industrialization. The low level of urban development results from the low level of industrialization. The best policies and strategies for governments at the central, regional, and local levels are to encourage and promote industrial development, especially in the minority resident areas.

Keywords Urbanization · Ethnic minority areas · Urban development · Industrialization · Industrial development

5.1 Introduction

China's urbanization rate has been rising rapidly with China's economic growth since the economic reform started in 1978. In a large and diverse country such as China, differences in economic and urban development between regions are expected. Differences between Eastern, Central and Western China are substantial even by the standards of other large countries (Davis and Henderson 2003; Zhang 2002; Zhang and Song 2003). For decades, the resource-rich west has been lagging behind China's coast in market-oriented reforms and openness to trade and investment. Disparities in urban development as well as income have widened

L. Si (✉)
Lanzhou University, Lanzhou, China
e-mail: silj@lzu.edu.cn

Z. Tang (ed.), *China's Urbanization and Socioeconomic Impact*,
DOI 10.1007/978-981-10-4831-9_5

between regions, mainly due to the spectacular progress of the coastal regions (Xie and Zhang 2004). While much attention has been paid to regional gaps in urban development, studies on regional urbanization of Chinese ethnic minority groups seem to be limited in the literature. In particular, little work has been done on the issue of minority groups in Western China (WB and DRCC 2014). How is urbanization going in Western China's minority areas? Is it special for minority regions in determinants of urban development? What policy implications can be derived regarding promoting urbanization in the minority regions of Western China? This chapter intends to close the gap in the literature by examining these questions, based on a case study of Linxia Hui autonomous prefecture and policy discussions of urbanization through industrialization.

The large interregional disparities in urban development have been a major concern of the central government since the late 1990s, since increasing income gaps between leading and lagging regions will eventually undermine social cohesion and stability. Moreover, lagging regions may drag down the overall growth rate of the national economy, as well as limit the expansion of the domestic market (Hamer and Linn 1987; Song and Zhang 2002). Many lagging regions in Western China contain large numbers of poor people, including minority groups. Since poverty incidence is more severe in western rural areas, economic progress will not only increase minority groups' income and urbanization, but also help ethnic harmony and national unity.

Industrialization drives urbanization when a country or region transforms from an agricultural economy to an industrial economy (Michaels et al. 2012; Zhang 2004). The huge industrial potential of the west is becoming essential to China for several reasons: (a) China is undergoing a transition from an export-oriented economy to one with more balanced growth and stronger domestic demand. Western China is being called to play a major role as a supplier of parts and components to manufacturing-based companies on the coast. (b) China has become a net importer of farm products, raising fears over food security. The development of the west's agro-industries may meet increased domestic demand, and thus reduce the dependency on foreign food imports. (c) Growing energy consumption poses a big constraint to China's industry; the development of the West's rich mining and gas resources could be a solution to meet domestic demand. (d) Coastal China may lose its comparative advantage in labor-intensive sectors as wages rise. The west needs to stand ready to attract national and international investors seeking relocation.

The rest of the chapter is organized as follows. Section two provides overall patterns of urbanization in Western China's minority regions, focusing on various types of urban development models. In Sect. 5.3, a case study of Linxia Hui autonomous prefecture in Gansu province is presented to investigate some details of urban development and future strategies in minority-group regions. More general policy implications at the central, regional, and local governments are discussed in Sect. 5.4, based on the view that industrialization is a key driver of urbanization. Summary and concluding remarks are given in the last section.

5.2 Overall Patterns of Urbanization in Western China's Minority Areas

China is composed of 56 ethnic groups. Among them, Han Chinese (about 1.25 billion) account for 91.59% of the overall Chinese population and the other 55 (about 115 million) make up the remaining 8.41%. As the combined population of these other minorities is far fewer than that of the Han, they form the 55 minorities of China. Though making up a small proportion of the total population, the 55 minority ethnic groups are distributed extensively throughout different regions, mainly in Western China, as shown in Fig. 5.1. In order to ensure that the 56 Chinese ethnic groups live together in harmony, the government introduced a series of policies, including ones to secure the equality and unity of ethnic groups, give regional autonomy to ethnic minorities and promote respect for the faith and customs of ethnic groups.

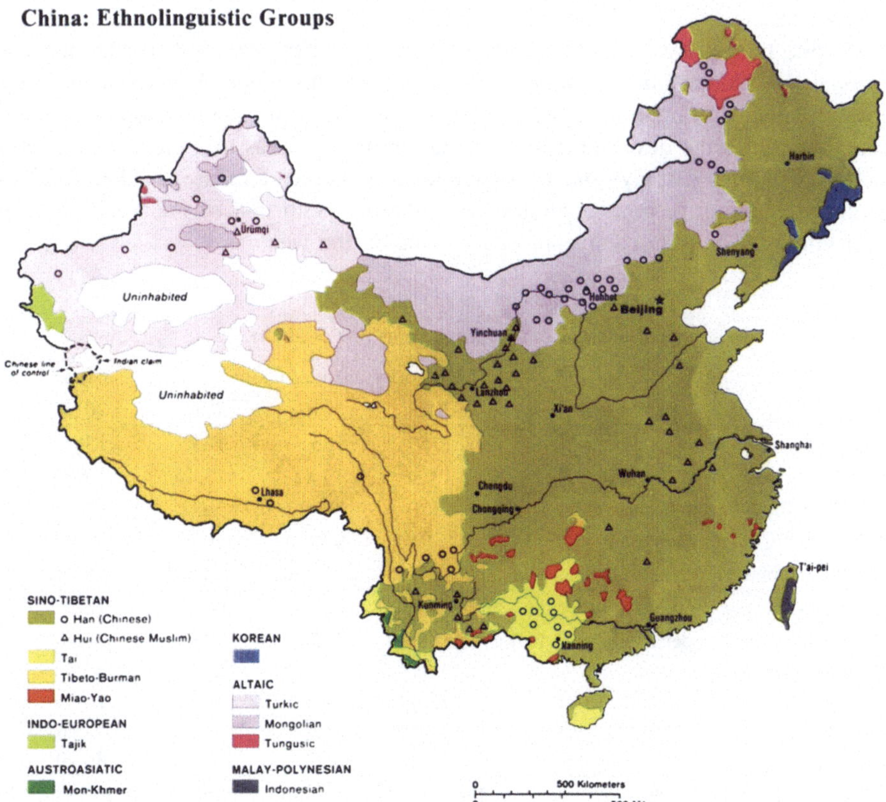

Fig. 5.1 Distribution of China's ethnic minority groups

Urbanization is driven by industrialization/economic development in developing economies like China. In less developed regions of China, poor conditions, in factors of endowments, location, and ecological environments, result in difficulties in economic growth, and lower urbanization levels could not contribute to economic development. How can we break down the vicious cycle of urbanization-economic development? Is it possible to start with urban development in promoting economic development? What are the characteristics of urbanization in China's backward economic regions? The government has launched several large-scale initiatives to address regional development inequalities. In early 2000, the State Council adopted the 'Great Western Development Strategy,' and launched the Western Regional Development Programs to accelerate physical investment in twelve regions in Western China, many of which are economically backward parts of the country.

The economic development of minority areas has a direct bearing on the living conditions and quality of the native dwellers and an important influence on the comprehensive development of the western areas. Table 5.1 presents basic economic indicators of minority areas and the country as a whole for the purpose of comparisons.

Despite better development in recent years, minority areas still lag behind the national level in regard to economic and social development. With most minority populations inhabiting the backward western areas in China, the development of the west determines the development of China's minority areas to a great degree, and such gap in turn displays the backwardness of the western areas. Therefore, to develop the minority regions should be combined with that of the west; and the most important is to develop minority regions in the west.

Table 5.1 Basis economic indicators of minority areas (2005–2013)

	Minority areas of China			China
	2005	2010	2013	2013
Population (in millions)	175	185	183	1361
Share of population in total (%)	13.38	13.82	13.46	100.00
GDP in billions of Chinese yuan	1570	3899	5932	59,524
Percentage of the country (%)	8.49	9.71	10.09	100.00
GDP per capita (in Chinese yuan)	8991	22,060	33,003	35,181
Ratio of GDP per capita to country	0.63	0.74	0.94	1.00
Gross fiscal revenue per capita (in yuan)	587	1758	3331	9496
Economic structure (%)				
Agriculture	21.01	15.90	15.24	10.00
Industry	40.87	48.24	48.16	43.90
Services	38.12	35.86	36.60	46.10

Notes Minority areas include 5 ethnic autonomous regions, 30 ethnic autonomous prefectures, and 120 ethnic autonomous counties, overlapping not counted

Sources China Statistical Yearbook (NBSC various years 2006–2014)

The new-type urbanization that China implements at present has provided minority regions in the west with great opportunities. Urbanization is closely related to a region's social and economic development, and economic development to urbanization. Except for Shannxi and Chongqing provinces, all 12 provinces and regions in the west are inhabited by minorities, as presented in Table 5.2. It is in these provinces that cities have a relatively lower level of urbanization. Besides, these provinces have an unbalanced development.

It can be concluded after comparing data from Table 5.2 that in all the ten western provinces, only Inner Mongolia (54.77%) has achieved a higher urbanization than the national average level. Guangxi, Gansu, Yunnan, Guizhou and Tibet all rank after 25; these have lowest level of urbanization in China. Differences also exist in the average growth of percentage points. From 2009 to 2014 there were nine provinces, except for Tibet, which realized over one percentage point growth per year; except for Inner Mongolia and Tibet, other provinces realized a higher level than the national average. The two provinces ranked 22nd and 27th among all the provinces. Other eight provinces ranked higher than the national average, among which Gansu, Yunnan, Ningxia and Qinghai grew faster, for although their urbanization was low at the beginning, they developed fast under the support of the government. This fact depicts the high efficiency of the new-type urbanization in the minority regions in the west.

Such common difficulties need to be solved in the urbanization of minority areas in the west, such as relatively backward economy, deteriorating ecological environment, insufficient infrastructure, poor education and transportation (Barrior et al. 2006; Brückner 2012). The urbanization types in such areas can be summed up as follows, according to their distinctions and development features:

Table 5.2 Urbanization and economic development of minority areas in 2009–2014

Region	Urbanization			GDP		
	Rate (%)	Rank	Average annual rise of percentage points in 2009–14	Rank	Value (100 million yuan)	Growth rate (%)
Inner Mongolia	59.51	10	1.22	22	17,770	7.8
Ningxia	53.61	18	1.50	12	2752	8.0
Qinghai	49.78	21	1.58	8	2303	9.2
Xinjiang	46.07	25	1.24	21	9273	10.0
Sichuan	46.30	24	1.52	11	28,537	8.5
Guangxi	46.01	26	1.36	19	15,673	8.5
Gansu	41.68	29	1.80	6	6837	8.9
Yunnan	41.73	28	1.54	10	12,815	8.1
Guizhou	40.01	30	2.02	2	9266	10.8
Tibet	25.75	31	0.70	27	921	10.8
China	54.77		1.30		635,910	9.1

Note GDP in Chinese currency, yuan
Sources China Statistical Yearbook 2010–2014 (NBSC 2011–2015)

Border-trade driven urbanization This type mainly functions in border areas, especially Xinjiang and Yunnan provinces. The economies in these areas are weak and urbanization lags behind more developed areas in the east of China. However, as a strategic barrier of the country, the multinational borders shoulder the responsibility of safeguarding peace and the territorial integrity of the country. Therefore, advancing urbanization in these areas has a self-revealing significance. Taking advantage of its unique geological location, locals living in borders in question can vigorously develop border trade, build strategically important cities and forge ahead on the border-trade driven urbanization mode.

Tourism-driven urbanization Endowed with abundant tourism resources, Ningxia, Guangxi and Guizhou provinces should utilize local resources to the fullest to build their emerging tourism-based service industry. Meanwhile, the realization of the lasting development in such areas depends on improved transportation, especially high-level roads in tourist spots, in order to link these spots and build cities prospering on tourism. More attention should be paid to the conservation of tourism resources and maintenance of ecological environments in the development of tourism.

Industry-driven urbanization The economy of Sichuan province is relatively strong in the west due to its rich natural resources, based on which the area may accelerate its second industry and follow a new-type industrialization path. The positive interaction between the new-type of industrialization and urbanization can be achieved by industry boosting the agriculture and service sectors.

Animal husbandry on grassland driven urbanization Inner Mongolia, Xinjiang, Tibet, Qinghai and Gansu are the major provinces in the country developing animal husbandry on grassland. Tibet and Qinghai provinces are sparsely populated, mainly by minorities despite their large area, with limited industrial development due to the location and topographical features. However, the geological position and climate features (e.g. rich grassland resources and little precipitation) make these areas suitable to develop agriculture and animal husbandry, which would raise the local's income and provide rich agriculture and animal products, as well as transfer the farmers to other industries and provide abundant laborers to the second and tertiary industries.

5.3 Case of Linxia Prefecture, Gansu Province

5.3.1 Overviews of Linxia's Urban Development

In order to offer a reference to the development of other minority regions, this paper will analyze the urbanization types in Western China. Linxia is a backward prefecture in Gansu. In 2014, the per capita GDP of Linxia was 10,166 yuan, and the urbanization rate was 29.57%, both lagging behind the average level of Gansu Province. In comparison with other minority regions, Linxia also lags behind in

Table 5.3 Urban and economic development of minority prefectures/counties in 2014

Prefectures/countries	Minority share	Regional GDP	Per capita GDP	Per capita GDP of farmers	Economic structure	Urbanization (%)
Linxia, Gansu	56.4	203.0	10,166	4127	19:27:54	29.57
Boer, Xinjiang	35.4	258.1	53,847	11,345	23:30:47	54.74
Liangshan, Sichuan	55.2	1314.3	28,556	8264	19:53:28	31.44
Wenshan, Yunnan	57.8	615.7	17,136	6998	23:41:36	35.5
Qiannan, Guizhou	55.9	801.8	24,791	7265	16:39:46	14.0
Guoluo, Qinghai	91.9	34.1	17,547	4827	18:45:37	23.68
Enshi, Hubei	55.0	612.0	15,063	7194	23:36:41	38.38
Xiangxi, Hunan	78.8	457.0	17,508	5260	15:34:51	39.9
Yanbian, Jilin	36.3	900.8	41,941	8466	8:51:40	67.6
Lianshan, Guangdong	59.0	28.34	23,617	9079	23:34:43	35.7
Jingning, Zhejiang	11.3	42.0	24,222	12,432	16:38:47	17.9

Notes Minority share is percentage of minority in total population; regional GDP is in 100 million yuan; per capita GDP is in yuan. Economic structure is shares of three sectors (agriculture, industry, and services) in percentage. The shares of minority population in total population are approximate based on estimations. The full name of Boer, Xinjiang is Boertala Mongol Autonomous Prefecture
Sources China Statistical Yearbook 2014 (NBSC 2015a, b, c)

Table 5.4 Urban development of Linxia prefecture, by town/county in 2014

Town/county	Population (in 10,000)	Urban population (in 10,000)	Urbanization rate (%)
Linxia town	25.59	17.00	66.4
Linxia county	41.12	5.72	13.9
Kangle	28.61	2.82	9.8
Yongjing	20.56	4.73	23.0
Guanghe	27.21	2.86	10.5
Hezheng	22.08	4.19	19.0
Dongxiang	35.15	5.06	14.4
Jishishan	27.56	2.93	10.6

Sources Gansu Statistical Yearbook 2014 (NBSC 2015b) and Gansu Social and Economic Statistical Yearbook (NBSC 2015c)

economic development (Table 5.3). The prefecture shoulders more pressure with limitations in its natural environment and resources.

The urbanization rate of Linxia is generally low, and differences exist in the urbanization of the town and countries, as reported in Table 5.4. The Linxia town's urbanization rate is 66.4%, the highest in the prefecture; and the rates of other counties in the prefecture are all less than 30% at the primary stage of urbanization.

The analysis above shows that the prefecture faces huge challenges in regards to urban development due to its low and imbalanced urbanization rate. Meanwhile,

Linxia's growth is economically and politically significant since it is a typical impoverished area with many minorities. There is a provincial, even national significance in developing new-type urbanization in Linxia. The following are some limitations faced by Linxia as to its urbanization:

Backward economic development A region's urbanization is determined largely by its economic development. However, economic indices of Linxia Prefecture are all behind the national average, ranking low among 14 towns and prefectures in the province and minority autonomous prefectures in the country, as shown in Table 5.5. The per capita GDP of the prefecture was 100,166 yuan in 2014, or 38.5% of Gansu's average and 22% of the national average. The per capita fixed asset investment was 10,210 yuan, or 40% of Gansu's average and 32% of the national average. The per capita total retail sales of consumer goods were 2700 yuan, or 29% of Gansu's average and 14% of the national average. The per capita fiscal income is 1163 yuan, or 24% of Gansu's average and 11% of the national average. In sum, all of the economic indicators are lower than the Gansu's average, and much lower than the national average.

Poor natural environments Linxia Prefecture is located in the three transition areas, i.e. the transition of the Loess Plateau, the transition of cold and warm, dry and wet climate, and the transition of agriculture and animal husbandry. Featuring plateaus, mountainous areas and loess hilly regions, Linxia has over-apparent natural disadvantages and sharp contrast between human and arable land (the per capita arable land is merely 1.09 mu). With a fragile agricultural basis, relatively dry climate and frequent natural disasters, Linxia is at the mercy of natural conditions to feed its population (Chao and Fang 2007). Besides, there are no sufficient reserves of mineral resources either.

Multiple social-cultural problems A minority autonomous prefecture located in the less developed northwest China with a fragile ecological environment, Linxia is confronted by multiple economic and social development challenges, including tackling religion issues, nationality issues, ecology issues and poverty alleviation, which pose more challenges to the urbanization of the area (Cao 2010). Local dwellers are conservative and lack of innovation and competition psychology, which is another barrier to the urbanization.

Table 5.5 Aggregated economic indicators of Linxia prefecture and its rank in 2014

	Value in 100 million yuan	Rank among 14 towns/prefectures in Gansu	Rank among 30 minority autonomous prefectures in China
GDP	202.97	13	21
Fixed asset investment	263.73	11	18
Local fiscal revenue	25.40	13	20

Sources Gansu Statistical Yearbook 2014 (NBSC 2015b), Gansu Social and Economic Statistical Yearbook (NBSC 2015c), and China Social and Economic Statistical Yearbook (NBSC 2015a)

Lack of development driving forces The problems of agriculture, famers and rural areas are prominent in Linxia. With a large impoverished population in rural areas, combined with the poor quality of its population, Linxia finds it challenging to realize agricultural industrialization and agricultural restructuring, making it difficult for agriculture to drive urbanization. Industry in the prefecture, weak as it is, has little effect in driving urbanization. The per capita industrial value added in 2014 of Linxia is only 10% that of the provincial average, or 5.3% of national average. Indistinctive industry at Linxia is of small scale and low standard, and the development of the tertiary industry is limited by a lack of promotion caused by a conservative mindset.

5.3.2 Strategies for New-Type Urbanization in Linxia

Due to a range of limitations and disadvantages, people in Linxia Prefecture should spare no effort in facilitating Linxia's urbanization through seizing chances and implementing policies that suit the unique local conditions. As a typical minority autonomous prefecture in the west of China, Linxia should develop the new-type urbanization with distinct minority characteristics, and present itself as an exemplar to other minority regions in the west. Therefore, it is suggested that the process starts from building an urbanization innovation demonstration zone. Special attention should be paid to the following aspects:

Industrial development Three industrial sectors should be encouraged. (a) Manufacturing, especially in the labor-intensive sectors. Due to industrialization as major driving force for urbanization, Linxia should strengthen industry projects and the construction of industrial parks based on resources and features of its counties, attract investments and support the leading industries, so as to boost the development of its industrialization and the non-public sectors of the economy. (b) Traditional services, specifically tourism. The fact that the prefecture has abundant tourism resources and minority culture and that the prefecture is located on the new silk road economic zone should be stressed in the promotion of local tourism, which could attract more tourists from both at home and abroad to appreciate the beautiful scenery and rich culture. As to catering, it is suggested to improve the quality and increase the variety of Muslim food to appeal to tourists. Meanwhile, a modern service industry developed selectively may provide new economic growth points and help the prefecture learn from eastern cities in the country. (c) Non-agricultural sector in rural areas. Agriculture is the major sector of Linxia; therefore, adopting policies to support and encourage township enterprises can absorb the surplus laborers in rural areas. As well, voluntary organizations by famers that can truly represent them and bring profit to them in a relatively short period should be encouraged to realize the transition of agricultural laborers to non-agricultural sectors.

Rural-urban migrations Two institutional reforms should be completed for promoting urbanization. (a) Reforming the household registration system and encouraging mobility between urban and rural dwellers. The reform in question has been an academic hotpot, but it has not been effectively solved. To realize migrant between urban and rural areas, the binary household registration management should be called to an end, and a united mechanism established instead. Besides, social insurance system should also be improved, such as unemployment insurance for non-agricultural employees, and medical insurance to guarantee the equal treatment. (b) Reforming the land acquisition and transfer system. As to the former, the prefecture government should investigate in a wide areas and plan scientifically and formulate phased planning of land exploitation, utilization and protection that suit local conditions. Government should also enhance the standard operation of land transfer, proactively promote the concepts involved, especially the legal awareness of farmers, and compensate the farmers who lose the land with reasonable economic and social benefits (Williamson 1988; Zhang and Song 2003)

Regional collaboration Urbanization is a long process and can never be completed overnight, and differences in economy require different methods. For Linxia Prefecture, mechanisms and strategies of urbanization should differ according to different counties to suit the appropriate urbanization types to the appropriate county. Meanwhile, positive interactions between counties should be realized and cooperation between the prefecture and other regions enhanced. One of the fundamentals in building new-type urbanization is coordination, which is to maximize the resource profits of counties and inject vigor into regional development. The connection between the prefecture and other cities and provinces should also be enhanced in its building of new-type urbanization so as to learn from others.

Incentives for minority development Building up innovation demonstration zones of new-type urbanization should be closely linked to the construction of the demonstration zone of "two commons" while properly dealing with harmonious coexistence of different minorities in the area. First, the "Linxia Spirit" should be promoted among different minorities, and multi-themed education events launched in religious circle for the purpose of harmony among the locals. Next is to improve the training and education of minorities and religious peoples, further enhancing their moral and cultural quality, and ensuring the social subsidy and living allowance of religious people. Finally, the religious events should be put on a reasonable and legally justifiable track that will make the administration of religion organized and standard.

5.4 Policy Implications for Urbanization Through Industrialization

While minority-group areas may differ from majority-group areas in many aspects, they do share in the main driver of urbanization: industrialization. Western regions with minority groups can learn from the experience of eastern regions in urbanization through industrialization. A gradual and timely diversification of the manufacturing sector towards the production of a selected number of higher technology goods and exports may help them promote urban development in the future. For sustained industrial development, reliance on static endowments such as primary resources and cheap labor is a good way to start, but this should be accompanied by building and enhancing technological capabilities to produce technology-intensive manufacturing. In sum, while increasingly targeting technology-intensive manufacturing, they should by no means ignore or discriminate against resource-based, labor-intensive, and low technology manufacturing.

Western China's rich natural resources and abundantly cheap labor give the regions great industrial potential. They may maintain a static comparative advantage in resource-based and labor-intensive manufacturing over the east in the years to come. The regions, however, have not exploited the full potential of their agro-industries. They need to move up the value chain, and increase the processing activities of their agro-industrial products.

Implications for central government *Education*. To reduce educational disparities between the east and the rest of the country, the central government can allocate additional funds to assist the regions left behind.

SME promotion. The central government can consider taking the following measures to promote small and medium enterprises (SMEs) in the manufacturing sector: targeting government funds, preferential measures and other promotional efforts at small enterprises only, not small and medium; ensuring balanced regional development, by allocating more funding to lagging areas; increasing the flexibility of interest rate ceilings so that banks can charge commercial rates to smaller enterprises; channeling SME development funds through commercial banks; unifying the government administration for urban and rural SMEs; improving the SME promotion law; and monitoring and evaluating SME promotion programs.

Implications for regional government *Focus on key determinants of industrial competitiveness*. The regional governments have the more important direct role to play to enhance industrial competitiveness. They need to focus on the key structural determinants of industrial performance (namely technological effort, foreign direct investment (FDI), modern infrastructure, and educated labor force). The most important measure may be to encourage the widespread development of technological efforts in all types of industries and firms of all sizes. Other important areas are effective investment promotion and SME development. In all three areas, the western regions must learn from their eastern counterparts and from successful examples abroad.

Develop manufacturing and technological capabilities of all firms Technological effort takes many forms, not just R&D, and includes activities such as purchase of machinery and turn-key plants, reverse-engineering and continuous improvements in process, product and logistics.

Investment promotion services Many western regions possess adequate and reliable infrastructure and skills for the manufacturing sector, and offer substantial labor cost advantages to attract more FDI. However, FDI will not automatically flow in unless the regions devote sufficient resources to publicize business opportunities to prospective investors. Western regions need to step up their investment promotion services by learning from their eastern counterparts and by learning from successful examples abroad.

SME promotion Since the vast majority of SMEs do not regard the existing technological support institutions as important for raising their manufacturing capabilities and competitiveness, the regional governments can take the following measures: focusing technology extension services on SMEs and revamp them to become proactive, encouraging universities and private and public training institutions to become more proactive in selling their services to the SMEs, encouraging business and industry associations to promote technological development, and facilitating access to business development services.

Implications for local government Local governments have a distinct role to play, complementary to the central government and regional authorities, to enhance the competitiveness of manufacturing firms located in their areas. The main areas of intervention include the local business environment and investment climate, the pro-active role of business associations, SME and cluster promotion, education and training and government services.

Business registration, regulations and inspections. Local governments can speed up business registration and keep regulations and inspections to a strict minimum to reduce the regulatory burden on entrepreneurs.

Contract enforcement. To improve the overall business climate, local business and industry associations can work closely with the local government to achieve an efficient and speedy local court system.

Business and industry associations as technology promoters. Local governments should promote and encourage the formation of local industry associations run by their own members. The associations should then be encouraged to promote manufacturing and technological upgrading of their members, and to invest in common facilities such as quality certification, information services, trade fairs and joint marketing.

SME promotion. Many changes have already been legislated for, and many biases against SMEs have been formally removed. Now the initiative is with local governments to become the focus for improving the enabling environment for SMEs. Local governments need to systematically reduce the cost of doing business in the areas under their jurisdiction and improve the attitude of staff regarding SMEs. They should facilitate the provision of BDS for small businesses, and provide guidance to SMEs on how to operate within the law, and maintain social and environmental standards.

Education and skills are the most important resource sought by SME after finance. Local governments are in effect responsible for providing most of the educated and skilled labor needed by SMEs. While government supervision remains a necessary ingredient, local providers of education and training must develop an intimate relationship with the SMEs so that the qualified labor is produced in line with SME needs. Local governments can also effectively take the lead in encouraging SMEs to retrain their staff in line with market developments and new technologies to enhance competitiveness.

Encourage natural SME clusters. Traditionally, local governments, and even regional governments, see themselves as rivals of with their neighboring local or regional economies. Cluster management seeks to overcome administrative boundaries and encourage the development of natural clusters that cross county, district, city and regional boundaries. Cluster management also needs a coherent overall administration for regional marketing, strengthening of institutional linkages, attracting qualified human resources, technology, and other inputs, and furthering the tacit knowledge available to the members of the cluster on product and process development. Cluster management seeks to organize a coordinated system of support to the cluster's enterprises to avoid the pitfalls of administrative fragmentation.

5.5 Conclusions

Based on international information and the national experience of urbanization and industrialization, this study examines urban development of minority areas in Western China. We first present an overall pattern of urbanization in the western China's minority areas, focusing on four urban development models in terms of driving forces: border trade, tourism, industry, and animal husbandry on grassland. Then we investigate Linxia prefecture of Gansu province as a case study in order to identify specific problems in urbanization. The factors resulting in low urbanization include poor natural endowments, backward economic development, multiple social-cultural problems, and lack of growth-driving forces. A proposal of future strategies for Linxia is also discussed, including promoting industrial development, encouraging rural-urban migration, and enhancing regional collaboration. Finally, this study draws some policy implications at central, regional and local governments, focusing on how to promote urbanization through industrialization.

China's impressive performance in overall urbanization and economic growth has been by now well documented. China's developmental successes, including urbanization, are largely due to rapid industrialization through manufacturing success, confirming the potential of harnessing industrialization for sustained development and urbanization. What is less well known, however, is that China's western minority areas have been less developed in both industrialization and urbanization relative to the eastern regions. The western minority areas appear to have focused on exporting more primary goods and less processed manufactured products and technology-intensive products. They upgraded their production structure, but this did not translate into technology-intensive products. As a result, urbanization has been not taking place as rapid as the eastern regions. We find the main cause for low urban development in minority areas is low industrialization, same as other areas with low urbanization. In other words, ethnic minorities are not a key factor in determination of urban development and economic growth.

References in English

Barrios, S., L. Bertinelli, and E. Strobl. 2006. Climatic change and rural-urban migration: The case of Sub-Saharan Africa. *Journal of Urban Economics* 60(3): 357–371.

Brückner, M. 2012. Economic growth, size of the agricultural sector, and urbanization in Africa. *Journal of Urban Economics* 71(1): 26–36.

Cao, H. 2010. Urban–rural income disparity and urbanization: What is the role of spatial distribution of ethnic groups? A case study of Xinjiang Uyghur autonomous region in western China. *Regional Studies* 44(8): 965–982.

Chao, B., and C. Fang. 2007. Water resources constraint force on urbanization in water deficient regions: A case study of the Hexi Corridor, arid area of Northwestern China. *Ecological Economics* 62(3): 507–517.

Davis, J.C., and J. V. Henderson. 2003. Evidence on the political economy of the urbanization process. *Journal of Urban Economics*, 53(1), 98–125.

Hamer, A.M., and J. F. Linn. 1987. Urbanization in the developing world: Patterns, issues, and policy. In *Handbook of Regional and Urban Economics*, Vol. II, ed. by E.S. Mills. Amsterdam: Elsevier-North Holland.

Michaels, G., F. Rauch, and S. J. Redding. 2012. Urbanization and structural transformation. *The Quarterly Journal of Economics* 127(2): 535–586.

Song, S., and K. H. Zhang. 2002. Urbanization and city-size distribution in China. *Urban Studies* 39(12): 2317–2327.

Williamson, J.G. 1988. Migration and urbanization. In *Handbook of Development Economics*, vol. I, ed. by Chenery, H. and Srinivasan, T.N. Amsterdam: Elsevier-North Holland.

Xie, J., and K. H. Zhang. 2004. Urban population in the reform era. In *Urban transformation in China*, ed. by Chen, Liu, and Zhang. Ashgate, pp 83–96.

World Bank and Development Research Center of China (WB and DRCC). (2014). *Urban China: Toward Efficient, Inclusive, and Sustainable Urbanization.* Washington, DC: World Bank.

Zhang, K.H. 2004. Evolution of Chinese urban transformation: 1949–2000. In *Urban Transformation in China*, ed. by Chen, Liu, and Zhang. New York: Ashgate, pp 25–39.

Zhang, K.H. 2002. What explains China's rising urbanization in the reform era? *Urban Studies* 39 (12): 2301–2315.

Zhang, K. H., and S. Song. 2003. Rural-urban migration and urbanization in China: Evidence from time-series and cross-section analysis. *China Economic Review* 13(4): 386–400.

References in Chinese

NBSC (National Bureau of Statistics of China). 2005–2015. *Zhongguo tongji nianjian 2004–2014 [China Statistical Yearbook 2004–2014].* Beijing: China Statistics Press.

NBSC. 2015a. *Zhongguo shehui he jingji tongji nianjian 2014 [China Social and Economic Statistical Yearbook 2014].* Beijing: China Statistics Press.

NBSC. 2015b. *Gsnsusheng tongji nianjian 2014 [Gansu Statistical Yearbook 2014].* Beijing: China Statistics Press.

NBSC. 2015c. *Gansusheng shehui he jingji tongji nianjian 2014 [Gansu Social and Economic Statistical Yearbook 2014].* Beijing: China Statistics Press.

Part III
Urban Development and Impact on Women and Environment

Chapter 6
Infrastructure Development and Urbanization in China

Chaosu Li, Yan Song and Yan Chen

Abstract The unprecedented infrastructure development in China has created huge opportunities for urban land development and economic activity. Recently, China has accelerated the construction of urban public infrastructure by investing as much as seven trillion Yuan ($1.03 trillion) during its 12th Five-Year Plan from 2011 to 2015. In this chapter, we provide empirical evidence on how different levels of infrastructure provision influence urbanization in China. By using a cross-sectional dataset from 650 Chinese cities, we examine the effects of infrastructure related determinants on urban expansion rates and urban land price. Additionally, we use the hedonic price model to explore the relationship between urban intra-infrastructure development and housing prices in the city of Shenzhen. The results indicate both intra- and inter-city infrastructure developments, including streets within cities, and inter-city express highways and railways connecting cities, have positive impacts on urban expansion. However, much of the convenience provided for intra- and inter-city commuters by streets, public transit and railways has not been capitalized into land price. In general, the findings clearly show that infrastructure has important effects on urban expansion rates, land prices, and subsequently, housing price. Finally, we examine whether recent infrastructure developments could help Chinese cities grow toward a sustainable future, and further discuss the challenges and critical issues associated with the current practice of infrastructure development in China.

Keywords Infrastructure development · Urbanization · China · Sustainability

C. Li (✉) · Y. Song · Y. Chen
University of North Carolina at Chapel Hill, Chapel Hill, USA
e-mail: chaosuli@live.unc.edu

Z. Tang (ed.), *China's Urbanization and Socioeconomic Impact*,
DOI 10.1007/978-981-10-4831-9_6

6.1 Introduction

Accompanied by continuous urbanization processes and market-oriented reform, China has been one of the world's fastest-growing economies with a per capita real income more than quadrupling since 1978. In this period, China has made substantial investments in infrastructure and improved access to services such as safe water, sanitation, electric power, telecommunications, and transport (Zhang 2011). More recently, China has accelerated construction of urban public infrastructure by investing as much as seven trillion Yuan ($1.03 trillion) during its 12th Five-Year Plan from 2011 to 2015.

It is generally believed that during the development process, infrastructure investments are quite necessary to alleviate infrastructure endowment related constraints and to facilitate economic growth (Démurger 2001; Gramlich 1994; Wu 2010). The adequacy of infrastructure, which can contribute to diversifying production, expanding trade, coping with population growth, reducing poverty, or improving environmental conditions, helps determine a country's success (World Bank 2004) by accommodating economic and urban growth (Calderón and Servén 2004). Thus, in recent years, infrastructure development still remains as one of the top priorities for the Chinese government.

Although there have been studies concerning the relationship between infrastructure development and economic growth (for example, Démurger 2001; Gramlich 1994; Wu 2010), as well as rural development (Fan and Zhang 2004) in China, the link between infrastructure and urban growth remains understudied. In this regard, it is somewhat surprising that infrastructure research has developed in isolation from the larger literature on urban growth. To shed light on this, in this chapter, we aim to discuss the links between infrastructure provisions and urban expansion, the relationship between levels of infrastructure and land price, and the relation between different intra-city infrastructures and housing price. Data and case studies from developed and developing cities in China are used to provide empirical evidence about the extent to which infrastructure service provisions affect urban development and shape development patterns. We also examine whether recent infrastructure development could help Chinese cities grow toward a sustainable future, and further discuss the challenges and critical issues associated with the current practice of infrastructure development in China.

6.2 Overview of Infrastructure Development in China

Since the economic reform and opening-up policy in 1978, China has made substantial investments in infrastructure, improving access to services such as clean water, sanitation, electricity, telecommunications, and transport (Economic Research Institute for ASEAN and East Asia 2007). Urban infrastructure investment in China has grown exponentially in the last several decades. From 1978 to

2008, urban infrastructure investment as a percentage of GDP fluctuated between 0.33 and 3.29%, while urban infrastructure investment as a percentage of total investment ranged between 1.79 and 8.02%. Despite this marked increase, infrastructure investment in China relative to both GDP and total investment was lower than it was in other developing countries, as reported in a World Bank Survey, and levels recommended by the U.N. (World Bank 2004). Although China spends about 50% of its GDP on fixed investment (compared to the world average of fewer than 20% or the US figure of 15%), only a small percentage is spent on urban infrastructure.

In the context of economic development and growing interregional trade, updated infrastructure became necessary. In this context, in the early 1990s, investment in infrastructure has been reasserted as one of the national major policy priorities (Démurger 2001). Especially in recent years, China's investment in infrastructure has increased, relieving economic and social development pressures caused by limited infrastructure. The heavy infrastructure investment in China in recent years is driven by the high demand for infrastructure services fueled by steady economic growth, and it is also partly related to the proactive fiscal policy adopted by the government to minimize the impact of the financial crisis through increased public expenditures in infrastructure (Liu 2010). Many problems still exist with current practices of infrastructure development. There is still an insufficient level of infrastructure in some regions, especially the western region despite the recent increase in investment. Insufficient investment in infrastructure could hinder urban and economic growth (Economic Research Institute for ASEAN and East Asia 2007).

It is also worthwhile to note that main policy regimes of the central government can act as an impetus to infrastructure developments. In recent years, following several policy regimes such as "Develop the West," "Revitalize Old Industrial Bases in the Northeast," and "Boost the Equalization of Public Services," infrastructure investments in interior areas have grown significantly. From 2003 to 2010, on average, 40.5% of China's railway investment was channeled to the west. Over the same period, road investment in the west comprised 32.7 percent of the national total. This heavy investment in the western region's transportation infrastructure has decreased businesses' transportation costs and promoted the redistribution of industry from coastal areas to the interior. The order of the investment amount spent on public services is eastern, western, central and northeast, from high to low. The east's higher financial capacity as compared to other regions accounts for its larger share of investment in public facilities, such as drainage systems within cities.

Since the following sections of this chapter will be mainly focused on urbanization and transportation infrastructure, it is useful to further examine the scope of transportation infrastructure investment in China. Since the late 1980s, investment in major urban infrastructure types, including railroads, roadways, aviation, and public facilities, has increased significantly with the rapid urbanization in China (Economic Research Institute for ASEAN and East Asia 2007). During the year 2003 and 2011, total investment in major transportation infrastructure accounted for between 13.2 and 17% of total urban investment, or 15.7% on average.

Contributing to the rise in government spending in 2009 was an increase in investment to address the financial crisis, resulting in a small peak in investment in railways and public facilities.

More specifically, railway mileage increased from 51,700 to 78,000 km, a total increase of 50% and an average annual increase of 1.4% from 1978 to 2007. During this period, road mileage tripled and civil aviation mileage increased 15-fold. According to the Interim and Long Term Railway Network Plan adopted by the State Council in 2004, the target is to add 120,000 km of railway to the nation's existing 91,000 km network by 2020 with an investment of 700 billion RMB in the 12th Five-Year Plan period between 2011 and 2015. The objective set in the Twelfth Five-Year Plan is to construct an additional 120,000 km of railway before 2015, 45,000 km of which will be high-speed. This is compared to China's current 13,000 km of high-speed railway. A high proportion of these planned infrastructure projects will be constructed to connect cities in the western region, such as from Xining to Lanzhou; or to connect cities in the west to the central or eastern regions.

Intra-urban railway transportation infrastructure is also developing at an accelerated rate. In Shanghai, for example, subway mileage has been planed and approved by the State Development Reform Commission to reach 850 km, which would far exceed the total subway mileage in New York or London. Spatially, these new intra-urban railways are concentrated. According to Freemark (2010), Ninety-five percent of urban railway transportation is concentrated in 11 provinces and cities in the east and is developing at an exceptionally rapid pace in the Yangtze River Delta.

6.3 Infrastructure, Urban Scale, and Urban Land Prices—A Cross-Sectional Analysis

This section aims to explore how infrastructure development in China has affected urban expansion and land prices. Many studies have examined the driving forces of urban land expansion across Chinese cities (He et al. 2011; Ke et al. 2009; Liu et al. 2005; Song and Zenou 2006) and have found that China's urban expansion had a high level of spatial differences, which resulted from different levels of demographic change, economic growth, and changes in land use policies and regulations (Liu et al. 2005). However, few attempts have been made to investigate how infrastructure provisions can affect urban expansion and urban land prices. Démurger (2001) provides empirical evidence on the links between infrastructure investment and economic growth in China using panel data from a sample of 24 Chinese provinces throughout the 1985 to 1998 period. The results indicate that besides differences in terms of reforms and openness, geographical location and infrastructure endowment did account significantly for observed differences in growth performance across space, and that transport facilities are a key differentiating factor in explaining the growth gap.

This section examines the links between infrastructure investment and urban growth; specifically, this section provides some empirical evidence on how different levels of infrastructure provision contribute to variations in urban scale and land price across Chinese cities. To do so, this paper applies a consolidated monocentric model that was previously-developed by He et al. (2011). The model is developed to account for both "closed" and "open" city features in a developing country, where permanent urban residents and migrants interact in the informal goods market and the land market and yield a distinctive equilibrium pattern.

In this section, the theoretical model (He et al. 2011) is applied to an empirical analysis of urban scales and land prices across all Chinese cities for the year of 2010. Table 6.1 describes the variables used in two regressions of urban scale and land prices. The dependent variables are urban scale and land price respectively in 2010. Of main interests, the analysis includes a set of variables accounting for infrastructure level in 2005: number of city buses per thousand residents (Bus), street length per resident (Street), number of express highways (ExpHwy), capacity of railroad centers (RRCenter), capacity of airports (AirPort), and percentage of infrastructure investment comparing to GDP. Together, these variables characterize the capacity of intra-city infrastructure levels and long range transport infrastructure in each city. It is hypothesized that greater levels of infrastructure provision and investments corresponds to better accessibility, hence larger cities, and higher land price. There are 660 officially designated cities in China. Excluding observations with missing data on key variables, 638 observations are retained for the urban scale equation. Data on land price is available only for prefecture or higher-level cities. Of these, 260 of the 280 have complete data and are used in the price equation. The data are extracted from the China City Statistical Yearbook 2011, China Statistical Yearbooks for Urban Construction 2011, and China Statistical Yearbooks for Land and Resources 2010.

The regressions include a set of control variables as suggested by previous studies (He et al. 2011), such as population (UrbPoP), average annual salary income of permanent residents (Salary), the average productivity of agricultural land (GDP_AgriLand) as a proxy for the price of agricultural land. In addition, a set of dummy variables are used to define city types, such as provincial capital cities (Capital), prefecture level cities (Prefecture), resource extraction cities (Resource), and cities in different regions (Central, or Western). For land price estimation, lagged land price (Price_lag) and land supply (Land_supply) are also included. These variables all have large standard deviations relative to the means and show great dispersion, suggesting significant disparities among Chinese cities in urban scale and land prices, and the attributing factors (Table 6.2).

The log-log form is used to estimate the urban scale and land price equations. The results are shown in Table 6.3.

The estimates show that urban infrastructure provision affects both urban expansion and land price. Specifically, in the urban scale regression, of the six variables that are used to account for infrastructure level, Street, ExpHwy, RRCenter and Infra_GDP have significant and positive parameter estimates while Bus and AirPort are not significant determinants of urban scale. This indicates that

Table 6.1 Variables and data sources

Variable name	Variable description	Units
Urban scale	Defined as $\sqrt{Built\_distr/\pi}$ where Built_distr is the area of the urban built district	km
Land price	Defined as land sale values divided by area (for details on variable construction see He et al. 2011)	10,000RMB[a]/ha
Bus	Number of city buses per thousand residents	NA
Street	Street length per resident	km/person
ExpHwy	Number of express highways passing through the jurisdictional territory	NA
RRCenter	For cities at the prefecture level and above, *RRCenter* is assigned number 0 if total railway passenger throughput was zero in year 2000; non-zero throughput values are grouped into six quantiles and numerical values 1–6 are assigned accordingly; for cities at the county level, *RRCenter* is assigned the value 1 if there is a railway station within 30 km from the urban center, and 0 otherwise	NA
AirPort	For cities at the prefecture level and above, *AirPort* is 0 if the total airline passenger throughput was zero in year 2001; non-zero throughput values are grouped into six quantiles and numerical values 1–6 are assigned accordingly; for cities in the county level, *AirPort* is assigned the ordinal values 0–4 if number of daily flight departures is no greater than 0, 200, 300, 500, or greater than 500 from airports within 100 km from the urban center	NA
Infra_GDP	Percentage of infrastructure investment comparing to GDP	NA
UrbPop	Population of permanent residents with non-rural residence permits in the jurisdictional territory	10,000
Salary	Average annual salary income of permanent residents	1000RMB[a]
GDP_AgriLand	Defined as $\frac{GDP\_Ag}{Urban\_area-Built\_distr}$ if $GDP\_Ag \neq 0$; otherwise as $\frac{GDP}{Urban\_area}$	10,000RMB[a]/km^2
Price_lag	Defined as *Price* in the previous year	10,000RMB[a]/ha
Land_Supply	Available land for transactions in the market (for details on variable construction, see He et al. 2011)	ha
Capital	Dummy for provincial capital cities or directly governed cities (30 in total)	NA
Prefecture	Dummy for prefecture level cities (249 in total)	NA
Resource	Dummy for resource extraction cities (16 in total)	NA
Central	Dummy for cities in the central region, including the following provinces: Anhui, Heilongjiang, Henan, Hubei, Hunan, Inner Mongolia, Jiangxi, Jilin, and Shanxi	NA
Western	Dummy for cities in the western region, including the following provinces: Chongqing, Gansu, Guizhou, Ningxia, Qinghai, Sha'anxi, Sichuan, Tibet, Xinjiang, and Yunnan	NA

Notes NA = not applicable
[a]RMB is the basic unit of the official currency of China

Table 6.2 Descriptive statistics

Variable name	Descriptive statistics			
	Mean	S.d.	Min	Max
Urban scale	3.46	2.03	0.94	21.45
Land price	698	540	28.49	3868.35
Bus	0.06	0.06	0.015	0.26
Street	8.25e−04	4.11e−04	1.67e−04	3.41e−03
ExpHwy	1.42	1.31	0.00	11.00
RRCenter	1.79	1.48	0.00	6.00
AirPort	0.84	1.76	0.00	5.00
Infra_GDP	2.69%	2.08%	1.97%	5.87%
UrbPop	55.31	110.34	2.01	1398.36
Salary	15.89	5.77	6.53	37.93
GDP_AgriLand	3.87e + 04	2.99e + 06	7.29	4.06e + 06
Price_lag	527	457	15.78	3564.71
Land_Supply	149	201	2.44	2048.90
Capital	0.046	0.210	0.00	1.00
Prefecture	0.383	0.486	0.00	1.00
Resource	0.025	0.155	0.00	1.00
Central	0.372	0.484	0.00	1.00
Western	0.194	0.395	0.00	1.00

Note For most variables, the statistics are calculated for the scale equation sample, which includes 638 cities. Statistics for Price, Price_lag, and Land_Supply are reported for the price equation sample, which includes only 260 cities

both intra- and inter-city transportation investments, including streets within cities, and inter-city express highways and railways connecting cities, have positive impact on urban growth. The general measure of infrastructure investment as a percentage of GDP is also positive and significant, indicating infrastructure's important role in stimulating urban growth. The estimates show that a 10% increase in Street increases the urban radius by 1.39%, a 10% increase in ExpHwy increases the urban radius by 0.78%, a 10% increase in RRCenter increases the urban radius by 0.39%, and a 10% increase in Infra_GDP increases the urban radius by 0.05%.

In the land price regression, of the six variables that are used to account for infrastructure level, ExpHwy, AirPort and Infra_GDP have significant and positive parameter estimates while Bus, Street and RRCenter are not significant determinants of urban land price. The insignificant estimate of Bus, Street and RRCenter suggest that much of the convenience provided for intra- and inter-city commuters by streets, public transit and railways has not been capitalized into land price.

It is necessary to point out that the variables of RRCenter and AirPort perform differently in the urban scale and land price equations. Variable RRCenter is significant in explaining urban scale while variable AirPort explains more price variations. The different results can be explained by the differences between China's rural-to-urban migrants and inter-city migrants. Rural-to-urban migrants,

Table 6.3 Regression results for urban scale and land price

Variable	Urban scale			Land price		
	Estimate	t value	Pr(> |t|)	Estimate	t value	Pr(> |t|)
(Intercept)	0.867*	2.285	0.02	2.750***	3.789	0.00
Bus	0.009	0.781	0.31	0.008	0.972	0.34
Street	0.139***	10.973	0.00	0.065	0.785	0.32
ExpHwy	0.078***	9.736	0.00	0.058*	2.164	0.03
RRCenter	0.039***	4.573	0.00	0.023	1.312	0.22
AirPort	0.004	0.950	0.32	0.121**	2.711	0.01
Infra_GDP	0.005**	2.627	0.01	0.004*	2.166	0.03
UrbPop	0.313***	20.990	0.00	0.237*	2.291	0.02
Salary	0.174***	7.472	0.00	0.681***	5.882	0.00
GDP_AgriLand	−0.021***	−5.909	0.00	0.028	1.112	0.27
$Price_{\_lag}$				0.389***	11.381	0.00
Land_Supply				−0.116	−1.333	0.18
Capital	0.135***	3.695	0.00	0.264*	2.289	0.02
Prefecture	0.164***	5.980	0.00	0.497***	3.762	0.00
Resource	0.045	1.335	0.18	−0.035	−0.282	0.78
Central	0.051**	2.672	0.01	0.0379	1.109	0.27
Western	0.03	1.110	0.22	0.058	1.255	0.22
Adj-R^2	0.816			0.606		
Wald test	24.5**			20.3**		

Note *** denotes $P < 0.01$; **$P < 0.05$; * $P < 0.1$

contributing to urban expansion, are more likely to use the railways than the airlines. Thus, capacity of railway infrastructure is valued more in affecting urban scale. On the other hand, inter-city migrants are usually better paid professionals. In a few highly developed Chinese cities, inter-city migrants have dominated hi-tech industry and financial business. Many white-collar migrants prefer air travel and thus capacity of aviation infrastructure exerts a much greater influence on urban land price (He et al. 2011).

Most of the other variables are consistent with expectations. From the urban scale regression, urban population plays the dominant role in determining urban spatial scale. The estimated elasticity of urban scale with respect to average income (Salary) is 0.17 and very significant. The estimates also provide evidence that government planning is important in affecting urban scale. Estimated coefficients for Capital and Prefecture are both significant and positive, indicating that holding everything else constant, a capital city and a prefecture level city is larger than an otherwise comparable county level city because of more governmental functions contained in capital and prefecture level cities. The estimated coefficient of the regional dummy Central is significant, indicating that cities in central China on average use slightly more land than those in the east.

From the land price regression, results also show that land price is very responsive to urban population and average income. *Ceteris paribus*, a 10% increase in average income induces a 6.8% increase in land price. A 10% increase in non-agricultural urban population drives up land price by 2.4%. Price_lag is significant, indicating that lagged land price induces an increase in the current price. Estimated coefficients for Capital and Prefecture are both significant and positive, indicating that holding everything else constant, a capital city and a prefecture level city has higher land price than an otherwise comparable county level city.

In summary, through examining the determinants of urban scale and land price across Chinese cities, it is evident that when controlling for other factors, greater urban infrastructure investment contributes to a higher level of growth of human settlements, and a higher level of land price. It is important to note that the analysis included in this section is a cross-sectional analysis. Therefore, the results only suggest that across cities, earlier investment in infrastructure is correlated with more expansive urban growth and higher land prices. It is also possible that earlier decisions on infrastructure investments were made because of expected urban and economic growth in selected cities (World Bank 2004). In the next section, time-series data will be used to explore how earlier infrastructure shapes land development at a later time.

6.4 Infrastructure and Urban Housing Price—A Hedonic Model

This section aims to explore the relationship between housing price and proximity to urban transportation infrastructure in Futian District, Shenzhen. Our hypothesis is that accessibility to intra-city transportation infrastructure would positively affect housing price. This hypothesis is tested using the hedonic price model. Typically, hedonic modelling is often used to estimate the implicit value of differences in property characteristics. In this case, we use hedonic model to estimate the externalized benefits provided by access to transportation infrastructure.

Previous research on hedonic price models of transportation infrastructure is quite extensive. Researchers have tested the relationship between property values and multiple distance metrics (Thériault et al. 1999). However, there are still limited studies concerning this topic in China. In effect, empirical hedonic models using housing price as a dependent variable are widely used. From previous studies, we can conclude that hedonic models often use structural (e.g., square footage, building age, number of rooms lot size), neighbourhood (e.g., accessibility to different facilities and infrastructures), and environmental characteristics (e.g., urban green space) as explanatory variables to model housing price (Champ et al. 2003; Morancho 2003; Seo et al. 2014). In this study, we include both environmental and neighbourhood characteristics in the neighbourhood variables and extract all the infrastructure related variables from neighbourhood characteristic and list them as

Table 6.4 Variables and data sources

Variable name	Variable description	Data source/ Units
Structural variables		
Salearea	Average living area of housing units	Various[a]/ Square meter
Far	Floor area ratio of the residential area	Various[a]/NA
Floor	Average floors of the buildings in the residential area	Various[a]/NA
Roomnum	Average room number of housing unit	Various[a]/NA
Orientation	Orientation of the buildings Defined as an ordinal variable, with values of 1, 2, 3, 4; 4 denotes best orientation (south-facing buildings)	Various[a]/NA
Housetype	Defined as an ordinal variable, with values of 1, 2, 3; 1 denotes low-rise multi-family apartment, 2 denotes high-rise multi-family apartment, 3 denotes single-family house	Various[a]/NA
Neighborhood variables		
Industry	Distance to nearest industrial estate	GIS calculation/Meter
Green_Sp	Distance to nearest urban green space	GIS calculation/Meter
Mid_Sch	Distance to nearest middle school	GIS calculation/Meter
Ele_Sch	Distance to nearest elementary school	GIS calculation/Meter
Hospital	Distance to nearest hospital	GIS calculation/Meter
Commer	Distance to nearest commercial area	GIS calculation/Meter
Infrastructure variables		
Dis_Hwy	Distance to nearest highway	GIS calculation/Meter
Dis_Expre	Distance to nearest main road	GIS calculation/Meter
Dis_Subway	Distance to nearest subway corridor	GIS calculation/Meter

Notes NA = not applicable

[a]Including planning bureau, multiple official websites and online documents

infrastructure variables. We calculate the distance to the nearest infrastructure based on geographic information systems (GIS). All the explanatory variables and data sources are listed in Table 6.4.

We systematically gathered the average sale price of each residential estate in Futian District, Shenzhen from multiple sources from official websites. Finally we collected 1123 valid samples. It is worthwhile to note that in order to control the time-variance of the housing price, we only gathered the sale price from September to November, 2015.

It is worthwhile to note that there always exist nonlinear relationships in hedonic price models. For instance, in our model, housing price would decrease at a decreasing rate with increasing distance to nearest facilities and infrastructures. We tried different functional forms and found that the semi-log form fit this study better

Table 6.5 Regression results of hedonic price model

Variable	Standard coef	*t* value	Pr(> |t|)
(Intercept)	2.763***	18.202	0.00
Structural variables			
Salearea	0.782***	22.812	0.00
Far	−0.091***	−5.098	0.00
Floor	0.036*	2.039	0.04
Roomnum	0.284***	6.920	0.00
Orientation	0.049*	2.201	0.03
Housetype	0.156***	5.608	0.00
Neighborhood variables			
Industry	−0.190	−1.120	0.26
Green_Sp	−0.008	0.325	0.75
Mid_Sch	0.046	0.897	0.37
Ele_Sch	0.070**	2.908	0.00
Hospital	0.053	1.630	0.10
Commer	−0.088**	−2.913	0.00
Infrastructure variables			
Dis_Hwy	−0.202***	−5.908	0.00
Dis_Expre	0.009	0.372	0.71
Dis_Subway	−0.256***	−9.092	0.00
R^2	0.754		
Adj-R^2	0.732		

Note *** denotes $P < 0.001$; **$P < 0.01$; * $P < 0.05$

compared to linear and translog forms of the hedonic price model. Thus we choose the semi-log hedonic price model to capture the declining effects of explanatory variables.

The regression results of our hedonic models are presented in Table 6.5. Overall, all the structural variables are significant and the coefficients of them all have expected signs. Measures of the living area of housing units, number of rooms, housing type, orientation of the buildings, average floors of the buildings, are positively related to the sale price of the residential estate. Not surprisingly, the floor area ratio is negatively associated with housing price. Many of the neighbourhood variables do not appear to be significant, probably because Futian District is located in the central city of Shenzhen, and there is not much variance in terms of proximity to industry estate, urban green space, schools, hospitals, etc. However, it is worthwhile to notice that proximity to commercial areas has a positive effect on the housing sale price. Most importantly, our main hypotheses on the amenity of proximity to intra-city transportation infrastructure are generally valid in this study. The accessibility effect of highways on housing price is positive, which indicates that the convenience provided by highway access has outweighed the disamenities such as noise. Moreover, proximity to subways is significant in increasing the housing price. Accessibility to urban main roads does not appear to have a significant effect on housing price, probably because the density of main road in Futian District is generally high.

To sum up, our hedonic valuation of intra-city transportation infrastructure is valid in the case of Futian District, Shenzhen, which demonstrates that intra-city transportation infrastructure has important positive effects on housing price.

6.5 Discussions and Conclusions

In recent years, to hedge against flagging economic growth, infrastructure investment continues to increase in China. This chapter provides empirical evidence that infrastructure has important effects on urban expansion rates, housing prices, and spatial land developments. Given this set of established links, it is thus especially important to examine whether recent infrastructure development could help cities grow toward a sustainable future. Despite the accelerated rate of infrastructure development, there are several issues associated with current practice of infrastructure development in China.

There is no denying the fact that the general level of infrastructure development in China is still low. Although infrastructure development has been advanced in developed cities in China, in many inland cities, the average infrastructure capacity per capita is comparatively low due to the large size of the population and the underdevelopment of infrastructure (Lin 2001). This insufficient level of infrastructure could impede efforts to accommodate both spatial and economic growth. There is a need to improve infrastructure, not only to facilitate economic growth (Sahoo et al. 2010), but also to overcome geographic barriers and increase western growth (Démurger et al. 2002). To address this issue, local municipalities, specifically the planning bureaus, need to design an infrastructure inventory system to have accurate understandings of existing and predicted capacities. By doing so, intelligence can be added to the infrastructure planning system to either avoid wasteful investment or to expand infrastructure development to accommodate urban and economic growth.

It is also evident that regional infrastructure development is imbalanced. Infrastructure in the eastern region of China is more developed (Loo 1999) compared with the western and the central regions despite the recent acceleration of infrastructure investment in the west. Such imbalance in the level of infrastructure across the regions is a barrier to the socioeconomic development of hinterland regions. In particular, many hinterland areas still have inadequate transportation infrastructures and other facilities like telecommunications, water supply, drainage, and electricity supply (Economic Research Institute for ASEAN and East Asia 2007; Li and Shum 2001). As improving regional equity is particularly important to maintaining social stability, measures need to be designed and implemented to lessen regional differences.

Financing sources for infrastructure provisions are still limited in China. On the one hand, increasingly decentralized central-local fiscal relations are allowing municipalities a great degree of freedom for resource mobilization through a wide range of mechanisms that greatly expand extra-budgetary revenue (Wu 1999); in other words, China has succeeded in addressing urban infrastructure backlogs by opening up new venues for financing. But simultaneously, there have been emerging financing problems prompted by debt-laden local governments in China in the aftermath of the global financial crisis (Tsui 2011). Several key institutions (the cadre evaluation system, the land management regime, and the banking sector) have created an environment that draws local governments into a trap of relying on unconventional sources, such as land transfer fees. The resulted high levels of debt may impede China's efforts to mitigate structural imbalances in its economy. The different administrative ranks of cities have significant variation in financial capacities. The ingenious nature of extra-budgetary and off-budgetary resource collection by local authorities has resulted in high levels of inter-city and intra-city inequalities, further producing imbalanced distribution of infrastructure (Démurger 2001; Wang et al. 2011). Efforts have been made to diversify financing sources. Much of foreign investments and commercial loans are used for infrastructure construction in response to insufficient public financing mechanisms. However, the repayment terms for infrastructure loans are relatively long, and the banks face the risk of incurring bad debts. In some regions, commercial bank loans account for 80% of the total investment in transportation (Economic Research Institute for ASEAN and East Asia 2007).

Moreover, there are many potential development management tools (such as land value capture and property taxes) that could offer market-oriented financing to infrastructure development in China. The value capture management tool allows the local government to cover partial or even all costs of public infrastructure investment and maintenance by income gained from real estate developments in surrounding station areas. Increases in land value induced by infrastructure development, as demonstrated in the case study in this chapter, now could be "captured" directly into government revenue by involving real estate development. Hong Kong has achieved a world-level success on building a self-profitable light-rail system using the value capture tool, which is called the "Rail & Property" model. According to Cervero and Murakami (2008), the "Rail & Property" model in Hong Kong is one of the best examples anywhere of applying the value capture principle to finance railway investments. Due to a range of institutional issues, in other areas of China, the planning, construction, management process of infrastructure development is not easily consolidated by one authority as in the Hong Kong case. Therefore, experiences with such tools are still limited and need to be expanded. The evidence on the link between infrastructure and land prices suggests that a more efficient land value capture tool can be designed to finance public infrastructure projects.

Using infrastructure projects to guide sustainable spatial development is challenging in most cities. The priorities set by many cities on infrastructure investment are to promote economic growth and attract private investment. Nevertheless, evidence has been provided to show that infrastructure does have an impact on urban scale and urban development patterns. However, when infrastructure development neglects other goals such as efficient urban form and sustainable communities, it could result in an unsustainable form of urban land development. There are several examples to illustrate this issue.

- Many transportation infrastructure projects allocate land uses according to arbitrarily planned geometries such as axes, cores, and circles. Legacies from past central planning schemes have granted more power to the governments in determining where to locate infrastructure in China. City image projects exemplify institutional interference in the process of city growth. The layout design for Ordos Kangbashi new town development (Fig. 6.1) is an example of highlighting city images and neglecting principles of sustainable design and planning: The new town is mainly supported by the high-level highway system. This layout of infrastructure falls short in promoting walkability, accessibility, and dense developments endorsed by smart growth principles.
- The current infrastructure planning system does not ensure effective mechanisms for guiding the timing, location, and intensity of urban developments. For instance, a bedroom community in Beijing, Huilongguan, is planned and constructed outside the fifth ring road and about 15 km from downtown Beijing. Huilongguan is characterized by its enormous residential capacity, housing about 0.3 million residents. However, there is no concurrency requirement in terms of transportation infrastructure connecting the community to the city core. With a rapid increase in the number of private passenger cars, the current level of access roads and services is insufficient for 0.3 million people. An additional concern with this suburban neighborhood is the lack of land use and

Fig. 6.1 Illustration of Ordos Kangbashi New Town

transportation integration. More than 60 percent of residents in Huilongguan commute to downtown or other areas in Beijing for their daily work. The community generates more trips (especially external trips during peak hours), which worsens the existing transportation system not only for the lower-occupancy travel mode (private passenger cars), but also for the higher-occupancy travel mode (bus transit). Current land use design does not consider the provision of more efficient modes of public transportation. Moreover, the current transportation infrastructure still suffers from the lack of coordinating connection between inter-regional transit (such as high speed rail) and intra-city transit (such as bus, subway), which also indicates that the location of transportation infrastructure nodes is not determined based on sustainability principles. Another similar case of this could be found in Fig. 6.2: an urban light rail station in Shenzhen is located near high-end residential developments, in which residents drive mostly.

This lack of incorporating sustainable principles in infrastructure development has caught the attention of China's planners and policy makers. The Ministry of Housing and Urban and Rural Development (MHURD) is calling for more efficient and green infrastructure development in the next era of urban growth. Existing infrastructure system and land developments in many local cities have been evaluated with the purpose of identifying unsustainable planning practices. Currently, national pilot programs of Low-carbon Cities and Transit Metropolis are pervasive in China; advanced planning techniques are being explored and developed to improve current infrastructure provision practices, in order to promote a more sustainable urbanization process.

Fig. 6.2 Illustration of an urban light rail station in Shenzhen

References

Calderón, C., and L. Servén. 2004. *The effects of infrastructure development on growth and income distribution* (No. 270). World Bank Publications.

Cervero, R., and J. Murakami. 2008. *Rail + Property development: A model of sustainable transit finance and urbanism*. UC Berkeley Center for Future Urban Transport: A Volvo Center of Excellence.

Champ, P.A., K.J. Bolye, and T.C. Brown. 2003. *A primer on nonmarket valuation*. Boston, MA: Kluwer Academic Publishers.

Démurger, S. 2001. Infrastructure development and economic growth: An explanation for regional disparities in China? *Journal of Comparative Economics* 29(1): 95–117.

Démurger, S., J.D. Sachs, W.T. Woo, S. Bao, G. Chang, and A. Mellinger. 2002. Geography, economic policy, and regional development in China. *Asian Economic Papers* 1 (1): 146–197.

Economic Research Institute for ASEAN and East Asia. 2007. *Infrastructure Development in China*. Available from http://www.eria.org/research/images/pdf/PDF%20No.2/No.2-part2-3.China.pdf.

Fan, shenggen., and X. Zhang. 2004. Infrastructure and regional economic development in rural China. *China Economic Review* 15(2): 203–214.

Freemark, Y. 2010. *China expands its investment in rapid transit, paving way for future urban growth*. Available from http://www.thetransportpolitic.com/2010/05/13/china-expands-its-investment-in-rapid-transit-paving-way-for-future-urban-growth/.

Gramlich, E.M. 1994. Infrastructure investment: A review essay. *Journal of Economic Literature* 32 (3): 1176–1196.

He, M., S. Ke, and Y. Song. 2011. A consolidated model of monocentric cities and an empirical analysis of urban scales and land prices in Chinese cities. *Journal of Regional Science* 51 (2): 371–398.

Ke, S., Y. Song, and M. He. 2009. Determinants of urban spatial scale: Chinese cities in transition. *Urban Studies* 46 (13): 2795–2813.

Li, S.M., and Y.M. Shum. 2001. Impacts of the national trunk highway system on accessibility in China. *Journal of Transport Geography* 9 (1): 39–48.

Lin, S. 2001. Public infrastructure development in China. *Comparative Economic Studies* 43 (2): 83–109.

Liu, J., J. Zhan, and X. Deng. 2005. Spatio-temporal patterns and driving forces of urban land expansion in China during the economic reform era. *AMBIO: A Journal of the Human Environment* 34(6): 450–455.

Liu, Z. 2010. Planning and policy coordination in China's infrastructure development: A background paper for the EAP Infrastructure Flagship Study. The ADB-JBIC-World Bank East Asia Pacific Infrastructure Flagship Study. Available from http://siteresources.worldbank.org/INTEAPINFRASTRUCT/Resources/855084-1137106254308/China.pdf.

Loo, B.P. 1999. Development of a regional transport infrastructure: Some lessons from the Zhujiang Delta, Guangdong, China. *Journal of Transport Geography* 7 (1): 43–63.

Morancho, A.B. 2003. A hedonic valuation of urban green areas. *Landscape and Urban Planning* 66 (1): 35–41.

Sahoo, P., Dash, R.K. and Nataraj, G. 2010. Infrastructure development and economic growth in China. Institute of Developing Economies (IDE) Discussion Paper No. 261, Available from http://www.ide.go.jp/English/Publish/Download/Dp/pdf/261.pdf.

Seo, K., A. Golub, and M. Kuby. 2014. Combined impacts of highways and light rail transit on residential property values: A spatial hedonic price model for Phoenix, Arizona. *Journal of Transport Geography* 41: 53–62.

Song, Y., and Y. Zenou. 2006. Property tax and urban sprawl: Theory and implications for US cities. *Journal of Urban Economics* 60 (3): 519–534.

Thériault, M., F. Des Rosiers and M.H. Vandersmissen. 1999. GIS-based simulation of accessibility to enhance hedonic modeling and property value appraisal: An application to the Quebec City Metropolitan area. Faculté des sciences de l'administration, Université Laval.

Tsui, K.Y. 2011. China's infrastructure investment boom and local debt crisis. *Eurasian Geography and Economics* 52 (5): 686–711.

Wang, D., L. Zhang, Z. Zhang, and S.X. Zhao. 2011. Urban infrastructure financing in reform-era China. *Urban Studies* 48 (14): 2975–2998.

World Bank. 2004. Infrastructure for development. World Development Indicators.

Wu, W. 1999. Reforming China's institutional environment for urban infrastructure provision. *Urban Studies* 36 (13): 2263–2282.

Wu, W. 2010. Urban infrastructure financing and economic performance in China. *Urban Geography* 31 (5): 648–667.

Zhang, C. 2011. The scale, structure and the efficiency of the infrastructure investment. *China Economic Observer* 28: 2–10.

Chapter 7
Women, Work, and Marriage: Challenges of Gendered Mobility in Urban China

Arianne M. Gaetano

Abstract Policies of the Chinese state during the post-socialist era have engendered demographic and socioeconomic changes that intersect with gender and class to both enable and restrict women's social mobility, autonomy, and independence. This chapter evaluates the impact of these changes on the social mobility of women in China's cities, drawing upon relevant literature and my own ethnographic studies of rural migrant women workers in Beijing and educated career women in Shanghai. My contribution illuminates the material and discursive constraints that obstruct these women's achievement of personal goals under conditions of structural inequality as China urbanizes.

Keywords Gender · Education · Migration · Employment · Social mobility · Marriage

7.1 Introduction

This chapter approaches China's urbanization from a feminist anthropological perspective to examine the intersections of gender with socioeconomic changes in the lives of upwardly mobile women in the city, specifically rural migrant workers and educated urban professionals. I draw upon relevant literature and ethnographic research I conducted in Beijing in the late 1990s and the 2000s among unmarried migrant women working in the service sector (see Gaetano 2004, 2008, 2015), and in Beijing during summer 2008 and in Shanghai during summer 2012 and summer 2015 among unmarried, highly educated, white-collar women (see Gaetano 2010, 2014). I argue that socioeconomic changes that have accompanied China's state-directed urbanization intersect with gender to create opportunities for, but also constraints on, social mobility and individualization through education, employment, and marriage. I explore the impact of these opportunities and constraints on

A.M. Gaetano (✉)
Auburn University, Auburn, USA
e-mail: amg0028@auburn.edu

Z. Tang (ed.), *China's Urbanization and Socioeconomic Impact*,
DOI 10.1007/978-981-10-4831-9_7

women's subjectivity, agency, and life course trajectory. The chapter thus illuminates the challenges for upwardly mobile women in a patriarchal society as they strive for social mobility and personal autonomy.

China's urbanization is orchestrated by the state "reform and opening" policies, which over the past few decades have entailed a shift away from the planned economy of socialism toward global neoliberal capitalism characterized primarily by marketization and privatization. Simultaneously, to achieve development goals, the state has enforced strict population planning that until very recently limited births among urban couples to just one child, and to two or fewer births among rural couples. To further raise population *suzhi* (素质), meaning "quality," or human capital development, the state has mandated and invested in compulsory public education while expanding higher education access. These policies and their consequences have engendered tremendous demographic and socioeconomic changes, which have profound yet different consequences for rural migrant and urban women alike.

Neoliberal economics stresses the importance of a flexible labor market and competition, and goes hand in hand with individualization, which emphasizes individual autonomy and independence from traditions and social institutions (Kim 2012). In the socialist period, work units and collectives provided for citizen's daily existence and determined their futures, and strove to regulate individual's thought and behavior. In post-socialist era, by contrast, the state condones and even encourages citizens to have private selves and indulge personal desires, so long as these do not directly conflict with their loyalty and obligations to the nation-state (see Rofel 2007; Yan 2011). As part of this trend toward individualization, Chinese women today quest for "a valued status," characterized by greater autonomy and control over their lives, including marriage, along with "the good life," generally associated with middle class lifestyles (Kleinman et al. 2011; Goodman 2016).

Regarding employment, reform and opening policies set into motion two seemingly contradictory trends: the outward labor migration of able-bodied working-age women (as well as men) from the rural areas, and the inverse migration of urban women from the public sphere of employment back to the private sphere. These two trends are in fact united as ways the state positions women as a reserve and flexible labor force to achieve economic goals. Both the cheap labor of migrant workers and the unwaged labor of urban women in the household help subsidize urban development. Such policies, along with occupational segregation by gender and gender discrimination in employment, contribute to a pronounced gender pay gap as well as the reinforcement of traditional gender norms. According to figures provided by the All-China Women's Federation, women's income as a percentage of men's income was 56% in rural areas and 67% in urban areas at the end of 2010 (Erdenebileg 2016). Gender inequality thus impedes women's social mobility and personal autonomy.

The population planning and education policies likewise have had gendered effects. An unintended consequence of the planned birth policies, in the context of cultural preference for sons and access to technologies of fetal sex identification and sex-selective abortions, are "missing girls": a severe male-female imbalance at birth that peaked in 2004 at 121 and fell to 115 in 2016 (CIA World Factbook; Loh and Remick 2015). At the same time, the policy and its attendant propaganda are credited with decreasing son preference, both in rural in urban areas. In rural areas, smaller family size plus government support for compulsory education has enabled more daughters to receive basic education alongside their brothers, narrowing the education gender gap (Hannum et al. 2008). In urban areas, where couples were restricted to just one child, parents transferred to their "only daughters" the emotional and material resources that formerly were distributed in favor of sons (Fong 2005). Along with rising urban incomes and the expansion of higher education, this has led to a surge in urban women's attainment of post-secondary degrees. Education is generally associated with empowerment, expansion of choices, and individualization, but its promise can be illusory for women in a context of gender inequality in employment as well as in intimate relations (Kim 2012).

In addition to migration, employment, and education, marriage remains a social mobility pathway for women, due to the traditional marriage market rule of female hypergamy. This has different implications for migrant and urban women in the context of urbanization and socioeconomic change. Migration for work connects rural women to superior prospective partners, including urban bachelors, but marrying away from home entails substantial risks. Meanwhile, time in the city decreases their prospects for a timely marriage to hometown fellows. Urban women's options in the marriage market paradoxically decrease with higher education and subsequent increase in socioeconomic status, as fewer men can meet cultural expectations of hypergamy. In China, marriage is a strong social norm, so failure to find a suitable partner is a grave matter for young women and their parents. It also concerns the state, which promotes and regulates marriage to ensure population quality and social stability.

The remainder of this chapter explores the contradictory circumstances of these distinct groups of upwardly mobile women pursuing "the good life" and "a valued status" as autonomous and independent individuals. I focus first on rural migrant women and next on educated urban women. The conclusion synthesizes the findings to draw lessons about urbanization, socioeconomic change, and the transformation of gender norms.

7.2 Rural Migrant Women Workers

Economic reform polices implemented in the 1980s and 1990s prioritized industrial and urban development, which in turn produced sectorial and spatial disparities that propelled farmers into factories and rural youth to cities in search of higher incomes. The vast urban migrant labor force, reaching 230 million people according to 2011 data (cited in Chan 2012), has been the backbone of China's massive accumulation of capital, especially through low-wage, low technology manufacturing. Young women from poorer, rural areas have been the predominant manual workers in foreign invested, export-oriented light industries clustered in Special

Economic Zones of urban coastal, and then inland, China. In China's largest cities such as Shanghai and Beijing, migrants comprise as much as 30% of the population. In cities, migrant women cluster in retail and service occupations of the non-state (i.e., private) and informal sector, enduring low wages, few employment benefits, and weak labor regulations. The outmigration of working-age men and women has greatly affected the rural social landscape too, causing a feminization of agriculture and problems of "left behind" wives and mothers of young children, the aged, and of school-aged children entrusted to the care of grandparents.

Migrant women's socioeconomic mobility is conditioned by gender as it intersects with institutionalized class inequality produced by China's system of household registration, or *hukou* (户口). The hukou system was implemented in the 1950s as part of the socialist planned economy to organize the allocation of labor, goods, and services. Households were classified as either agricultural (rural) or non-agricultural (urban), and this hukou status was inheritable and difficult to change, except by order of the state; it effectively determined individuals' residence, occupation, and even citizenship. The hukou system privileged urban workers and residents; through the institution of the work unit (*danwei*), they enjoyed free education, guaranteed job placement, subsidized housing, medical care, and a pension after retirement. Rural farmers and residents belonged to self-sufficient agricultural collectives, and thus were still vulnerable to vagaries of nature for their economic well-being.

The implementation of reform and opening policies weakened the hukou system by allowing the temporary migration of rural residents to work in urban areas and industrial development zones. But it continued to construct a dual labor market by restricting most migrant workers to the non-state sector and even excluding them from certain occupations, thus relegating them to low-wage, low-skill, undesirable (e.g., dangerous and/or dirty) jobs, and limiting their access to urban welfare benefits, including medical, housing, education, employment, and pension. The system was also used, and abused, as a political tool to control migrants in the city while denying them legal rights of urban citizenship. Regulations required migrants to register with police and to purchase and carry valid employment and residence permits, and police enforced these regulations through raids and stop-and-frisks. Police and other bureaucrats, as well as employers and landlords, preyed upon migrants through these and similar fee and fine schemes. A combination of low wages, arbitrary fines or fees, and lack of legal rights created a migration trap that kept migrants at work in the cities without accruing sufficient savings to return home. Thus, the household registration system reinforced a labor market and citizenship duality between urban residents and migrant workers, to the relative disadvantage of the latter.

In the mid-2000s, government discourse underwent a sea change by acknowledging migrants as contributors, rather than impediments, to economic and social development of both rural and urban areas. Policy initiatives followed to address migrants' civil and social rights, such as the elimination of occupational restrictions, permit fees, arbitrary fines, and illegal mistreatment (e.g., detention and repatriation, wage withholding, etc.), as well as the extension of trade union membership, labor laws, and employment benefits to migrant workers. Popular representations of migrant workers likewise changed from negative, stereotyped depictions of their poverty, ignorance, and deviance to a more sympathetic focus on migrants' industriousness, morality, and hardship, as well as advocacy for government responsibility for their social and civil rights (Sun 2014). However, fundamental structural inequalities persist that limit migrants' ability to claim their rights, even as these are increasingly recognized on paper.

Gender inequality intersects with the hukou system to further restrict migrant women's socioeconomic mobility, autonomy, and independence. The dual labor market maintained through the hukou system helps to maintain a migrant workforce that is cheap and flexible: stuck in menial jobs without the benefits of urban welfare, most migrants are ineligible for legal urban residence, which requires the purchase of a home or other investment. Rather, they remain dependent on their families, and thus rural households bear the costs of social reproduction of the migrant workforce. Although socialism did improve rural women's lives by addressing gender inequality in the public sphere, it did not dismantle traditional gender ideology and roles in the domestic sphere. Thus women continue to shoulder primary responsibility for social reproduction in the household, including housework and childrearing. Migration has further exacerbated this aspect of gender inequality, as wives, particularly young mothers, are "left behind" by their migrant husbands as they are responsible not only to tend to young children and the elderly, but increasingly also to farm the family land.

These gender ideologies and divisions of labor spillover into the public sphere of employment. Stereotyped for "innate" feminine traits of nimble fingers and docility, women from rural areas have been the preferred workers on the assembly lines of foreign invested, export-oriented light industries clustered in Special Economic Zones of coastal, and later inland, China. In China's largest cities such as Shanghai and Beijing, young migrant women cluster in retail and service jobs, such as waitressing and domestic service, that similarly require feminine talents forged by domesticity. Wages in these occupations are lower than those earned by male migrant workers, who tend toward more lucrative heavy industry, construction, and transport. Women are also less likely than men to be hired for or promoted to technical and supervisory positions. They are especially vulnerable to sexual harassment and abuse by typically male bosses, and to discriminatory job termination due to pregnancy. Such jobs also expose them to industrial pollutants and cleaning agents that are especially harmful to women's reproductive health. Long hours of repetitive manual labor, poor nutrition, subpar living conditions in crowded dormitories or rented rooms away from city centers, along with homesickness and alienation, all pose proven physical and mental health risks.

Nonetheless, young migrant women parlay gender stereotypes into material and social advantage. The term "eating spring rice" (*chi qingchunfan* or 吃青春饭) refers to leveraging of youth, appearance, and femininity and/or sexuality for socioeconomic return. At the level of the individual, such a trade-off can be very empowering and effective. Indeed, the young migrant women of my study, who were working in hotel, restaurant, and domestic services, even exaggerated their youthful naiveté and feminine deference to win the favor of employers or supervisors in expectation of improving work relations and conditions. From a broader perspective, however, eating spring rice is merely a "bargain with patriarchy" rather than a challenge to it. Young migrant women have few employment options other than feminized occupations like domestic service, catering, sales, entertainment, beauty industry, or sexual services. Paradoxically, these occupations are stigmatized because of an association with servility and/or illicit sex (i.e., premarital, extra-marital, commercial, etc.) and hence immorality. Migrant women who elect to undertake these jobs do so at the risk of a tainted reputation, which may harm their own self-esteem and also their family's status as measured by more conservative rural standards. Again, the migrant women workers of my study often dissembled when discussing their occupations with kin or co-villagers, to protect their reputations as chaste maidens, and to shield their family from harmful gossip.

Young rural women seek to migrate for a host of reasons. As filial daughters, they wish to earn their own keep and relieve their families of an extra mouth to feed, and to raise funds to support family members' education or medical expenses. Yet they also desire to see the world and gain life experience, which requires relocating to urban centers as these are considered the centers of modernity and globalization. My own and others' research shows that earning independent income and generating remittances for their families, as well as exposing co-villagers to new opportunities and information, increases rural daughters' value and status among their kin and their bargaining power in their own families. Further, the urban environment equips migrant women with new knowledge about "modern" consumer practices, which they apply to their own bodies and lifestyles for their own pleasure, to boost their self-esteem, and to feel a degree of control and mastery. They can also benefit socially and materially by learning how to better assimilate to urban culture. For example, by adopting a more urban appearance and demeanor, which is more feminine and sexualized, migrant women may avoid being singled out, stereotyped, and stigmatized as a "country bumpkin," menial laborer, and/or as an outsider to the city. Cultivating a modern feminine self-image also expands migrant women's employment options in a labor market that especially values youth, beauty, femininity, and sexuality. Such techniques can enable individual migrant women workers to improve their work conditions or increase their wages by shifting occupations. However, they do so at the expense of reinforcing gender norms that undergird gender inequality and they cannot fully overcome their marginalization in urban society without broader changes in the political economy.

Migration profoundly alters young migrant women's life course by raising expectations and possibilities for their future as determined by marriage. Marriage is nearly universal in China and is also closely associated with procreation. Rural migrant women desire to marry to fulfill traditional social expectations; indeed, marriage and motherhood are essential to women's gender identity, personhood, and passage to adulthood. According to China's predominant tradition of patrilineal kinship, women ultimately belong to their husband's kin group. Unmarried women are a rarity who are ostracized as "old maids" (*lao guniang* or 老姑娘), and childless women may also be stigmatized. Pragmatically, marriage is key to women's future economic security. A migrant woman would be hard-pressed to support herself long-term either in the city or in the countryside. Migrant work is precarious and it provides very limited social insurance, if any. Migrant women workers are vulnerable to both gender and age discrimination. In general, women are not expected to work past age 55, the official retirement age for women in the public sector. Further, marriage is the primary means by which women acquire property, especially in rural areas, where daughters' inheritance rights are not well enforced (Sargeson 2012). Marriage is a prerequisite for bearing offspring, which is important for future security. Childbearing outside of marriage is socially unacceptable and legally complex. The traditional intergenerational contract and value of filial piety, whereby children are expected to provide for their parents in old age, persists and is even enshrined in the constitution, promoted in propaganda, and enforced through law.

Migration impacts rural women's vision of the ideal marriage and enables many of them to choose their own marital partner, independent of parental influence, even as it restricts their prospects due to marriage postponement. Young migrant women hope for a marriage that meets their romantic and practical aspirations. They firmly reject agriculturalists as prospective spouses. They desire someone who has been a migrant worker, with whom they can communicate about shared experience, and because it indicates ambition and grit as well as future potential, as he should have acquired marketable skills, technical training, and/or work experience. Migration also provides many opportunities to meet and date fellow migrants. Through their workplaces and residences, whether in dormitories or in migrant enclaves, young migrant women come into contact with many more prospective partners than would be available at home. Away from the watchful eyes of parents, with some discretionary income, they can experiment with dating and enjoy leisurely courtship. Studies indicate that migrant women have more liberal views on premarital sex than their non-migrant peers, and are knowledgeable about prevention of STD and HIV. However, they are also at greater risk of unwanted pregnancy. As migrant women devote years to working away from home, they tend to marry later than their non-migrant peers. But postponing marriage is risky. As a woman ages, she has fewer potential mates available to her. Also, she risks aging out of the marriage market, as men prefer to marry women slightly younger than themselves. Moreover, due to conservative gender norms and the misogynist stigma against young woman living and working independently of male kin and protectors, migrant women must carefully manage their reputations to avoid rejection by suitors who associate their lifestyle with immorality.

Marrying a legal urban resident, with local hukou and housing, provides rural migrant women the right and the means to remain in the city. But the possibility of this sort of status hypergamy is limited by actual and perceived social and class differences between migrants and urban residents, by urban prejudice against outsiders, and by opportunity. Such marriages tend to occur between exceptional migrant women and men considered economically and socially inferior by standards of the urban marriage market, such as having low levels of education and income. To some extent, rural women have an advantage over other women in this marriage market, because they are thought to embody more traditional feminine virtues of diligence, thrift, obedience, and purity. But they are also looked down upon as ignorant and shifty. In Shanghai in recent years, about 20,000 marriages each year occur between natives and outsiders; due to a traditional preference for (female) hypergamy, it is likely that a majority are between Shanghai men and women from other cities, towns, or villages (Cheng et al. 2011). Migrant women who marry "up" in this fashion are not likely to enter the middle class, but their offspring might, as the family has access to subsidized housing, medical insurance, and education.

Choosing a marital partner independently of parents and from among a large pool of candidates encountered through migration affords rural migrant women potential to fulfill modern expectations for a companionate marriage, autonomy, and social mobility. In my own study, migrant women who married in this non-traditional way were able to continue living and working in the city after marriage. However, the precariousness of their jobs and lack of affordable housing and education meant they were often separated from their spouse and/or child, the latter typically left in the care of elderly relatives in the countryside. Unlike the traditional daughter-in-law living with and under the control of in-laws, my informants who married fellow migrants had autonomy and greater independence. Those who married into the city usually co-resided with in-laws, who in turn provided care for the grandchild. In all cases, married women continued working, and used their earnings to support both their birth families and their in-laws, and so maintained autonomy while earning respect and gratitude. Their lives also reflected acceptance of many middle-class values, such as having just one child, emphasizing education, and buying a home.

Rural migrant women spend their youth laboring away from their villages and parents, "eating bitterness" (*chiku* or 吃苦) and learning in the school of life. Their inferior social and economic status relative to urban residents, which results from the dual labor market and their lack of urban hukou-based citizenship, combined with gender inequality in employment, precludes them from remaining single or settling in the city. Yet their outlook on marriage is quite positive as it aligns with their desires to fulfill traditional social expectations as well as to pursue of the good life through social mobility. They do attain a degree of control over their marital choices and post-marital lives, though the demands of the labor market for flexible workers can lead to temporary breakup of the conjugal or nuclear household, causing emotional distancing and stress among family members. They do not reject traditional gender roles in the family, yet their independent income and physical distance from in-laws helps to preserve their autonomy and independence, and exercise filial piety as they wish. Interestingly, in regard to marital choice, migrant women have much more freedom and a larger pool of available bachelors than do single women from Shanghai, who tend to experience greater parental intervention in their marriage choices, and have a smaller pool of potential mates, as I explain in the next section.

7.3 Highly Educated Urban Working Women

Particularly regarding education, young urban women are privileged beneficiaries of post-socialist reform and opening policies. Throughout China since the 1990s, women's educational attainment has been steadily increasing (Attané 2012). In recent years, the gender gap in compulsory education levels (i.e., grades 1–9) has all but closed (Hannum et al. 2008; Li et al. 2015). Further, with the expansion of higher education begun in 1998, the proportion of women in tertiary (post-secondary) education has also risen, such that more than half of tertiary graduates in 2013 were women (World Bank 2016). Overall, women's "human capital stock" is still significantly less than men's; women on average receive one year less of education than men (Hannum et al. 2008; Attané 2012). Yet education favors urban youth, especially those from wealthier cities. Thus, highly educated young urban women are an elite group who can capitalize on their privilege to attain professional employment and secure their place in the emergent middle class. However, their socioeconomic advancement as well as individualization are hampered by gender segmentation and discrimination in the labor market, as well as by pressure to conform to traditional gender roles and norms regarding marriage and family, all of which reflect and reinforce a broader resurgence of societal gender inequality (Fincher 2014).

Women's "liberation" (*jiefang* or 解放) from family patriarchy through participation in employment was a hallmark of socialism. By the late 1970s, nearly 90% of working-age women in cities were in the workforce (Erdenebileg 2016). Yet since 1990, despite post-socialist economic growth, women's overall labor force presence has been declining (Maurer-Fazio et al. 2007). According to the national census, the rate of employment for women between ages 20–59 was 84.3% in 1990 and only 73.6% in 2010 (Erdenebileg 2016). Urban working-age women's share of the labor force has decreased most dramatically, from 77.4% in 1990 to 60.8% in 2010 (Ibid). Part of the decline is attributable to China's transition from a labor-intensive economy to a goods-and-services economy, but government policies and gender ideologies are also significant factors in this imbalance (Ibid). The decentralization of industry has given greater freedom and flexibility to managers, who may exercise gender discrimination (Maurer-Fazio et al. 2007). The economic restructuring of underperforming and inefficient state-owned enterprises, required of China to join the WTO, resulted in over 30 million job losses between 1995 and 2000 (Ibid). Women were disproportionately made redundant, often at the peak of their productive years, and had greater difficulty finding re-employment (Ibid.; Liu 2007).

In contrast to revolutionary socialist propaganda, official discourse today emphasizes urban women's gender roles in the domestic sphere. For example, the state supports retraining of women workers in feminized fields like household economics, reinforcing traditional gender roles and divisions of labor (Zheng 2000). Meanwhile, the government has withdrawn much of its support for working mothers with young children such as subsidized healthcare and childcare (Zhang and Maclean 2012). Housework and child rearing duties are unequally shared between the sexes; even among two-income earning couples, women's share is larger (Hannum et al. 2008). Urban women are also pressured to meet new middle-class standards of consumption. Although some can afford to hire others (usually migrant women) as substitutes for their own domestic labor, they are nonetheless expected to shoulder new responsibilities of "household management" and "scientific mothering"—attentive parenting to ensure their offspring's physical fitness and educational success (Zhu 2010). In the media, career women are often portrayed as bad mothers (Zhang and Sun 2014). No wonder urban working women feel challenged to balance a career with marriage and family.

In the urban labor market, as in the migrant labor market, gender inequality is reflected in a pronounced gender pay gap, that is only partly explained by women's overall lower level of education and work experience relative to men (Zhang et al. 2008). The horizontal and vertical segregation of occupations by gender, a characteristic of the economy that has increased since socialism, accounts for some of the discrepancy (Liu 2007; Zhang et al. 2008). For example, women are more likely found in occupations considered "light" and "unskilled" (Ibid). Women also face blatant gender discrimination in hiring and promotion (Zhang et al. 2008). Employers reportedly avoid hiring young women who have not yet married or had children so as not to incur the expense of state-mandated paid maternity leave or child care costs (Ibid). Similarly, some women report being fired at pregnancy. Gender stereotypes and a masculine business culture may also impede women's advancement to managerial and leadership positions (Zheng 2000). For example, women are perceived as less suited to business travel and socializing with clients after office hours. Compounding gender inequality, the official retirement age for women is five years earlier than for men, which reinforces the message that women are less integral to the public sphere than men.

Finally, research indicates that much of the gender pay gap in the urban labor market is due to a "marriage and child penalty," as working mothers cut back on hours or opt out, or are pushed out, of the labor force (Zhang et al. 2008). Women's primary responsibility for household duties is a contributing factor to the gender wage gap (Hughes and Maurer-Fazio 2002). Married women's income is just 77% that of married men's (Ibid). Importantly, the gender pay gap is virtually non-existent between unmarried men and unmarried women workers (Zhang et al. 2008). Moreover, it is smaller at the very top of the income scale, and unmarried women actually outpace single men in income and employment rates (You et al. 2016). Nonetheless, for most employed urban women, continued social mobility and long term economic security requires marriage, even as it paradoxically contributes to women's overall lower earnings relative to men (Kam 2015).

As with rural women, marriage is the primary means by which urban women accrue property, a significant form of wealth in urban China (Fincher 2014). In cities like Shanghai, municipal policies restrict home purchases by those without local hukou to couples only. Many of the highly educated professional women whom I interviewed already owned property in Shanghai purchased with parental help. Others fully expected to receive an intergenerational wealth transfer at marriage, when their parents would contribute to the purchase of a marital abode. However, upon marriage, urban women (and their parents) often cede legal rights to property by allowing their husbands to claim formal ownership, in accordance with the traditional expectation that the groom provide the marital home. By law, ownership is determined by documentation (e.g., property deeds) rather than financial contributions, so adherence to this patriarchal convention is particularly harmful to women in the event of divorce (Fincher 2014).

Moreover, marriage is a deeply held value for most Chinese and strong social norm from which few individuals wish to deviate. Indeed, the post-socialist trend of individualization has not obviously weakened marriage and family as it arguably has in much of the West; in China, marriage is still nearly universal (Jones 2007). Only a small fraction of the Chinese population is never married, and that percentage has not increased in the past 30 years. According to 2005 statistics, at age 40–44, virtually all females were married and only 5% of males were still single (Yong and Wang 2014). Yet, since the 1990s, the average age at first marriage in China has steadily risen (Cheng et al. 2011). Especially in the large cities, a growing proportion of youth remains single into their late 20s and beyond. In Shanghai for example, the average age of first marriage rose from 28.8 to 30.1 for men and 26.5 to 28.1 for women between 2010 and 2013, as reported by the Civil Affairs Bureau.[1]

Highly educated young women feel the greatest pressure to marry and start a family just at the point when they are establishing their careers. That pressure is intensified by the combination of traditional gender norms that organize the marriage market, parental concern, and conservative government propaganda and popular media that admonishes women who postpone marriage. As explained above, China's marriage market reflects pervasive expectations for women of status hypergamy and age hypergamy. The former reflects traditional, patriarchal gender norms, whereby society perceives men who "marry up" as emasculated. The latter reflects a "gender double standard of aging," whereby men prefer to marry younger women; together these proscriptions create a marriage squeeze particularly for highly educated women over the age of 30 (Ji 2015). Indeed, the conundrum is illustrated by 2010 census data, which show that regardless of gender, the higher the individual's educational attainment, the higher the likelihood of remaining unmarried. But, for individuals at all educational levels, the increases in this likelihood are larger for women than men (You et al. 2016). Further, research shows it is "education per se" and not the time spent pursuing it or the income that results from it that is "the main obstacle to marriage for well-educated women" (You et al. 2016: 7–8). This suggests that educated urban women are not disadvantaged simply by their later entry into the marriage market, but rather by men's outright rejection of women with higher education levels as potential partners (You et al. 2016).

In accordance with normative marriage market expectations, parents wish for their precious only daughters to marry at the expected time and to someone of

---

[1]Per shanghaidaily.com.cn, accessed on 2/28/2014.

higher socioeconomic status (To 2015). Some parents, particularly those with only daughters, endeavor to locate prospective partners for their children by participating in "matchmaking corners," government-sponsored events typically held in public spaces such as Shanghai's People's Park, where they can exchange information about their single children with other parents (Zhang and Sun 2014). State propaganda and popular discourse further compound the pressure on educated urban women. Since the late 2000s, the media has focused much attention on them, even warning that those who postpone marriage beyond age 27 will become, literally, "leftover women" (*shengnü* or 剩女). Some scholars worry that this derogatory label and the government's campaign against marriage postponement will lead ever younger women to make hasty and regrettable marital choices, and be less empowered to insist on their legal rights to joint ownership of marital property (Fincher 2014).

My research among highly educated urban career women indicates that most aspire to marry, but they are ambivalent about it. Those whom I interviewed were rather hesitant to marry because it involves an inevitable transition to adulthood without sufficient time to enjoy their relatively carefree and independent youth. Marriage entails the acceptance of a host of new obligations associated with marital and reproductive roles, for which they would need to develop special domestic skills along with interpersonal and emotional competencies. Although they sought spouses who would participate equally in housework, they also recognized that women typically shoulder a disproportionate share of domestic duties. In China conventionally, childbirth follows within one or two years of marriage, and childrearing exacts a huge sacrifice from mothers especially. Eldercare support is an additional responsibility that looms on the far horizon, and which is increasingly shouldered by women (Evans 2008). "Only daughters" (i.e., those born under the one-child birth planning policy) have an additional burden, as they must attend to the caretaking needs of their own parents in addition to their in-laws. Marriage and motherhood thus promise to constrain a woman's social world, decreasing time and energy for peer relationships and leisure pursuits.

Another reason that educated urban women feel ambivalent about marriage is due to their rejection of many conservative gender norms that guide the marriage market and influence prospective partners' expectations, and their concerns about the stability of the institution of marriage in the current market society. As among rural women, the ideal marriage envisioned by highly educated urban women is a companionate marriage between equals. Although the urban women in my study desired romance in their relationships, especially at the courtship stage, in marriage they did not seek passionate love, based only on mutual attraction and chemistry, because they anticipated it to be short-lived. Rather, they intended to build a marriage from a longer-lasting mutual affection, or "mature love." They eschewed unruly passions, but they desired their spouse to have a degree of "EQ"—emotional competency, to facilitate mutual communication. They were turned off by potential partners who displayed chauvinism, arrogance, and excessive concern about superficial appearances and reputation (i.e., "face" [*mianzi* or 面子]). They wished their future spouse to be supportive of their career and to share in housework and childrearing duties. They also sought a partner who would not care about his bride being slightly older than him in age, or more educated, or from a higher-status family. Finally, while they expected their partner to have a college degree and respectable employment and income, they avoided those who were too materialistic. They admired a man willing to split the wedding costs and allow his bride to maintain her own property assets. In a nutshell, they opposed the man who seeks a "soft and passive" (*wenrou* or 温柔) traditional housewife, and yet were wary of the man who seeks only his own pleasure and fortune and shirks his traditional familial obligations. Unfortunately, most men they had met did not share their rather gender egalitarian views. A general consensus among highly educated women in my own research, as well as in studies by To (2015) and Ji (2015), was expressed to me by one interviewee, a 26-year old Ph.D. holder and Shanghai resident. She said: "A lot of guys are self-centered. They are miserly. They are not very tolerant. They will tell you how a woman should be, that she should do household chores, that she should be pliant."

In summary, highly educated urban women desire to marry for personal satisfaction and in order not to disappoint their parents, with whom "only children" especially hold very close emotional bonds. However, they are also ambivalent about marriage. First, there is a mismatch between societal and parental expectations of status and age hypergamy and their own aspirations for a more gender egalitarian marriage. Second, they suspect that their aspirations for a "valued status"—for autonomy and a companionate marriage—will be compromised in post-marital life, due to societal expectations to conform to certain inflexible gender roles and the lack of external supports that would enable them to better maintain their independence after marriage. In short, highly educated urban women face "an ongoing dilemma: to lower their expectations of education and labor market outcomes to fit the traditional wifely role, or to persevere in their educational and career pursuit [but forego marriage]" (You et al. 2016: 36).

7.4 Conclusion

Clearly, state policies and their consequences have complicated influence on the upward mobility, autonomy, and individualization of both young migrant women workers and urban professionals, albeit not uniformly due to their different positions in the social structure. Social mobility is an aspirational ideology that is associated with urban middle class lifestyles. It is more difficult, perhaps impossible, for rural migrants to attain due to their inferior economic resources and social exclusion. In contrast, educated urban women are afforded ample opportunity and resources to be upwardly mobile, but they face many obstacles in pursuing their aspirations to fulfill both filial obligations and personal desires for companionate marriage.

Social mobility pathways are gendered in that they reflect but also challenge gender ideologies and roles. Significantly, post-socialist China is undergoing a resurgence of traditional, patriarchal gender norms. Upwardly mobile women are perceived as out of place and improper, because they are not confined to a domestic role and even compete with men in the public sphere. As they appear to transgress essentialist gender roles and ideals, young migrant women workers and highly educated urban career women alike may face societal stigmatization. Rural migrant women are frequently relegated to low-status jobs that tarnish their reputations because of associations with servility or sex. Yet, they derive personal satisfaction from their experiences of migration and work, and they are empowered to exercise greater autonomy regarding marriage and family roles. Educated single urban women are stigmatized as "leftover women." In both official media and popular culture, they are depicted negatively, as too fickle and materialistic, as if they alone are responsible for their failure to marry. In fact, their single status is largely due to the rigid gender norms that underpin the marriage market and guide potential partner's expectations. Societal gender inequality that forces such women to have to choose between career and family roles compounds their ambivalence toward marriage. Some may capitulate to gender norms and accept "traditional" unequal marriages, but others will seek alternatives that allow them to maintain their independence, including marrying "down," abroad, or foregoing marriage altogether (see examples of such strategies in Fincher (2014), To (2015), and Gaetano (2014)).

The individualization of both rural migrant women and educated urban career women is incomplete, as they all are bound by filial obligations. Yet, migrant women's improved social status—accrued through wages, work experience, and temporary urban residence, allows them to negotiate the intergenerational contract to their own advantage. Similarly, educated urban women may accept parental interference in marital decisions due to their desire to please their parents, yet they have the wherewithal to refuse an unsatisfactory proposal. As urban only daughters, their financial security may not depend on marriage, and their parents may be more concerned about their happiness than their marital status.

References

Attané, I. 2012. Being a woman in China today: A demography of gender. *China Perspectives* 4: 5–15.

Central Intelligence Agency (CIA). 2016. The world factbook China. https://www.cia.gov/library/publications/resources/the-world-factbook/geos/ch.html. Accessed December 12, 2016.

Chan, K.W. 2012. Migration and development in China: Trends, geography, and current issues. *Migration and Development* 1 (2): 187–205.

Cheng, Y., X. Han, and J.K. Dagsvik. 2011. Marriage pattern in the city of Shanghai. *Chinese Sociology and Anthropology* 43 (4): 74–95.

Erdenebileg, Z. 2016. Holding up half the sky? Assessing the current state of female employment in China. *China Briefing* (July). www.china-briefing.com. Accessed August 1, 2016.

Evans, H. 2008. *The subject of gender: Daughters and mothers in urban China*. Lanham, MD: Rowman and Littlefield.

Fincher, L.H. 2014. *Leftover women: The resurgence of gender inequality in China*. London: ZED Books.

Fong, V.L. 2005. *Only hope: Coming of age under China's one-child policy*. Stanford, CA: Stanford University Press.

Gaetano, A.M. 2004. 'Filial daughters, modern women': Migrant domestic workers in Beijing. In *On the move: Women and rural-to-urban migration in contemporary China*, ed. A.M. Gaetano, and T. Jacka, 41–79. New York: Columbia University Press.

Gaetano, A. M. 2008. Sexuality in diasporic space: Rural-to-urban migrant women negotiating gender and marriage in contemporary China. *Gender, Place, and Culture*, 15(6): 629–645. Special issue on heterosexuality and migration in Asia edited by Katie Walsh, Hsiu-hua Shen, and Katie Willis.

Gaetano, A.M. 2010. Single women in urban China and the 'unmarried crisis': Gender resilience and gender transformation. *Lund University Working Papers in Contemporary Asian Studies 31*, Lund, Sweden: Center for East and Southeast Asian Studies, 1–21.

Gaetano, A.M. 2014. 'Leftover women': Postponing marriage and renegotiating womanhood in urban China. *Journal of Research in Gender Studies* 4 (2): 124–149.

Gaetano, A.M. 2015. *Out to work: Migration, gender, and the changing lives of rural women in contemporary China*. Honolulu: University of Hawai'i Press.

Goodman, D.S.G. 2016. Locating China's middle classes: Social intermediaries and the party-state. *Journal of Contemporary China* 25 (97): 1–13.

Hannum, E., J. Behrman, M. Wang, and J. Liu. 2008. Education in the reform era. In *China's great economic transformation*, ed. L. Brandt, and T. Rawski, 215–249. Cambridge: Cambridge University Press.

Hughes, J.W., and M. Maurer-Fazio. 2002. The effects of marital status, education, and occupation on the female/male wage gap in China. *Pacific Economic Review* 7 (1): 137–156.

Ji, Y. 2015. Between tradition and modernity: 'Leftover' women in Shanghai. *Journal of Marriage and Family* 77: 1057–1073.

Jones, G. 2007. Delayed marriage and very low fertility in Pacific Asia. *Population and Development Review* 33 (3): 435–478.

Kam, L.Y.L. 2015. The demand for a 'normal' life: Marriage and its discontents in contemporary China. In *Routledge handbook of sexuality studies in East Asia*, ed. M. McLelland, and V. Mackie, 77–86. New York: Routledge.

Kim, Y. 2012. Introduction. In *Women and the media in Asia: The precarious self*, ed. Y. Kim, 1–27. New York: Palgrave MacMillan.

Kleinman, A., Y. Yan, J. Jun, S. Lee, E. Zhang, T. Pan, F. Wu, and J. Guo. 2011. Introduction. In *Deep China: The moral life of the person*, ed. A. Kleinman, Y. Yan, J. Jun, S. Lee, E. Zhang, T. Pan, F. Wu, and J. Guo, 1–25. Berkeley: University of California Press.

Li, H., P. Loyalka, S. Rozelle, F. Wu, and J. Xie. 2015. Unequal access to college in China: How far have poor, rural students been left behind? *The China Quarterly* 221: 185–207.

Liu, J. 2007. Gender dynamics and redundancy in urban China. *Feminist Economics* 13 (3): 125–158.

Loh, C., and E.J. Remick. 2015. China's skewed sex ratio and the one-child policy. *The China Quarterly* 222: 295–319.

Maurer-Fazio, M., J. Hughes, and D. Zhang. 2007. An ocean formed from one hundred rivers: The effects of ethnicity, gender, marriage and location on labor force participation in urban China. *Feminist Economics* 13 (3–4): 159–187.

Rofel, L. 2007. *Desiring China: Experiments in neoliberalism, sexuality and public culture*. Durham, NC: Duke University Press.

Sargeson, S. 2012. Why women own less, and why it matters more in rural China's urban transformation. *China Perspectives* 4: 35–42.

Sun, W. 2014. *Subaltern China: Rural migrants, media, and cultural practices*. Lantham, MD: Rowman and Littlefield.

To, S. 2015. *China's leftover women: Late marriage among professional women and its consequences*. London and New York: Routledge.

The World Bank database. 2016. Percentage of graduates from tertiary education who are female, China, 2013. http://data.worldbank.org. Accessed December 12, 2016.

Yan, Y. 2011. The changing moral landscape. In *Deep China: The moral life of the person*, ed. A. Kleinman, Y. Yan, J. Jun, S. Lee, E. Zhang, T. Pan, F. Wu, and J. Guo, 36–77. Berkeley: University of California Press.

Yong, C., and F. Wang. 2014. (Re)emergence of late marriage in Shanghai: From collective synchronization to individual choice. In *Wives, husbands, and lovers: Marriage and sexuality in Hong Kong, Taiwan, and urban China*, ed. D.S. Davis, and S.L. Friedman, 97–117. Stanford: Stanford University Press.

You, J., Yi, X., and Chen, M. 4 2016 April. Love, life, and 'leftover ladies' in urban China. MPRA Paper No. 70494. Munich Personal RePEc Archive. https://mpra.ub.uni-muenchen.de/70494/. Accessed December 12, 2016.

Zhang, Y., and M. MacLean. 2012. Rolling back of the state in child care? Evidence from urban China. *International Journal of Sociology and Social policy* 32 (11/12): 664–681.

Zhang, J., and P. Sun. 2014. When are you going to get married? Parental matchmaking and middle class women in contemporary urban China. In *Wives, husbands, and lovers: Marriage and sexuality in Hong Kong, Taiwan, and urban China*, ed. D.S. Davis, and S.L. Friedman, 118–144. Stanford: Stanford University Press.

Zhang, Y., E. Hannum, and M. Wang. 2008. Gender-based employment and income differences in urban China: Considering the contributions of marriage and parenthood. *Social Forces* 86 (4): 1529–1559.

Zheng, W. 2000. Gender, employment, and women's resistance. In *Chinese society: Change, conflict, and resistance*, 1st ed, ed. E.J. Perry, and M. Selden, 158–182. London: Routledge.

Zhu, J. 2010. Mothering expectant mothers: Consumption, production, and two motherhoods in contemporary China. *Ethos* 38 (4): 406–421.

Chapter 8
Understanding Chinese Environmental Risk Perceptions from 1995–2015

Wanyun Shao

Abstract China has experienced a dramatic economic growth accompanied by a massive environmental degradation over the past four decades. This unprecedented level of environmental devastation has taken a toll on both public health and economic development. Being faced with severe environmental pollution, how does the Chinese public perceive its environment? In this chapter, by utilizing data from two sources including the World Values Surveys (WVS) and Pew Research Center Global Attitudes Surveys, the author first describes the general trends of Chinese environmental views from 1995–2015, and then examines how Chinese public perceptions of air pollution, water pollution, and global climate change fluctuated between 2008 and 2015 based on the Pew Global Attitudes Surveys. Additionally, the author uses the 2013 Pew Global Attitudes Survey to depict geographic variations of environmental perceptions across the population-concentrated region. Lastly, the author analyzes the 2013 Pew survey and reveals that income is the most consistent positive factor determining perceptions of air pollution, water pollution, and global climate change. Meanwhile, the second most dominant factor is education that has positive effects on both perceptions of water pollution and global climate change. The author concludes this chapter by summarizing the findings and indicating policy implications of these results. Moreover, the author suggests that future studies of Chinese environmental perceptions should consider a more comprehensive list of explanatory variables including contextual variables such as objective environmental measures and economic indicators.

Keywords China · Environmental degradation and protection · Economic growth · Global climate change

W. Shao (✉)
Auburn University at Montgomery, Montgomery, USA
e-mail: wshao@aum.edu

Z. Tang (ed.), *China's Urbanization and Socioeconomic Impact*,
DOI 10.1007/978-981-10-4831-9_8

8.1 Background

A significant economic growth has been witnessed in the post-reform China. Consequently, hundreds of millions of people have been lifted out of poverty. In Fig. 8.1, Zhu (2012) demonstrates the rapid growth of GDP per capita of China compared to that of the United States over the period from 1952 to 2009. Economic development and the process of urbanization often go hand in hand (Henderson 2003). City clusters, consisting of large contiguous cities with many satellite cities in the proximity, serve as crucial engines for rapid economic growth in China (Shao et al. 2006). Based on empirical data from 110 countries, Chen et al. (2013a) divide the entire period from 1960 to 2010 into three phases, each of which represents a rapid decline stage (1960–1978), a stable ascension stage (1979–1995), and a rapid promotion stage (1996–2010) respectively. At the rapid promotion stage, the annual growth rate of urbanization in China exceeds that of the world excluding China by as many as 1.2% (refer to Fig. 8.2). The urbanization process in China started to take off at an unprecedented rate in the mid 1990s and converged to the world average urbanization level in 2010, as demonstrated in Fig. 8.3.

The rapid economic development accompanied by urbanization is not without downsides. The average 10% annual GDP growth in China for the last decade is taking a toll on its environment and public health (Xu 2014). The unprecedented intensity and scale of environmental problems have even dwarfed Chinese leaders' sincere efforts to tackle them (Liu and Diamond 2005). These problems include but are not limited to: air pollution, water pollution and shortage, increasing frequency and scale of human-induced natural disasters, interrupted river flow, depleted fisheries, desertification, salinization, soil erosion, trash accumulation, and cropland losses (Liu and Diamond 2005). Air pollution and surface water pollution have become issues of great concern to many urban residents (Shao et al. 2006).

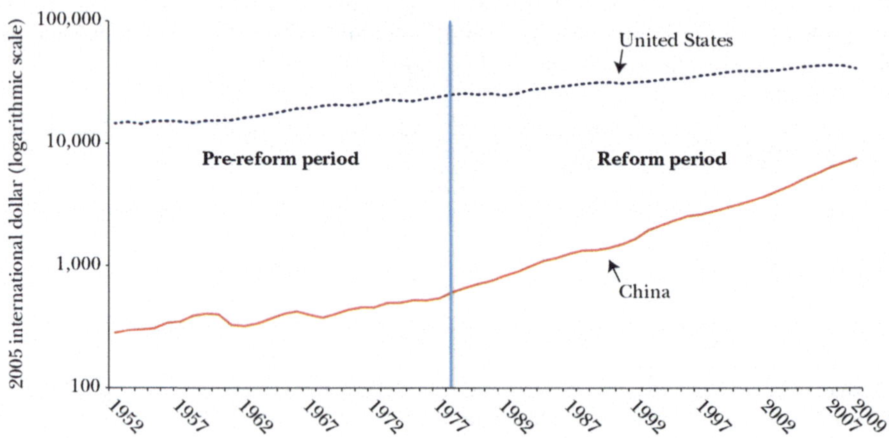

Fig. 8.1 GDP per capita of China and US: 1952–2009. *Source* Zhu (2012)

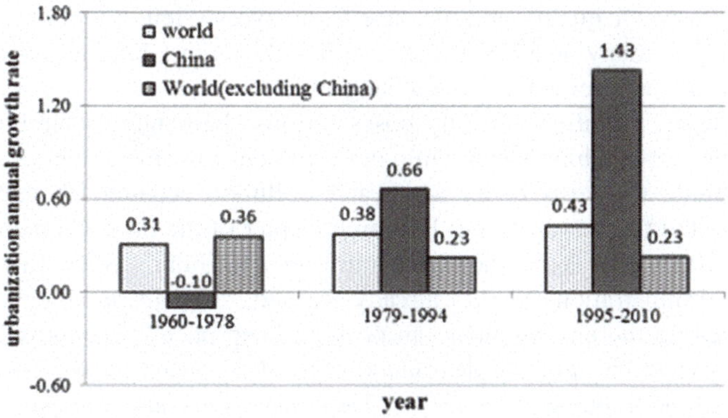

Fig. 8.2 Comparison of China's Urbanization and the World in 1960–78, 1979–94, and 1995–2010. *Source* Chen et al. (2013a)

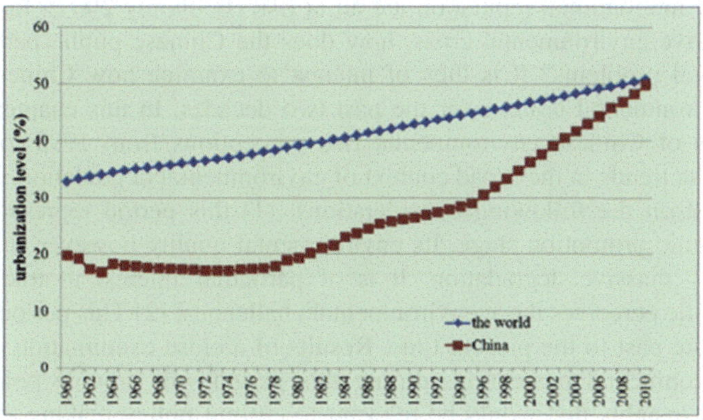

Fig. 8.3 The evolution of China's urbanization and the world average in 1960–2010. *Source* Chen et al. (2013a)

According to Chen et al. (2013b), 500 million residents of Northern China are estimated to lose more than 2.5 billion years of life expectancy due to air pollution. The impact of air pollution on public health is further compounded by an aging population and rapid urbanization (World Bank and the Development Research Center of the State Council 2013). Industrial and municipal wastewater in conjunction with agricultural and aquacultural runoffs contributes to the constant deterioration of water quality in most Chinese rivers (Liu and Diamond 2005). Over 75% of the river water that flows through the urban areas is deemed to be undrinkable (Economy 2007). Digestive cancer mortality is found to be closely correlated with water quality and distance from rivers (Hendryx et al. 2012). As a matter of fact, as many as 81% of the cancer villages in China are located within 5 km from a major river (Gong and Zhang 2013).

Environmental pollution not only poses serious challenges to the public health but also slows down China's economic development to some extent. According to the World Bank, the costs of air and water pollution account for 8.6% of GDP (World Bank and the Development Research Center of the State Council 2013). As early as in 2005, Pan Yue, then vice minister of China's State Environmental Protection Administration (SEPA) already warned, "The [economic] miracle will end soon because the environment can no long keep pace" (Economy 2007).

This massive environmental degradation has also caused growing social unrest among the Chinese public (Xu 2014). Demonstrations and protests against the construction of chemical plants can be witnessed in many places. Some residents take their dissents to the street. Public outrage over environmental issues has been growing and appears to build a momentum for a green movement (Gilbert 2012).

As China's environmental quality worsens, its economy, public health, social stability and international reputation are all at risk (Economy 2007). In the face of such a massive environmental crisis, how does the Chinese public perceive these environmental problems? It is thus of interest to examine how Chinese perceive various environmental issues over the past two decades. In this chapter, I present some trends of Chinese environmental risk perceptions from 1995 to 2015 and describe these trends in the broad context of environmental degradation. I select this period based on the following considerations: (1) this period represents China's rapid economic promotion stage. Its environmental quality however suffers a correspondingly massive degradation. It is of particular interest to track how the Chinese public perceives these environmental challenges; (2) This period represents the immediate past to the present time. Results of a close examination on Chinese public environmental perceptions during this period will provide policy makers with crucial insights that would be relevant to current policy making efforts.

The data used in this chapter are compiled from two major sources including the World Values Surveys and Pew Research Center. The World Values Survey (WVS) is a global network of social scientists who study changing values and their impacts on social and political life (www.worldvaluessurvey.org). Pew Research Center (Pew) is a nonpartisan fact tank based in the United States, which conducts public opinion surveys around the world (www.pewrsearch.org). This research effort aims to provide a glimpse into the evolution of Chinese environmental risk perceptions in the past two decades by demonstrating descriptive statistics based on WVS and Pew survey data. Furthermore, geographic distributions of environmental views and some socio-demographic factors that determine variation in Chinese environmental risk perceptions are explored.

8.2 Public Views Toward the Relationship Between Economic Development and Environmental Protection

China's miraculous economic ascension in conjunction with unprecedented environmental degradation presents an especially interesting case study for scholars of environmental perceptions. According to Maslow's theory of human motivation (1943), humans tend to satisfy physiological needs that are the physical requirements for survival before turning to other needs such as safety, love/belonging, esteem, and self-actualization. The economic growth has helped hundreds of millions of Chinese meet with their basic physiological needs by providing them with adequate material goods such as food. Following Maslow's theoretical reasoning, the Chinese supposedly feel positive about China's economic development when they personally experience material abundance. What happens when the environmental pollution has reached a point where it constitutes a substantial threat to many survivals? When the air becomes non-breathable and water becomes undrinkable, would the Chinese reevaluate the relationship between economic growth and environmental protection. In other words, when other physiological needs such as air and water cannot be satisfied, would the environment attract more public attention than the economy?

From 1995 to 2012, the World Values Survey asked four nationally representative samples of Chinese respondents which should be given priority between environmental protection and economic growth. Figure 8.4 (left) displays the general trend of Chinese opinion toward these two issues over the 17-year period. Chinese have consistently been in favor of environmental protection over economic growth, with more than half of the population giving priority to protecting the environment. Over time, the Chinese support for environmental protection has slightly increased from 51.3 to 56.6%. The Chinese public views towards environment and economy during this period conform to Maslow's theory. While the economic growth has satisfied most basic physiological needs for food, the environmental degradation has jeopardized the quality of air and water, two other

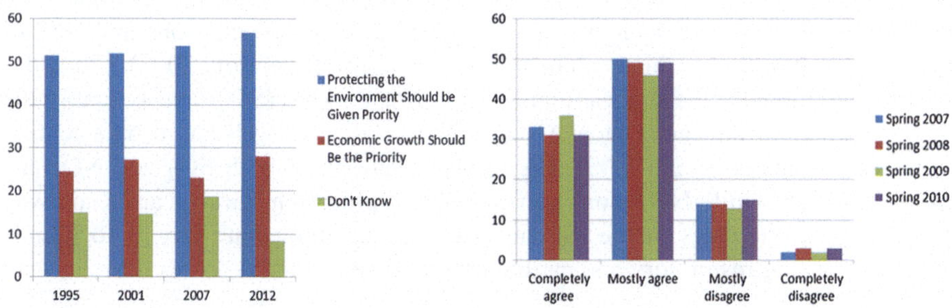

Fig. 8.4 Chinese views toward environmental protection and economic growth: from 1995–2012 based on World Values Surveys (*left*); from 2007–2010 based on Pew Research Center Global Attitudes (*right*)

essential physiological needs. Accordingly, the Chinese public exhibited increasing preference of environment over economy with the environmental condition worsening from 1995–2012.

Pew Research Center in its Global Attitudes Surveys asked respondents a similar but differently-worded question about the relationship between the environment and economic growth during the period from 2007–2010. One crucial difference between the World Values Surveys and Pew Global Attitudes Surveys on this question is that the Pew datasets are non-national samples with disproportionate representation of the urban population. When asked, "Please tell me whether you completely agree, mostly agree, mostly disagree or completely disagree with the following statement…Protecting the environment should be given priority, even if it causes slower economic growth and some loss of jobs," approximately, one third of Chinese respondents completely agree with this statement, and nearly half of them mostly agree with the statement (see Fig. 8.4 right). Less than 20% of respondents either mostly disagree or completely disagree with this statement. The variation from year to year remains small during this period.

Both the WVS and Pew surveys together depict a picture that a majority of the Chinese favor environmental protection over economic growth in recent times. In addition, the public support of environmental protection manifested in their opinions has been stable over the past two decades. This may reflect that environmental pollution has raised universal awareness of environmental problems among the Chinese public, which may be further translated into public concerns and policy support intentions.

8.3 Public Perceptions of Air Pollution

China's maintained fast economic growth rate is extensively built on energy-intensive construction of infrastructure which demands thermal-power generation, pig-iron and cement production (Zhang et al. 2012). Especially, coal consumption provides a substantial proportion of China's energy needs (Economy 2007). This heavy reliance on coal is also largely blamed for the environmental devastation. By estimate, as many as 90% of sulfur dioxide emissions and 50% of particulate emissions in China can be traced to coal use (Economy 2007). China has become undoubtedly the biggest emitter of sulfur dioxide (SO_2) and probably the biggest emitter of nitrogen oxides ($NO_x = NO + NO_2$) as well based on scientific estimates (Vennemo et al. 2009). High concentrations of both SO_2 and NO_x can lead to acid rain while NO_x alone can cause eutrophication (Gruber and Galloway 2008). Fine particulates in the air can pose serious immediate threats to human health by causing respiratory and cardiovascular diseases (EPA 1997). PM 2.5[1] and

[1]Fine particles in air that measure less than 2.5 μm in diameter.

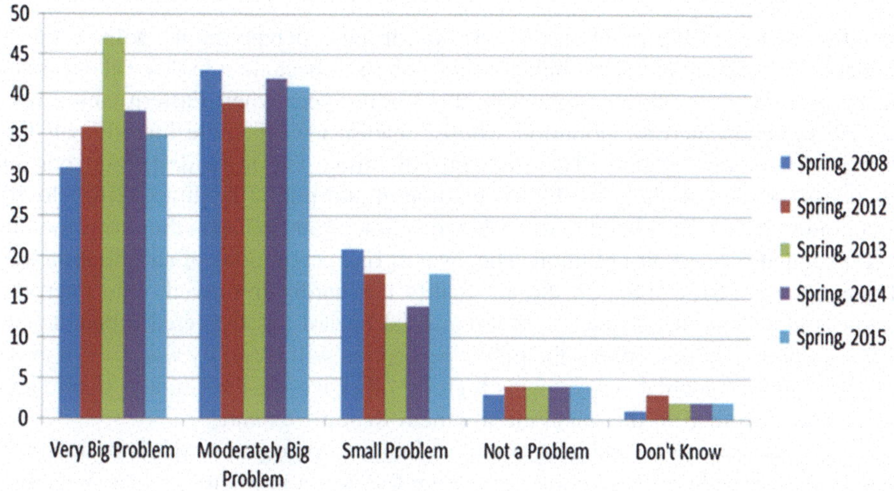

Fig. 8.5 Chinese risk perceptions of air pollution from 2008–2015, based on Pew Research Center Global Attitudes Series

PM 10[2] are adopted by the World Health Organization as crucial metrics to control PM levels (Holland et al. 1999). PM 2.5 is especially notorious for causing chronicle diseases. The concentrations of PM 2.5 in many Chinese cities are well above the proposed standards (Zhang et al. 2012). The health consequence of air pollution is dire at a large scale. For instance, as of 2001, 3.4% of the total deaths in China were premature caused by urban air pollution according to the World Health Organization (WHO) (Zhang and Smith 2007). More recent estimates depict an even grimmer picture that 13% of urban deaths may be premature owing to air pollution according to the World Bank (2009). Welfare damage caused by air pollution increased from $22 billion in 1975 to $112 billion in 2015 (Matus et al. 2012). Young children are particularly susceptible to adverse effects of air pollution which can lead to reduced fetal and child growth, developmental impairment, and increased risk of cancer (Millman et al. 2008).

Under the imminent threat of air pollution, how does the Chinese public perceive air pollution? Pew Global Attitudes Survey asked the Chinese respondents about their views toward air pollution in the year 2008. Pew resumed this question in 2012 and repeated this question every year ever since. As Fig. 8.5 demonstrates, a majority of Chinese, which is disproportionately represented by urban residents in this Pew series, has consistently viewed air pollution as either a very big problem or moderately big problem during the period from 2008–2015. Furthermore, the public perception of air pollution is heightened in 2013. Nearly half of the respondents who mostly resided in urban areas viewed air pollution as a very big problem. 2013 is also the year when the proportion of respondents viewing air

[2]Fine particles in air that measure less than 10 μm in diameter.

pollution as a very big problem exceeds that of those perceiving air pollution as a moderately big problem. This indicates air pollution became a highly salient issue in that year. Upon a closer inspection, 2013 is the year when Eastern China witnessed unprecedented air pollution whose "readings went, quite literally, off the charts" (Economist 2013). The outbreak of smog led to widespread societal repercussion such as daily livelihood disruption and public facilities being closed (Economist 2013). This heightened risk perception of air pollution thus corresponds well to actual risks of air pollution. The level of risk perceptions of air pollution has dropped since 2013, although the air quality has hardly improved. One interpretation is that: once the objective environmental hazard has triggered a heightened level of public risk perception, the public perception will naturally wane down even when the environmental risk remains high. In other words, the Chinese public has become accustomed to the harsh environment to some extent.

To further investigate the geographic variation of perceptions of air pollution, I recode this variable on four-point scale from 0 ("Not a problem") to 3 ("Very big problem") and average the points based on each province. Figure 8.6 displays the spatial variation of perceptions of air pollution with the red color indicating the highest level and yellow color suggesting the lowest level of concern for air pollution among residents.

As Fig. 8.6 illustrates, residents in northern provinces including Heilongjiang, Jilin, Hebei, and Inner Mongolia have expressed heightened risk perceptions of air pollution. In addition, a majority of residents in Sichuan of southwest China, Jiangsu of the east coast and Guangdong of the southeast coast perceive air pollution as a very big problem as well. According to a recent study applying Kriging interpolation to derive pollution maps for eastern China, the actual air pollution is widespread across northern and central China (Rohde and Muller 2015). The spatial distribution of perceived air pollution more or less reflects the actual air pollution except for residents in Sichuan and Guangdong who express unusually high level of risk perception. This suggests that a more in-depth study should be conducted to reveal the determinants of the spatial difference between perceived and real air pollution.

8.4 Public Perceptions of Water Pollution

Extensive use of fertilizers in agriculture and careless dumping of manufacturing wastes have led to severe water quality deterioration in China (Ebenstein 2009). According to the World Bank (2006), about 70% of the river water is unsafe for human consumption. The deep groundwater pollution is also found to be ubiquitous (Han et al. 2016). China's groundwater and surface water have been regarded as among the most polluted water sources in the world (Shapiro 2012). 200 million Chinese are estimated to lack access to safe water sources (Tao and Xin 2014). In addition to acute water-borne diseases such as typhoid and diarrhea, water pollution can lead to digestive cancers (Ebenstein 2009). 60,000 Chinese die

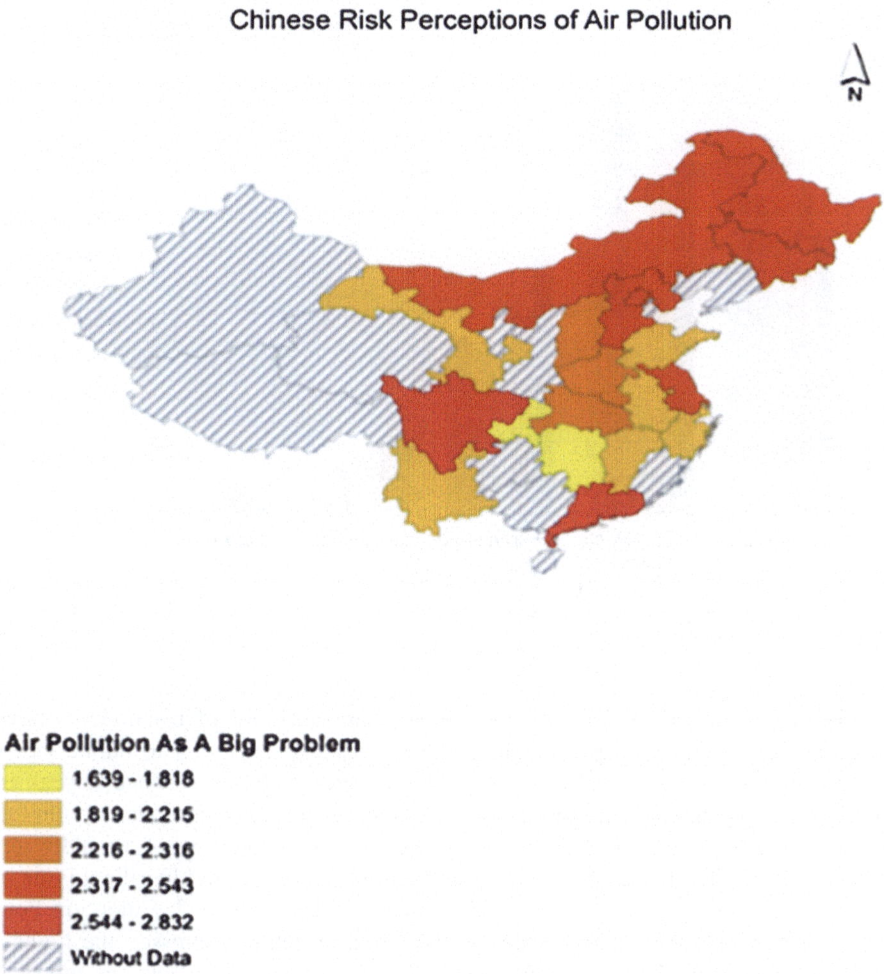

Fig. 8.6 Chinese risk perception of air pollution based on Pew Global Attitudes Survey, 2013

from diseases related to water contamination (Qiu 2011). 11,000 water quality-related emergencies have broken out since 1995 (Han et al. 2016). As a consequence, many Chinese citizens take their outrage and dissent to the streets in the form of demonstrations and protests. Annually, thousand of civil unrest incidents are estimated to be related to water pollution (Gilbert 2012).

Confronting such widespread and serious water pollution, how does the Chinese public view this issue in general? In addition to air pollution, Pew Global Attitudes Surveys asked Chinese respondents about their views toward water pollution during the same period. As Fig. 8.7 illustrates, compared to air pollution, the Chinese public expresses a lower level of concern for water pollution. This may be due to air's ubiquitous presence and air pollution's visibility both of which make it hard

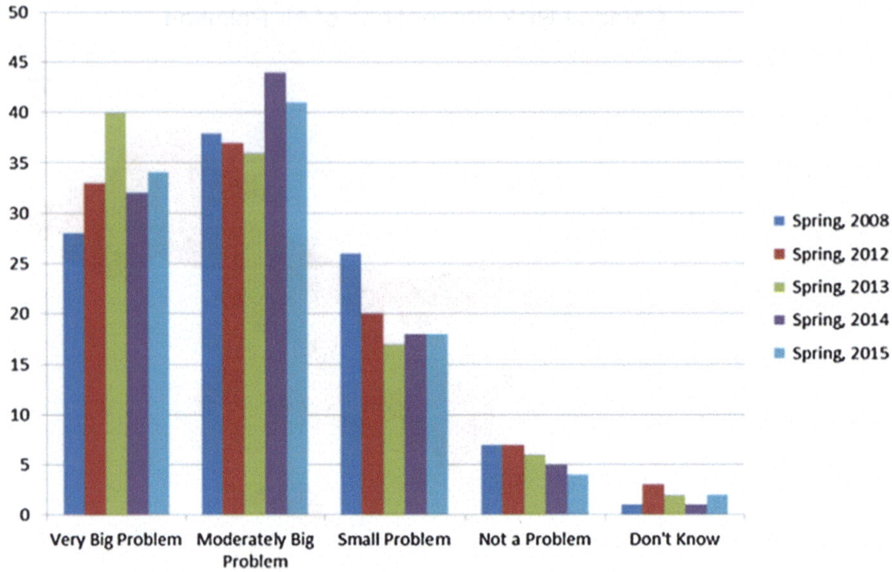

Fig. 8.7 Chinese risk perceptions of water pollution from 2008–2015, based on Pew Research Center Global Attitudes Series

for the public to ignore. Nevertheless, more than one third of respondents have viewed water pollution as a very big problem since 2012. Similar to public views toward air pollution, the public perception of water pollution reached a peak in 2013. 40% respondents who mostly resided in urban areas regarded water pollution as a very big problem. The combination of heightened perceptions of air and water pollution in 2013 indicates environmental pollution became a highly salient issue in that year. Environmental pollution has received widespread media attention both inside and outside China. Accordingly, the Chinese public expressed the highest level of concern for both air and water pollution to respond to both the physical environment—air and water pollution, and information environment—extensive media reports on these environmental issues.

Using the same method to create average scores of risk perceptions of air pollution, I demonstrate the geographic distribution of public perceptions of water pollution in 2013 (please see Fig. 8.8). Much different from the spatial pattern depicted in Fig. 8.6, northern provinces except for Heilongjiang display moderate levels of concern for water pollution. Similar to Fig. 8.6, residents in Sichuan, Jiangsu, and Guangdong are more likely to perceive water pollution as a very big problem compared to urban residents elsewhere.

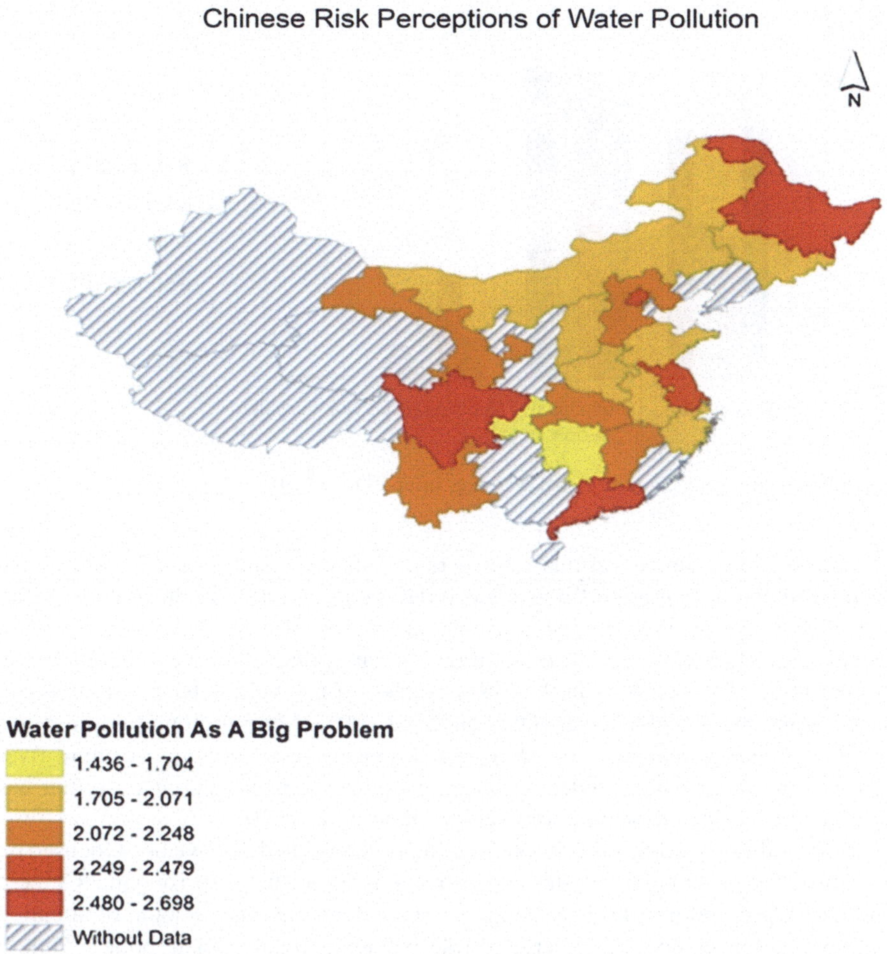

Fig. 8.8 Chinese risk perception of water pollution based on Pew Global Attitudes Survey, 2013

8.5 Public Perceptions of Global Climate Change/Warming[3]

The tremendous economic growth in China has substantially contributed to large amounts of carbon dioxide emissions (Wang et al. 2011). As the world's most populous country and a major emitter of greenhouse gases, China has experienced significantly adverse impacts of climate change. The nationwide surface air

[3]Climate change and global warming are two terms with different connotations in the scientific literature. However, these two terms are used interchangeably in the public discourse. Given

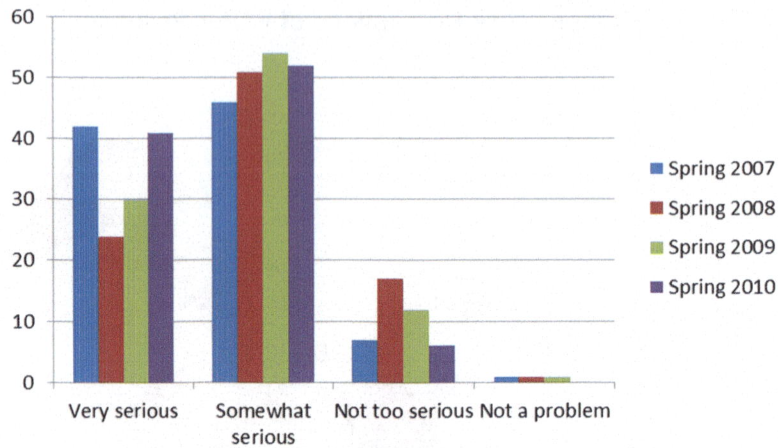

Fig. 8.9 Chinese perception of global warming from 2007 to 2010

temperature increases at various rates across China over the past 100 years have been attributed to rising greenhouse gas (GHG) concentration in the atmostophere, and 27% of the average annual warming in the last 50 years has been traced to urbanization (Ren et al. 2012). In addition, climate change has been identified as a driving force of the no-flow in the lower reaches of the Yellow River and frequent floods along the Yangtze River (Qian and Zhu 2001). More profound implications of climate change remain to be seen. For instance, the uncertainty of future river runoff in northern China under a changing climate worsens the anxiety that has already plagued this especially dry region (Piao et al. 2010).

Most studies on public perceptions of climate change to date have been focused on the United States and other western countries. It is somewhat surprising that Chinese public risk perceptions of this issue have not received the same amount of attention and enthusiasm given China's crucial role in international climate policy. Only a few empirical studies have examined the determinants of Chinese perceptions of climate change. A recent study found that climate change belief among Chinese can be attributed to perceived experiences with extreme weather events, higher level of education, lower level of income, and other socio-demographic factors (Dai et al. 2015).

Between 2007 and 2010, Pew Global Attitudes surveys asked a Chinese nationally representative sample every year the same question about global warming, "is global warming a very serious problem, or somewhat serious, not too serious, not a problem?" Figure 8.9 demonstrates that a majority of Chinese consistently viewed global warming as a moderately serious problem. Unlike being

(Footnote 3 continued)

that this chapter is concerned with public perceptions, these two terms are used interchangeably here.

a polarized issue in the United States (McCright and Dunlap 2011; Shao et al. 2014, 2016), a vast majority of Chinese regarded global warming as either a very or somewhat serious problem. In 2013, Pew Global Attitudes survey asked respondents a question related to global climate change, "do you think that global climate change is a major threat, a minor threat or not a threat to our home country?" 39 and 36% of the respondents viewed global climate change as a major threat and a minor threat, respectively. Only 14% of them did not regard this issue as a threat to China. Clearly, the Chinese public has displayed an overall moderate level of concern for global warming/climate change.

Based on the survey responses, I depict the spatial distribution of Chinese views towards global climate change in Fig. 8.10. Residents in northern China tend to show a moderate level concern for climate change, whereas residents in central China display a slightly higher level of concern for this issue. The province of Guangdong once again stands out as a region where heightened public perceptions of climate change is exhibited. Interestingly, the spatial variation of actual temperature change in the past 100 years demonstrates that the most significant warming has been witnessed in the northern part of North China and less warming and even a cooling trend before the early 21st century have been observed in southwest China (Ren et al. 2012). The conspicuous spatial discrepancy between perceptions of climate change and actual effects of climate change suggests that more extensive investigations need to be conducted in the future.

8.6 Understanding Determinants of the Environmental Risk Perceptions

I present variations in Chinese risk perceptions of air and water pollution, and global climate change on both temporal and spatial dimensions in the preceding sections. Naturally, then the question would be: what factors contribute to the variations in their environmental risk perceptions? In this section, I first provide a brief literature review on the socio-demographic base of environmental risk perceptions. I then examine the effects of socio-demographic characteristics on perceptions of air pollution, water pollution and global climate change by using the 2013 Pew Global Attitudes survey dataset. Last I present the results of these analyses.

The effects of social characteristics including gender, age, race, education, and income on environmental perceptions have been studied extensively in the United States over the past three decades (Vanliere and Dunlap 1980; Jones and Dunlap 1992; Dietz et al. 1998). First, the literature suggests that men generally tend to judge risks less than women. Some scholars attribute this gender gap to the different supposed societal roles that men and women assume (Davidson and Freudenburg 1996). Specifically, scholars argue that women express a higher level of concern for the environment because they tend to be nurturers and care providers. In comparison, men who are more likely to be involved with industry tend to give

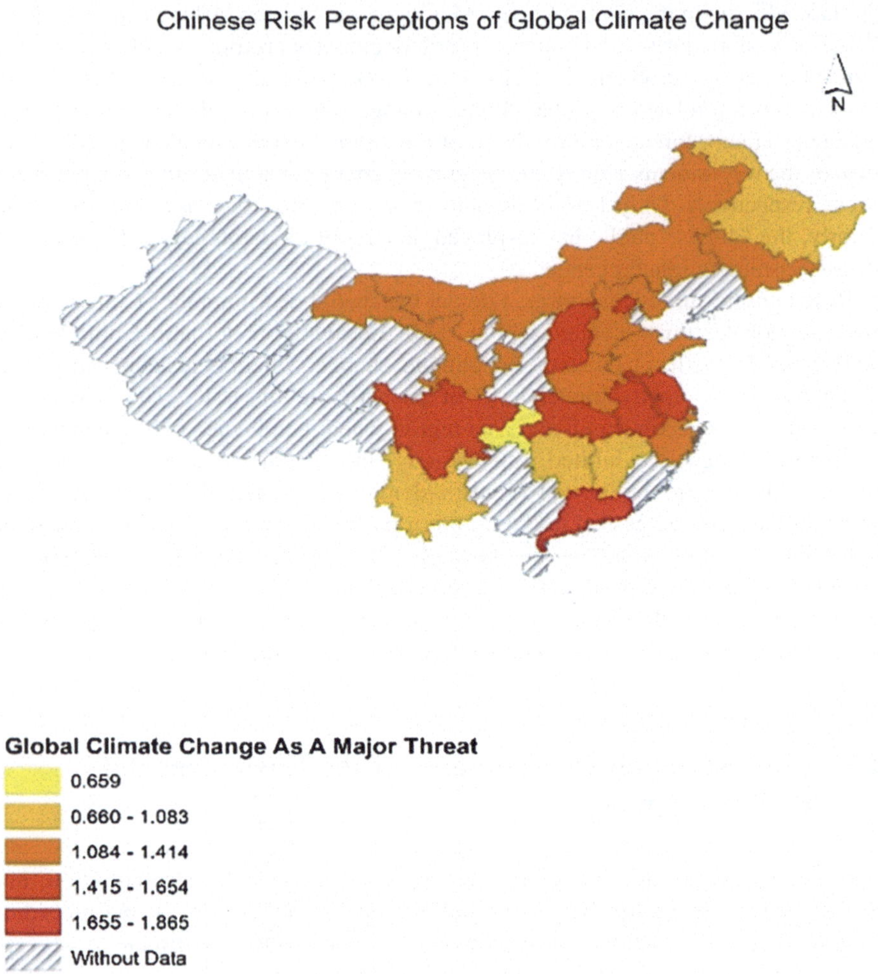

Fig. 8.10 Chinese risk perceptions of global climate change based on Pew Global Attitudes Survey, 2013

more consideration to economical tradeoffs when judging environmental risks. In modern times, an increasing number of women are involved in economic production activities and industry, though they continue to assume major household responsibilities and make more personal sacrifices than men for their families (Hochschild 1989). Age is usually found to be a strong negative predictor on environmental concern (Vanliere and Dunlap 1980). Vanliere and Dunlap (1980) attribute the age difference in environmental concern to cohort effects. Hamilton et al. (2010) regard the age difference as a result of the integration of environmental topics into modern school curricula driven by the 1970s environmental movement. Moreover, many consequences of environmental problems such as sea level rise take time to fully manifest. This delay poses more threats to younger generations (Hamilton 2008).

Characteristics pertaining to social class have been usually assumed to be positively associated with environmental concern. This assumption is again based on hierarchy of human needs proposed by Maslow (1943), suggesting that basic material needs (i.e., food, shelter, and economic stability) have to be satisfied before secondary needs such as arts, self-actualization, and environmental quality (Vanliere and Dunlap 1980). Therefore, individuals associated with higher social class tend to show more concern for the environment than those who are still struggling to have their basic needs met. Among the basic socio-demographic characteristic, education and income are most closely related to social class, indicating that individuals with higher education and income should show more concern for the environment (Vanliere and Dunlap 1980).

Here, I include gender, age, education, and income in models explaining variations in Chinese perceptions of air pollution, water pollution, and global climate change. Gender is coded as 1 (female) and 0 (male). Age ranges from 18 to 84. Education is represented from 1 to 8 with larger number indicating higher level of education. Household income is coded from 1 to 22 with larger number representing higher level of income. In addition, because environmental problems tend to be more acute in the urban setting and place can have significant effects on environmental views (Hamilton et al. 2010, 2014), I include two dummy variables to represent city and town with the control group being rural, and speculate that people who live in the cities are more likely to perceive environmental risks given that environmental problems such as air pollution are more acute and visible in cities.

Because the three dependent variables are categorical and ordered by nature, three ordered-logit regression models are estimated to explain variations in Chinese risk perceptions of air pollution, water pollution, and global climate change. Table 8.1 demonstrates the results. Pseudo R^2 is quite low across all three models, indicating the limited explanatory power of socio-demographic characteristics. This also suggests that future studies should take into consideration a more comprehensive list of independent variables such as geographic indicators to represent the objective measures of environmental risks, attitudinal variables such as views towards science and scientists, and the information environment such as media reports on environmental issues.

Income stands out as the most consistent factor exerting significant influence on all three risk perceptions. Specifically, individuals with higher levels of income tend to view air and water pollution, and global climate change as big problems and major threat, respectively. The results about income confirm the hypothesis that the environment may be a "luxury" that only financially well off individuals can afford to worry about. Correspondingly, the policy implication is that the government at varying levels needs to allocate more resources to help educate low-income individuals about risks associated with environmental pollution. The positive effect of income on perceptions of global climate change in particular is contradictory to a previous study (Dai et al. 2015). This is not surprising given that mixing results about income are also found in the literature on American public perceptions of

Table 8.1 Ordered-logit regression models explaining variations in Chinese risk perceptions of air pollution, water pollution, and global climate change

	Air pollution		Water pollution		Global climate change	
	b	z	b	z	b	z
Gender	−0.044	−0.63	−0.063	−0.92	0.005	0.06
Age	−0.005	−1.50	−0.008	−2.68**	−0.002	−0.58
Education	0.038	1.02	0.087	2.35**	0.198	4.96***
Income	0.039	3.51***	0.042	3.73***	0.049	4.35***
City	0.264	2.66***	0.143	1.49	0.024	0.23
Town (Control rural)	0.107	1.03	−0.107	1.03	−0.197	−1.53
N	3067		3065		2820	
Pseudo R^2	0.010		0.011		0.016	

*** $p < 0.001$; ** $p < 0.01$; * $p < 0.05$

climate change. This suggests that more rigorous empirical studies based on different datasets should be conducted to reveal a clear relationship between income and perceptions of climate change.

The second most consistent factor is education. More education is related to higher likelihood for one to perceive high levels of risks with water pollution and global climate change. The results of education conform to the prior hypotheses. Individuals with a higher level of education have better access to information on environmental problems and are more aware of these issues. This awareness can accordingly translate into concern. Similar to the implication of income, concerted educational efforts need to be targeted at less educated communities. For instance, more educational programs can be launched to deliver scientific facts about environmental problems to individuals with lower level of education.

The theoretical suppressing effect of age on environmental concern only manifest in risk perceptions of water pollution. Younger individuals are more likely to regard water pollution as a big problem. Last, city dwellers are inclined to perceive the severity of air pollution. This result reflects that air pollution in cities has reached a severe level so that residents are collectively more concerned about this issue than their rural counterparts. Meanwhile, it may well be due to the fact that urban residents have more access to information. The information sources can be newspapers, magazines, TV, or simply other individuals. Many city residents are known to have mobile-phone apps that can help them keep up with the air pollution readings (Economist 2013). The supposed place effect on environmental views fails to show in perceptions of water pollution and global climate change.

8.7 Conclusion

In this chapter, I examine the trends of Chinese environmental views in general and specific views toward air pollution, water pollution, and global climate change based on two series of survey data from 1995 to 2015. Generally, in the face of unprecedented environmental degradation at a massive scale, the Chinese exhibit a high level of environmental concern. During the period of rapid economic growth in conjunction with massive environmental degradation, Chinese consistently rank environmental protection higher than economic development. Public outrage and dissent over some local governments' preference of business to environment have already been expressed in the form of protests and demonstration across China. This sends a crucial message to the Chinese political leadership that environmental protection should be the new priority on the political agenda, especially with the signs of environmental pollution becoming increasingly conspicuous which further invites more public scrutiny. Some evidence suggests that the Chinese government does seriously take into consideration the public concern for environmental pollution. The recent aggressive effort on clean energy led by the Chinese government clearly displays its determination to shift from the heavy reliance on fossil fuel (Bradsher 2010).

Spatial patterns of environmental views demonstrate that there are geographic variations in how residents perceive environmental issues. Residents in Sichuan of the southwest, Guangdong of the southeast coast and Jiangsu of the east coast consistently display heightened risk perceptions for all three environmental issues. These findings encourage future studies to further explore the geographic factors that determine environmental views given that place characteristics can have demonstrable effects on personal environmental views (Hamilton et al. 2010, 2014). For instance, future studies should incorporate objective measures of air quality, water quality, and climate change, and examine how these geographic factors shape public environmental perceptions. Previous studies that are focused on the United States find that environmental risk perceptions do not always accurately reflect objective risks (Shao and Goidel 2016; Shao et al. 2016; Shao 2016). Is this finding also applicable in China? More studies are certainly needed to examine this relationship between objective and perceived environmental risks in China. Additionally, geographic factors refer to not only natural environments but also socio-economic-demographic conditions. General contextual characteristics such as rates of population growth and resource-industry employment are found to be correlated with environmental views in rural areas of the U.S. (Hamilton et al. 2010, 2014). Would the same effects be observed in China? Moreover, the province of Guangdong presents itself as an interesting case study. The environmental quality in Guangdong has been consistently ranked as among the best in China. The residents however have demonstrated exceptional levels of risk perceptions of environmental issues. Is this due to the fact that Guangdong is one of the wealthiest provinces in China and its residents tend to be financially satisfied and well educated? Previous research conducted in the U.S. does suggest that macroeconomic condition such as unemployment rate at the county level is significantly related to concern for global warming (Kahn and Kotchen 2011) and personal support for environmental rules (Hamilton et al. 2010). Future studies should incorporate geographic socio-economic-demographic indicators when estimating models of environmental perceptions and policy support.

Furthermore, three ordered-logit regression models reveal that household income is the most consistent factor determining environmental risk perceptions. This result confirms Maslow's theory of human motivation. Environmental quality is a luxury that only well off people can afford to worry about. The other social class relating factor education manifests its significant effects on views toward water pollution and global climate change. In addition, younger people are more inclined to view water pollution as a big problem. Last, city dwellers are more likely than rural residents to perceive air pollution as a big problem, which may reflect the severity of air pollution in cities. Again, more rigorous studies need to be conducted to further examine the relationship between their environmental perceptions and socio-demographic characteristics.

To sum up, this chapter presents one of the initial efforts to look into the evolution of Chinese environmental views from 1995 to 2015. Further, it conducts ordered-logit regression models examining the effects of socio-demographic characteristics on all three environmental views. Nevertheless, the research agenda on Chinese environmental perception is far from being complete. A more comprehensive list of independent variables should be considered in the future studies. Variables related to values, attitudes, and predispositions are found to play an influential role in determining one's environmental views in the U.S. (Shao et al. 2014, 2016). Due to the limitation of using an existing survey data, the relationship between Chinese environmental perceptions and this group of variables is not explored in this chapter. Future studies may consider designing original questionnaires including attitudinal items. In addition, objective measures of environmental quality should be directly compared to subjective perceptions of these environmental issues to explore the geographic variations. Geographic socio-economic indicators should be also considered. Another limitation of this chapter is the use of the 2013 Pew Global Attitudes survey for analysis. This survey oversampled urban dwellers. Although weighting technique is applied in this study, the results are subject to bias. Future studies therefore should be based on a more balanced data sample.

References in English

Bradsher, K. 2010, January 31. China is leading global race to make clean energy. *The New York Times*, A1.

Chen, M., M. Liu, and X. Tao. 2013a. Evolution and assessment on China's urbanization 1960-2010: Under-urbanization or over-urbanization? *Habitat International* 38: 25–33.

Chen, Y., A. Ebenstein, M. Greenstone, and H. Li. 2013b. Evidence on the impact of sustained exposure to air pollution on life expectancy from China's Huai River policy. *Proceedings of the National Academy of Sciences of the United States of America* 110 (32): 12936–12941.

Dai, J., M. Kesternich, A. Loschel, and A. Ziegler. 2015. Extreme weather experiences and climate change beliefs in China: An econometric analysis. *Ecological Economics* 116: 310–321.

Davidson, D.J., and W.R. Freudenburg. 1996. Gender and environmental risk concerns—A review and analysis of available research. *Environment and Behavior* 28 (3): 302–339.

Dietz, T., O.C. Stern, and G.A. Guagnano. 1998. Social structural and social psychological bases of environmental concern. *Environment and Behavior* 30 (4): 450–471.

Ebenstein, A. 2009. The consequences of industrialization: Evidence from water pollution and digestive cancers in China. *The Review of Economics and Statistics* 94 (1): 186–201.

Economist. 2013. *Beijing's air pollution: Blackest day*. Retrieved from http://www.economist.com/blogs/analects/2013/01/beijings-air-pollution. Last accessed: March 17, 2017.

Economy, E.C. 2007. The great leap backward? *Foreign Affairs* 86 (5): 38–59.

Environmental Protection Agency (EPA) United States of America. 1997. *The benefits and costs of the Clean Air Act 1970 to 1990*. Washinton, DC: US EPA.

Gilbert, N. 2012. Green protests on the rise in China. *Nature,* 488: 261–262.

Gruber, N., and J.N. Galloway. 2008. An earth-system perspective of the global nitrogen cycle. *Nature* 451: 293–296.

Hamilton, L.C. 2008. Who cares about polar region? *Arctic, Antarctic, and Alpine Research* 40: 671–678.

Hamilton, L.C., C.R. Colocousis, and C.M. Duncan. 2010. Place effects on environmental views. *Rural Sociology* 75 (2): 326–347.

Hamilton, L.C., J. Hartter, T.G. Safford, and F.R. Stevens. 2014. Rural environmental concerns: Effects of position, partisanship, and place. *Rural Sociology* 79 (2): 257–281.

Han, D., M.J. Currell, and G. Cao. 2016. Deep challenges for China's war on water pollution. *Environmental Pollution* 218: 1222–1233.

Henderson, J.V. 2003. The urbanization process and economic growth: The so-what question. *Journal of Economic Growth* 8 (1): 47–71.

Hendryx, M., J. Conley, E. Fedorko, J. Luo, and M. Armistead. 2012. Permitted water pollution discharges and population cancer and non-cancer mortality: Toxicity weights and upstream discharge effects in US rural-urban areas. *International Journal of Health Geography* 11: 9.

Hochschild, A.R. 1989. *The second shift: Working parents and the revolution at home*. New York: Penguin Group.

Holland, M., J. Berry, and D. Forster (eds.). 1999. *ExternE: Externalities of energy. Vol. 7: Methodology 1998 Update*. Luxembourg: European Commission.

Jones, R.E., and R.E. Dunlap. 1992. The social bases of environmental concern-have they changed over time. *Rural Sociology* 57 (1): 28–47.

Kahn, M.E., and M.J. Kotchen. 2011. Business cycle effects on concern about climate change: The chilling effect of recession. *Climate Change Economics* 2 (3): 257–273.

Liu, J., and J. Diamond. 2005. China's environment in a globalizing world. *Nature* 435 (30): 1179–1186.

Maslow, A.H. 1943. A theory of human motivation. *Psychological Review* 50: 370–396.

Matus, K., K. Nam, N.E. Selin, L.N. Lamsal, J.M. Reilly, and S. Paltsev. 2012. Health damages from air pollution in China. *Global Environmental Change* 22 (1): 55–66.

McCright, A.M., and R.E. Dunlap. 2011. The politicization of climate change and polarization in the American public's views of global warming, 2001-2010. *Sociological Quarterly* 52 (2): 155–194.

Millman, A., D. Tang, and F.P. Perera. 2008. Air pollution threatens the health of children in China. *Pediatrics* 122 (3): 620–628.

Pew Research Center. http://www.pewresearch.org/. Last accessed: March 17, 2017.

Piao, S., P. Ciais, Y. Huang, and J. Fang. 2010. The impacts of climate change on water resources and agriculture in China. *Nature,* 467 (2): 43–51.

Qian, W., and Y. Zhu. 2001. Climate change in China from 1880 to 1998 and its impact on the environmental condition. *Climatic Change* 50: 419–444.

Qiu, J. 2011. China to spend billions cleaning up groundwater. *Science* 334: 745.

Ren, G.Y., Y.H. Ding, Z.C. Zhao, J.Y. Zheng, T.W. Wu, G.L. Tang, and Y. Xu. 2012. Recent progress in studies of climate change in China. *Advances in Atmospheric Sciences* 29 (5): 958–977.

Rohde, R.A., and R.A. Muller. 2015. Air pollution in China: Mapping of concentrations and sources. *PLoS ONE* 10 (8): e0135749. doi:10.1371/journal.pone.0135749.

Shao, W. 2016. Are actual weather and perceived weather the same? *Journal of Risk Research* 19 (6): 722–742.

Shao, W., and K. Goidel. 2016. Seeing is believing?—An examination of perceptions of local weather conditions and climate change among residents in the U.S. Gulf Coast. *Risk Analysis* 36 (11): 2136–2157.

Shao, M., X. Tang, Y. Zhang, and W. Li. 2006. City clusters in China: Air and surface water pollution. *Frontiers in Ecology and the Environment* 4 (7): 353–361.

Shao, W., B.D. Keim, J.C. Garand, and L.C. Hamilton. 2014. Weather, climate, and the economy: Explaining risk perceptions of global warming, 2001-2010. *Weather, Climate, and Society* 6 (1): 16.

Shao, W., J.C. Garand, B.D. Keim, and L.C. Hamilton. 2016. Science, scientists, and local weather: Understanding mass attitudes toward global warming. *Social Science Quarterly* 97 (5): 1023–1057.

Shapiro, J. 2012. *China's environmental challenges*. Cambridge: Polity Press.

Tao, T., and K. Xin. 2014. Public health: A sustainable plan for China's drinking water. *Nature* 511: 527–528.

Vanliere, K.D., and R.E. Dunlap. 1980. The social bases of environmental concern-a review of hypotheses, explanations, and empirical evidence. *Public Opinion Quarterly* 44 (2): 181–197.

Vennemo, H., K. Aunan, H. Lindhjem, and H.M. Seip. 2009. Environmental pollution in China: Status and trends. *Review of Environmental Economics and Policy* 3 (2): 209–230.

Wang, S.S., D.Q. Zhou, P. Zhou, and Q.W. Wang. 2011. CO_2 emissions, energy consumption and economic growth in China: A panel data analysis. *Energy Policy* 39: 4870–4875.

World Bank. 2006. *Water quality management policy and institutional considerations*. Discussion Paper, Washington, D.C.: The World Bank.

World Bank. 2009. *Cost of pollution in China*. Washington, D.C.: The World Bank.

World Bank and the Development Research Center of the State Council, P. R. C. 2013. *China 2030: Building a modern, harmonious, and creative society*. Washington, D.C.: The World Bank.

World Values Survey (WVS). http://www.worldvaluessurvey.org/wvs.jsp. Last accessed: March 17, 2017.

Xu, B. 2014. *China's environmental crisis*. New York: Council on Foreign Relations.

Zhang, J., and K.R. Smith. 2007. Household air pollution from coal and biomass fuels in China: Measurements, health impacts, and interventions. *Environmental Health Perspectives* 115: 848–855.

Zhang, Q., K. He, and H. Huo. 2012. Cleaning China's air. *Nature* 484: 161–162.

Zhu, X. 2012. Understanding China's growth: Past, present and future. *Journal of Economic Perspectives* 26 (4): 103–124.

References in Chinese

Gong, G., and T. Zhang. 2013. Zhongguo ai zheng cun shi kong fen bu bian qian yan jiu [Temporal-spatial distribution changes of cancer village in China]. *Zhongguo renkou ziyuan yu huanjing* 23: 156–164.

Chapter 9
Urbanization, Industrialization, and Sustainable Development in China: Converging Paths?

Jonathan Harrington

Abstract Many policymakers and citizens alike point to cities as major culprits in China's ecological decline. Roads are clogged with vehicles, the air is often foul and unhealthy to breathe and waste piles up in mountainous landfills, robbing farmers of productive land. However, cities can also be powerful engines for sustainable development (可持续发展). This chapter will attempt to answer the following questions: First, what factors are driving China's urbanization and industrial strategy? Second, what does the concept of sustainable development mean in the Chinese context? Third, what measures are being taken at the national level to encourage sustainable development? Fourth, what challenges does the national government face in promoting sustainable development and environmental policy enforcement at the local level? Finally, what are the prospects for further deepening sustainable development as an integral part of China's overall revitalization strategy?

Keywords China urbanization · Sustainable development · China environmental policy · Global ecopolitics · China economic reform

9.1 Introduction

In recent years, the world's teeming masses have been on the move. At no point in human history have so many people migrated within and across borders. Where are all these people going? They are pulling up stakes from their family villages and moving to cities. The turmoil, prosperity and triumph of the first industrial revolution spawned the growth of great historical metropolises such as London, Paris and Rome. However, in the second decade of the 21st Century, seven of the top ten largest metropolitan areas are in the developing world. China is at the epicenter of

J. Harrington (✉)
Troy University, Troy, USA
e-mail: jhharrington@troy.edu

Z. Tang (ed.), *China's Urbanization and Socioeconomic Impact*,
DOI 10.1007/978-981-10-4831-9_9

this mega-trend. Shanghai and Beijing are both on the top-10 list. Over 20% of China's population lives in urban communities of 1,000,000 or more (UNDP 2015).

China's breakneck urbanization has been accompanied by astounding economic growth. In just a few short decades, China has transformed from a rural agricultural economy to an urbanized high tech manufacturing powerhouse. Since the beginning of China's reform period in 1978, Chinese GDP has grown from $148 billion to 10.3 trillion U.S. dollars at current market prices (UNDP 2015). The poverty rate has declined to around 10%. Life expectancy has risen from 66 to 75 years (it was 43 in 1960). Most Chinese now have access to basic amenities of modern life; electricity, decent housing, access to trained health care professionals and smartphones (Chen 2015; Ang 2016).

However, China's growth has generated numerous negative externalities. Many cities struggle to provide adequate services, infrastructure and employment to their fast-growing populations. Rural-urban, regional and intra-urban wealth gaps have grown. Over concentration of heavy industry and weak enforcement of environmental regulations has seriously damaged local ecosystems and endangered public health (Shapiro 2012; Nadin et al. 2016a).

Fortunately, these challenges have not gone unnoticed by government, industry, citizens and the international community. Over time, planners, policymakers and private industry have explored numerous strategies to preserve the benefits of urban agglomeration while also mitigating its potential negative effects (World Bank 2013). Since the late 1980s, one of the most influential concepts driving this discussion is sustainable development (and Chinese environmental/ecological variants). The purpose of this analysis is to trace the evolution of sustainable development dialogues and related policy and enforcement responses within the context of China's urbanization story.

9.2 China's Urbanization/Development Model

During the first 30 years of PRC history, China experienced relatively low levels of urbanization relative to other developing states. In 1949, only 10% of the population lived in urban areas (Zhang 2004). Initially, the new regime implemented a Soviet-style heavy industrial command and control economic model. Millions of workers migrated to new manufacturing bases. However, late 1950s policies which focused on collectivized agricultural production and rural industrialization (ex. Great Leap Forward) generated negative political, social and economic problems which arrested growth in urbanization (Zhang 2003; Spence 2012). The period during and immediately after the Cultural revolution (1966–1977) also exhibited almost no growth in urbanization (Banister 1987).

China's post-Mao leadership took a different approach. Reformers allowed China to transition to a more traditional model of industrialization which centered on urban manufacturing. Deng Xiaoping promoted the Four Modernizations; agriculture, industry, national defense and science and technology (Baum 1980; Naughton and Tsai 2015).

Urbanization was adopted as a core strategy to integrate China's peasants into the modern economy and improve living standards. Urban agglomeration placed workers in close proximity to manufacturers. Agricultural reform significantly increased agricultural productivity. The availability of surplus labor reduced costs for producers. Density allowed for more efficient provision of basic infrastructure including water, electricity, sewage, roads, and rail. Public services including education, healthcare, social welfare could be provided more efficiently. Large concentrations of firms encouraged the development of local supply chains, technology transfer and support for legal, management, marketing and other service firms. Density allowed construction of office skyscrapers and multi-family dwellings. Urbanization encouraged the development of local markets for manufactured goods and services (Lippit 1987; Naughton and Tsai 2015). Cities could also provide numerous leisure/cultural amenities including museums, theaters and retail centers that were not available in rural communities (Zhang 2004).

The Deng administration adopted a new regional development strategy which favored certain coastal cities/provinces. Large coastal cities exhibited comparative advantages in land, capital, technology, infrastructure and access to foreign markets (MacFarquhar 2011; Spence 2012). Other cities such as the Special Economic Zones of Zhuhai, Shenzhen and Shantou were mostly built from scratch (Lippit 1987). It was postulated that allowing these areas to get rich first would generate wealth that could then be used to develop other parts of the country.

Government administrators encouraged worker migration through incremental reform of China's household registration, or *hukou*, system. Millions were granted legal status to work in coastal cities, but the lure of higher paying jobs encouraged many more to immigrate without permission. By 1990, more than 100 million Chinese had joined the ranks of China's floating population (Solinger 1999). The availability of this teeming pool of cheap labor is one of the main reasons why China became the world's low cost producer of consumer goods.

9.2.1 Limits to Development

There is little doubt among scholars and policymakers that urbanization and industrial concentration are major drivers behind China's high GDP growth. Urban resident incomes are, in general higher, than their rural counterparts. Urbanites generally have better access to basic services, job opportunities and consumer options. However, progress has been very uneven. Much of the new wealth creation has gone to a handful of coastal cities that were already relatively well off before the reform period (MacFarquhar 2011). Inequality not only exists among cities and regions, but also within cities themselves. Workers with specific skills who are more suited to competing in a high tech, increasingly globalized economy have fared far better than their less fortunate peers. This phenomenon is not unique to China, but the magnitude of inequality is more pronounced than in many other parts of the world (Chen 2015).

Beyond fostering uneven development and exacerbating wealth inequality, China's industrial model has created numerous negative health and ecological externalities. A downside of industrial centralization is that high polluting heavy industries like coal-fired electricity generation and steel production generated highly concentrated air, water and toxic emissions that damage ecosystems and endanger public health. Most cities lacked the basic infrastructure to provide adequate sewer, electricity, transportation and housing to the massive influx of rural workers who were searching for a better life (Economy 2010; Shapiro 2012).

9.3 Global Eco-politics, State Environmentalism and Sustainable Development

In the area of environmental management and protection, China really started from scratch. The Mao Administration had virtually no environmental laws or regulations (Shapiro 2012; Ross 1988). China's reentry into the United Nations provided Chinese scientists and diplomats new opportunities to engage with their Western foreign counterparts for the first time. In 1972, China sent a delegation to the United Nations Conference on the Human Environment in Stockholm, Sweden. This was the starting point of China's participation in global eco-politics (Gilley 2012; Economy 2001).

Unlike most developed countries, China followed a top-down approach to generating awareness, developing and implementing environmental policy. Policymakers' relative inexperience with environmental management created opportunities for China's scientific "epistemic communities" to play a key role in disseminating environmental science, technology, laws and regulations and values to China's elites (Harrington 2005). These scientists played an outsized role in increasing elite awareness, especially given the fact that there were no civil society environmental movement actors or related pressure groups to advocate change. Harrington (2005) refers to this phenomenon as "state environmentalism." Other terms such as "Authoritarian Environmentalism" have been variously used to describe the appearance of government environmental responses in the absence of public pressure groups (Beeson 2010; Gilley 2012).

Three major sources for China's new environmental information, laws and regulations included U.N. development agencies (especially the World Bank and United Nations Development Program (UNDP), government to government communications (ex. U.S. Environmental Protection Agency and the China State Environmental Protection Agency) and foreign business interests (Mol and Carter 2006). Foreign businesses required legal and regulatory guidance to set up their Chinese operations. Also, the near-term urgency of responding to environmental threats in China's fast growing cities created domestic demand for change. Consequently, by the early 1990s, China had developed a full gamut of rules and regulations as well as a small national environmental bureaucracy to oversee environmental management and advise senior leadership on environmental matters (Silk and Ross 1987; Ma and Ortolano 2000).

9.3.1 Enter Sustainable Development…

It was during this period of creative sharing and communication among multitudes of Chinese and foreign actors that the concept of "sustainable development" burst onto the international stage. The World Commission on Environment and Development established a committee to delve more deeply into the link between environmental protection and socio-economic development (Blewitt 2014). The outcome of their deliberations was a document entitled *Our Common Future* which is credited with first coining the term "sustainable development." The report notes that sustainable development is "development that meets the needs of the present generation without compromising the ability of future generations to meet their own needs" (Bruntland 1987). Harrington (2008) notes that this concept includes three major elements: "First, it links economy, environment and equity into one comprehensive decision-making process. Second, it emphasizes long-term change and its impact on intergenerational equity. Third, it recognizes natural resource scarcity and the limited carrying capacities of ecosystems" (Harrington 2008, 17). Since its original formulation, the phrase sustainable development has become one of the core driving concepts guiding both environmental and development discourses among international agencies, domestic governments, NGO activists and academics (Sachs 2015; Cobbinah et al. 2015).

Sustainable development offered an important addition to existing Chinese discourses about China's future path. More than a decade of 10% per year GDP growth was taking an increasingly noticeable toll on China's environmental conditions, especially in urban areas. Industrial demand for raw materials exceeded domestic supplies. In 1992, China became a net importer of oil. Senior leaders called for a massive expansion of coal production to fuel the growing energy needs of consumers and industry (Stensdal 2014). Chinese leaders also approved construction of the Three Gorges Dam Project and dozens of new nuclear power plants. One of the main objectives of President Jiang Zemin's declared late 1990s "Go West" campaign was to open up China's Western provinces to mining and resource extraction. Cities struggled to provide basic services to new residents. Pollution and related health problems were on the rise. In other words, the time was ripe for exploring new ideas (Ye 2013).

By the early 1990s, the concept of sustainable development began to garner attention among senior Chinese policymakers. In 1992, Premier Li Peng spoke at the United Nations Conference on Environment and Development (UNCED) meeting in Rio de Janeiro. China expressed support for three initiatives under consideration, the Framework Convention on Climate Change (UNFCCC), the Convention on Biological Diversity (CBD) and Convention of Forestry (Harrington 2005;

Economy 2001). A related outcome of the meeting was "Agenda 21," an aspirational document which encouraged member states to develop their own domestic plans to promote sustainable development. China published its own "Agenda 21" report in 1994 (Lewis 2013; Stensdal 2014). The country became an active participant in all future Committee of the Parties (COP) meetings for the three conventions. China also eventually signed (in 2002) the Kyoto Protocol.

The world welcomed Chinese engagement, especially on the issue of climate change. China's participation in the climate change regime compared favorably to that of the George W. Bush Administration (2001–2009) which famously pulled the United States out of the Kyoto process in 2001 (Conrad 2012). China's defense of the 2015 Paris Agreement, which commits signatories to deeper cuts in greenhouse gas emissions (GHGs), has garnered widespread support around the world (Lewis 2013; Harrington 2016). Again, China's promise to decrease energy intensity by double digits and stop the absolute growth of GHG emissions by 2030 compares favorably with the Trump Administration which has stated it does not intend to fulfill American promises to make similar cuts.

Another interesting outcome of continuing debates about sustainable development and related concepts was that cities took on a more prominent role as potential new engines for sustainable growth. Growing concerns about carbon emissions and related energy consumption broadened the discussions beyond pollution abatement to larger issues about China's entire fossil-fuel based development model. Numerous studies done in the West revealed that properly planned cities are more energy efficient and generate lower carbon emissions per capita than other types of communities. Sustainability precepts regarding social and intergenerational equity were also appealing (Dhakal 2009; Nadin et al. 2016b).

9.3.2 *Ideas Versus Implementation*

Parallel to these policy debates, Chinese leaders developed a wide array of laws and associated bureaucratic structures to regulate environmental pollution. National level policy implementation was administered by the State Environmental Protection Agency (SEPA), which was founded in 1987 (it was administratively upgraded and renamed the Ministry of Environment in 2007). SEPA was responsible for coordinating national environmental policies with other ministerial bodies and setting targets for various pollutants (Jahiel 1998).

Both funding for and implementation of enforcement actions was mostly relegated to local governments. Local Environmental Protection Bureaus (EPBs) were delegated official enforcement powers such as issuing pollution permits, levying environmental fees and taxes and even closing down operations for serious environmental offenses. However, EPB mandates often conflicted with competing local bureaucracies and private firms, many of which prioritized income and job growth over pollution. Chinese regulatory pragmatism required that EPBs also weigh the implications of enforcement actions on the health of firms, ownership characteristics and related social and political factors (Ma and Ortolano 2000; McElwee 2011). The primary consequence of this highly decentralized system was (and is) that enforcement varied considerably by community and region. This delinking of national policymaking and local enforcement capacity has greatly complicated Chinese policymaker efforts to promote and enforce environmental and related sustainable development policies at the local level (Economy 2010; Mai and Franscesch-Huidobro 2015). These basic components of this enforcement system are still in place today.

9.4 "Harmonious Society," the "China Dream" and Sustainable Development

In the first few years of the new century, international discussions about sustainable development deepened. The UNDP-led Millennium Development Goals (MDG) agenda explicitly included environmental sustainability as one of eight core goals that developing nations should strive to achieve. China played a prominent role at the Rio-plus-10 Summit in South Africa where nations, businesses, governmental organizations and citizens reaffirmed their commitment to sustainable development (UNDP-China 2015). Premier Zhu Rongji's speech, which supported the goals of the Summit, contrasted sharply with U.S. Secretary of State Colin Powell's address, which signaled U.S. backtracking on many sustainable development commitments, especially those relating to climate change (Harrington 2005). China joined other countries in signing the Johannesburg Plan of Implementation which urged states to quicken the pace of elaborating national, regional and local sustainable development policies (World Bank 2013).

These discussions later culminated in the creation of more expansive agreements, the *Agenda for Sustainable Development* and the *Sustainable Development Goals*. China played a major part in drafting this new initiative which commits nations to end poverty, end hunger, greatly expand access to affordable clean energy provide clean water and sanitation at all, gender equality, income equality and promote sustainable cities and communities (and other things) by 2030 (UNDP-China 2015).

9.4.1 Hu-Wen Reforms

In 2003, the Hu-Wen administration adopted the phrase "harmonious society" (和谐社会) as a guiding concept for their new administration. This concept offered a more expansive articulation of development which called for greater social harmony, wealth equity and restoring balance to human relations with the natural world (Gang 2011; McElwee 2011; Song and Woo 2008). This concept is connected to the term "great harmony" (*datong*), a traditional concept rooted in old Confucian norms. From this picture of the past comes the sense that the wheel of equilibrium and harmony has been running in Chinese society for over 2000 years (Scott 2013).

These conceptual linkages were expressed in concrete terms in China's 11th Five Year Plan (2006–10) which clearly articulates the need for economic transformation. Of particular concern was reducing fossil fuel energy consumption and related carbon emissions. The growing interest in climate change was also driven by governmental studies which revealed the threat that global warming poses to China's future development (Nadin et al. 2016; Lin et al. 2006). The concepts of environmental protection and harmonious development were merged into a much more comprehensive strategy of ecological modernization (Guo et al. 2013; Kuhn 2016).

The 11th Five Year Plan established a series of hard targets for reducing energy intensity (20%), total discharge of major pollutants (10%) and increasing forest coverage. It also increased government investment in developing renewable energy industries and deploying renewable energy infrastructure. A new Ministry of Environment was created. Many new pilot projects, including the Top-1000 Enterprise Program and the Low Carbon Cities program were established and funded to encourage implementation. In 2009, China announced a commitment to reduce CO_2 emissions per unit of GDP by 40–45% by 2020 (Yu 2014). These policy goals were passed down to all levels of government. Cities were tasked with developing strategies to meet the new requirements. In the aggregate, China achieved its Plan targets. However, there was considerable variance in performance at the local level. Conflicting local government priorities, lack of policy coordination and the underfunding of EPBs continued to weaken enforcement (Kostka and Hobbes 2012; Koehn 2016).

China's 12th Five Year Plan (2011–2015) included sixteen targets relating to sustainable development including energy intensity (15% reduction), carbon intensity (18% reduction), SO_2 (15% reduction) and non-fossil fuel use (15% increase) (Kennedy and Johnson 2016). It also called for major new investments in clean energy and electric vehicle development. During this period, China became the world's biggest producer of solar panels and wind power generators (Ng et al. 2016). Growth of these industries revealed that it is indeed possible to simultaneously achieve economic growth, create jobs, expand exports and reduce environmental harms.

9.4.2 The "Chinese Dream"

President Xi has echoed and expanded on the harmony and sustainable development themes. He has promoted the "China Dream" (中国梦) concept which emphasizes two-way interdependence, win-win outcomes, development, cooperation, harmony and peace. He also has more strongly emphasized the need for China to both pursue peaceful development while also protecting its legitimate rights and interests. He further noted the need to develop policies that correspond to its rising prominence in world affairs (Swaine 2014). Other Chinese sustainable development related terms include "green development" (绿色发展), "ecological civilization" (生态文明), "green growth" (绿色增长), and "beautiful China" (美丽中国) and "Circular economy" (循环经济) all of which highlight the prospects of achieving ecological renewal, reducing inequality, recycling and balanced economic growth (Kuhn 2016; Seligsohn and Hsu 2016).

The 13th Five Year Plan and numerous other policy documents continue to place cities at the center of economic reconstruction. China's urbanization rate is expected to rise to 60% (from 56% in 2015) by 2020 (NPC 2016). However, despite all the discussion about sustainable development and related concepts over the past 20 years, city administrators still vary significantly in their ecological performance and basic understanding of sustainable development concepts. Multiple recently published comparative studies reveal that there is no universal agreement about the components and expected outcomes of sustainable development among local policymakers. For instance, there is no standardized national strategy for specifying specific, measurement indicators for SD. Shen and Zhou (2014) identify eight different sustainable development indicator systems that have evolved over the past 15 years. There is little coordination among the various institutes and government bodies that developed the indicators. Each system varies considerably in both the number and emphasis of indicators. City planners are unclear about which one to use (Tan et al. 2017). More often than not, uncertainty is the hand maiden of inaction.

9.4.3 Deepening International Cooperation

On the international front, U.S. President Barak Obama and Chinese President Xi Jinping reached an agreement to commit both countries to reduce carbon emissions. For the first time, China committed to stop absolute growth in GHG emissions by 2030 (Hart, Zhu and Ying 2015; Slater 2015). Both joined more than 100 other nations in signing the Paris Agreement at COP 21 of the UN Framework Convention on Climate Change in December, 2015.

In recent years, cities have been given more leeway to pursue cooperative agreements with their peers in other countries and directly participate in international organizations that promote sustainable development. Two organizations that have been active partners with Chinese cities include ICLEI—Local Governments for Sustainability (ICLEI) and the World Resources Institute. ICLEI is one of the largest international networks of local governments that focuses on sustainability. It has more than 1000 member governments from 85 countries (ICLEI 2015b).

ICLEI has been instrumental in creating a local government climate roadmap which highlights the efforts of local governments to promote sustainable development. It ensures recognition of the role of local governments, provides opportunities for engagement and cooperation as well as the technical resources that local governments need to set sustainability goals and track their progress in meeting those goals (ICLEI 2015a).

The World Resources Institute and the World Business Council on Sustainable Development have also provided a leadership role in providing the tools and expertise necessary for cities to tackle carbon emissions. In cooperation with Chinese partners, a Greenhouse Gas Protocol has been customized to allow Chinese cities to inventory, track and reduce carbon emissions (WRI 2013; Fong 2016).

9.5 Conclusion

In a few short decades, China has risen from relative international obscurity to one of the great powers of the world. If current trends continue, Chinese GDP will surpass that of the United States before 2025. Most of this growth has occurred in cities. Since 1978, China's urbanization rate has risen from 20% to almost 60%. Cities are also responsible for more than 70% of China's GHG emissions. However, China's political leaders have increasingly come to the realization that China must rebalance its development to be more inclusive, redistributive and ecologically sensitive (World Bank 2013).

Unfortunately, there is still dissonance between the relatively high standards of national policies, laws and regulations and the capacity and willingness of many cities to implement them (Hart et al. 2015). Overall divergence between national polices and local capacity for enforcement continues to be a challenge. Most funding for environmental enforcement is provided by local governments. Cities have widely varying resources and capacities, especially between the wealthy megalopolises of Guangzhou-Shenzhen, Shanghai and Beijing-Tianjin, and less developed inlands cities/provinces. As has been the case with get rich first cities taking initiatives to invest in Inland regions, these early beneficiaries of Deng's reform policies should also take the lead in disseminating environmental ideas, technology and values (Lo 2014). China has also greatly benefitted from international collaborations and this should continue. Chinese production of cleantech products has permitted faster dissemination of alternative energy capacity worldwide (Lewis 2012).

At some point, it may indeed possible to "decouple" economic growth and environmental degradation, but not with status-quo approaches. It is imperative for China (and other countries) to pursue a more sustainable development model, with cities in the lead, if they are going to help each citizen fulfill their "Chinese Dreams" for healthy and happy lives full of opportunity, both now and in the future.

References

Ang, Y. 2016. *How China Escaped the Poverty Trap*. Ithaca: Cornell University Press.

Banister, J. 1987. *China's Changing Population*. Palo Alto: Stanford University Press.

Baum, R. 1980. China's four modernizations. In *China's four Modernizations: China's New Technological Revolution*, ed. R. Baum, 1–22. Boulder: Westview Press.

Beeson, M. 2010. The coming of environmental authoritarianism. *Environmental Politics* 19 (2): 276–294.

Blewitt, J. 2014. *Understanding Sustainable Development*, 2nd ed. London: Routledge.

Bruntland, G. 1987. *Our Common Future*. Oxford, UK: Oxford University Press.

Chen, W. 2015. China's development path: Joys and worries. In *East Asian Development: Twenty-First Century Perspectives*, ed. S. Hua, and R. Hu, 177–194. London: Routledge.

Cobbinah, P., M. Erdiaw-Kwasie, and P. Amoateng. 2015. Rethinking sustainable development within the framework of poverty and urbanization in developing countries. *Environmental Development* 13: 18–32.

Conrad, B. 2012. China in Copenhagen: Reconciling the "Beijing climate revolution" and the "Copenhagen climate obstinacy". *The China Quarterly* 210: 435–455.

Dhakal, S. 2009. Urban energy use and carbon emissions from cities in China and policy implications. *Energy Policy* 37 (11): 4208–4219.

Economy, E. 2001. The impact of international regimes on Chinese foreign policy-making: Broadening perspectives and policies…but only to a point. In *The Making of Chinese Foreign and Security Policy in the Era of Reform: 1978-2000*, ed. D. Lampton, 230–253. Palo Alto: Stanford University Press.

Economy, E. 2010. *The River runs Black: The Environmental Challenge to China's Future*. Ithaca: Cornell University Press.

Fong, W.K. 2016. Twenty-three Chinese cities to cut peak carbon emissions by 2030. *World Resources Institute Insights*. Retrieved from http://www.wri.org/print/44163.

Gang, F. 2011. *The Economics of Climate Change in China: Towards a Low Carbon Economy*. Washington, DC: Earthscan.

Gilley, B. 2012. Authoritarian environmentalism and China's response to climate change. *Environmental Politics* 21 (2): 287–307.

Guo, X., D. Marinova, and J. Hong. 2013. China's shifting policies towards sustainability: A low-carbon economy and environmental protection. *Journal of Contemporary China* 22 (81): 428–445.

Harrington, J. 2005. Panda diplomacy: State environmentalism, international relations and Chinese foreign Policy. In *Confronting Environmental Change in East and Southeast Asia: Eco-Politics, Foreign Policy and Sustainable Development*, ed. P. Harris. New York: United Nations Press.

Harrington, J. 2008. *The Climate Diet*. London: Earthscan.

Harrington, J. 2016. China, global ecopolitics and Antarctic governance: Converging paths? *Journal of Chinese Political Science* 2016 (September): 1–20.

Hart, C., Y. Zhu, and J. Ying. 2015. *Mapping China's Climate Policy Formation Process*. Beijing: The Embassy of the Federal Republic of Germany.

ICLEI. 2015a. *Local government climate roadmap*. Retrieved from Bonn: http://www.iclei.org/index.php?id=1197.

ICLEI. 2015b. *ICLEI China partnerships*. Retrieved from http://eastasia.iclei.org/iclei-east-asia/iclei-china.html.

Jahiel, A. 1998. Organization of environmental protection in China. *China Quarterly* 149: 83–103.

Kennedy, S., and C. Johnson. 2016. *Perfecting China INC: The 13th Five Year Plan*. Washington DC: Center for Strategic and International Studies.

Koehn, P.H. 2016. *China Confronts Climate Change: A Bottom-Up Perspective*. London: Routledge, Taylor & Francis Group.

Kostka, G., and W. Hobbs. 2012. Local energy efficiency policy implementation in China: Bridging the gap between national priorities and local interests. *China Quarterly* 211: 765–785.

Kuhn, B. 2016. Sustainable development discourses in China. *Journal of Sustainable Development* 9 (6): 158–167.

Lewis, J.I. 2012. *Green Innovation in China—China's Wind Power Industry and the global Transition to a Low-Carbon Economy*. New York: Columbia University Press.

Lewis, J. 2013. China's environmental diplomacy: Climate change, domestic politics and international engagement. In *China Across the Divide: The Domestic and Global in Politics and Society*, ed. Foote, 200–225. New York: Oxford University Press.

Lin, E. et al. 2006. *National Assessment Report on Climate Change: Climate Change Impacts and Adaptation*. Beijing: National Climate Center Retrieved from http://en.cnki.com.cn/Article_en/CJFDTOTAL-QHBH200602001.htm.

Lippit, V. 1987. *The economic development of China*. White Plains: M. E. Sharpe.

Lo, K. 2014. China's low-carbon city initiatives: The implementation gap and the limits of the target responsibility system. *Habitat International* 42: 236–244.

Ma, X., and L. Ortolano. 2000. *Environmental Regulation in China: Institutions, Enforcement and Compliance*. New York: Rowman and Littlefield.

MacFarquhar, R. 2011. *The Politics of China: Sixty Years of the People's Republic of China*. Cambridge: Cambridge University Press.

Mai, Q., and M. Franscesch-Huidobro. 2015. *Climate Change Governance in Chinese Cities*. London: Routledge.

McElwee, C.R. 2011. *Environmental Law in China: Managing Risk and Ensuring Compliance*. Oxford; New York: Oxford University Press.

Mol, A., and N. Carter. 2006. China's environmental governance in transition. *Environmental Politics* 15 (2): 149–170.

Nadin, R., S. Opitz-Stapleton, and J. Wei. 2016. Understanding China's adaptation challenges. In *Climate Risk and Resilience in China*, ed. R. Nadin, S. Opitz-Stapleton, and Y. Xu, 37–60. London: Routledge.

Nadin, R. O.-S. Sarah, and J. Wei. 2016b. Understanding climate risk and building resilience. In *Climate Risk and Resilience in China*, R.O.-S. Nadin, Sarah, and X. Yinlong (ed.), 299–326. London: Routledge.

Naughton, B., and K.S. Tsai. 2015. *State Capitalism, Institutional Adaptation, and the Chinese Miracle*. Cambridge: Cambridge University Press.

Ng, S., N. Mabey, and J. Gaventa. 2016. *Pulling Ahead on Clean Technology: China's 13th Five Year Plan Challenges Europe's Low Carbon Competitiveness*. Retrieved from https://www.e3g.org/docs/E3G_Report_on_Chinas_13th_5_Year_Plan.pdf.

NPC. 2016. *China NPC 13th Five-Year Plan*. Beijing: National People's Congress of China.

Ross, L. 1988. *Environmental Policy in China*. Bloomington: University of Indiana Press.

Sachs, J. 2015. *The Age of Sustainable Development*. New York: Columbia University Press.

Scott, D. 2013. Soft language, soft imagery and soft power in China's diplomatic lexicon. In *China's Soft Power and International Relations*, ed. H. Lai, and Y. Lu, 39–63. London: Routledge.

Seligsohn, D., and A. Hsu. 2016. How China's 13th Five-Year Plan addresses energy and the environment. Chinafile.com. Retrieved from https://www.chinafile.com/reporting-opinion/environment/how-chinas-13th-five-year-plan-addresses-energy-and-environment.

Shapiro, J. 2012. *China's Environmental Challenges*. Malden, MA: Polity Press.

Shen, L., and J. Zhou. 2014. Examining the effectiveness of indicators for guiding sustainable urbanization in China. *Habitat International* 44 (2014): 111–120.

Silk, M., and L. Ross. 1987. *Environmental Law and Policy in the People's Republic of China*. New York: ABC-CLIO.

Slater, H. 2015. Insights: China's carbon emissions targets and the Paris COP. *China Carbon Forum Newsletter* 2015 (October): 1–3.

Solinger, D. 1999. China's floating population. In *The Paradox of China's Post-Mao Reforms*, ed. M. Goldman, and R. MacFaraquhar, 220–240. Cambridge, MA: Harvard University Press.

Song, L., and W.T. Woo. 2008. *China's Dilemma: Economic Growth, the Environment and Climate Change*. [Canberra]; [Washington, D.C.]; [Beijing, China]: ANU E Press: Asia Pacific Press; Brookings Institution Press; Social Sciences Academic Press (China).

Spence, J. 2012. *The Search for Modern China*. New York: W. W. Norton.

Stensdal, I. 2014. Chinese Climate-Change Policy, 1988-2013: Moving on up. *Asian Perspective* 38 (1): 111–135.

Swaine, M. 2014. Xi jinping's address to the central conference on work relating to foreign affairs: Assessing and advancing major power diplomacy with Chinese characteristics. *China Leadership Monitor,* 46.

Tan, Y., H. Hu, L. Jiao, J. Ochoa, and L. Shen. 2017. A study of best practices in promoting sustainable urbanization in China. *Journal of Environmental Management* 193 (2017): 8–18.

UNDP. 2015. *Human Development Report: Work for Human Development*. UNDP.

UNDP-China. 2015. *China, the Millennium Development Goals and the Post-2015 Development Agenda*. Retrieved from Beijing: https://issuu.com/undp-china/docs/undp-ch-mdgpaper-post2015.

World Bank and Development Research Center of the State Council. 2013. *China 2030: Building a Modern, Harmonious and Creative Society*. Washington D.C.: World Bank Publications.

WRI. 2013. *Greenhouse Gas Protocol Tools*. World Resources Institute: Washington D. C.

Ye, W. 2013. Chinese perspectives on the environment and sustainable development. In *Issues in Contemporary Chinese Thought and Culture* (1 online resource, 218 pages).

Yu, L. 2014. Low carbon eco-city: New approach for Chinese urbanization. *Habitat International* 44: 102–110.

Zhang, K. 2003. What explains China's rising urbanization in the reform era? *Urban Studies* 39 (12): 2301–2315.

Zhang, K. 2004. The evolution of China's urban transformation: 1949-2000. In *Urban Transformation in China*, ed. A. Chen, G. Liu, and K. Zhang, 25–39. Aldershot, UK: Ashgate Publishing.

Part IV
Urbanization and Impact on Rural Clans, Rural Clan Culture, and Villages

Chapter 10
Changes with Chinese Characteristics: Rural Clan Culture, Clan Communities, and Kinship Relations During Urbanization

Zongli Tang

Abstract This research examines urbanization and its impact on rural clan culture and clan communities, emphasizing normative changes with regard to clan sentiment, family values, filial piety, ancestor worship, decent relations, gender relations, marital relations, patriarchal power, and rituals, which have been long neglected by pioneer studies. As revealed, urbanization has weakened traditional influence among villagers especially the well-educated youths. But the impact is limited in scope and intensity. Migrant workers are still in their rural roots. The current urban development is not sufficient to completely separate them physically and mentally from native clan communities. Traditional culture remains not only in their memory but also in their daily life. China's urbanization is distinguished from European model thanks to changed technological environment today. New technical conditions in transportation and information make the distance between migrant workers and their villages relatively shorter. Migrant workers' spiritual communication with their family members, relatives, and local clans is not loosened. Their various links with home-villages do not cut off, but continue to be close and smooth. Urban effects move slowly on them. In the survey, a majority of the respondents expressed traditional viewpoints regarding ancestor worship, *xiao* (or filial piety), loyalty, clan rituals and clan genealogy, reflecting historical continuity of culture. Although villagers are shifting from the big *jia* to the small *jia*, and individualism is rising, *jia,* being the foundation of the Chinese society and Chinese culture, continues to be of more importance than individuals. Cultural changes bear strong Chinese characteristics.

Keywords Clan culture · Ideological modernization · Urbanization · Rural areas · Anhui

---

Z. Tang (✉)
Auburn University at Montgomery, Montgomery, USA
e-mail: ztang@aum.edu

Z. Tang (ed.), *China's Urbanization and Socioeconomic Impact*,
DOI 10.1007/978-981-10-4831-9_10

10.1 Introduction

In this chapter, clan is referred to *zongzu* (宗族). To discuss clan and clan culture, we must first figure out what *zongzu* is. In *Baihutong* (《白虎通》) Ban Gu said, "*Zong* (宗) means persons who are respected. They are the common ancestors respected by their descendants." Further, he said, "Zu (族) means a group of people who live together." According to *Erya · Shiqin*, (《尔雅·释亲》) "A group of families based on patrilineal descent is called *zongzu* (宗族)." Thus, in understandings of the ancient Chinese, *zongzu* is a group of people or a group of families based on patrilineal descent and living together. *Zongzu* was the basic unit of traditional Chinese society, which can be considered a clan society. Chinese traditional culture that grew up in this society can be referred to as a *zongzu* culture, which mainly consists of ethics and morals in regulating the behavior of *zongzu* members. While these patrilineal-centered people or families settling in a village or nearby villages can be defined as a local *zongzu* community, their management and administration system can be defined as the local *zongzu* organization.

The above terms that would not have been difficult to understand have become complicated after introducing Western concepts. In Western textbooks, two relevant terms exist concurrently: clan and lineage. Lineage is defined as a demonstrated descent, and clan as a stipulated descent. While lineage members can trace the actual generational links between themselves and ancestors, clan members cannot (Kottak 2010; Parkin 1997). Freedman (1966) challenged this definition and provided his own explanation. According to him, the critical difference between the two is commonwealth. Lineage members retain commonwealth, and clan members do not. This new interpretation generated a debate among anthropologists between the 1960s and the 1970s. Fried (1970) insisted that the only difference between clan and lineage was still genealogical or descent system. His standpoint essentially reflects the opinion expressed by most textbooks as mentioned above.

In every Chinese-English dictionary, lineage is translated as *zongxi* or *xuetong*, implying blood relationship or descent, and clan as *zongzu* or *jiazu*, referring to an organized group of families that share common ancestors. Therefore, the two terms in Chinese represent different but interrelated perspectives. The former focuses on descent relationships among group members, and the latter emphasizes an entity or community that is built upon blood relationships. In a broad sense, clan is considered a social system, and lineage is a component or a characteristic of the system. Perhaps due to the above reasons, Chinese scholars' research papers (written in English), especially during the period between the 1930s and the 1940s, used to take the term "clan" and paid more attention to socioeconomic characteristics and group patterns (Fei 1939; Lin 1947; Hsu 1948; Lang 1946). In this research, we use clan in a sense representing a social system or a traditional rural community whose members possess a common surname, a clear descent link, and the common wealth.

China's clan, or *zongzu* system, has attracted attention from scholars in various fields, such as anthropology and sociology. Chronologically, their research can be classified into three stages. The first stage, ranging from the 1930s to the 1940s, was characterized by the work of Wu Wenzao and Fei Xiaotong, two pioneers that introduced ethnographic methods into China. They, along with many others, primarily engaged in the so-called late imperial clan pattern that dominated the Qing dynasty (1616–1911). The second stage, ranging from the 1950s to the 1970s, was strongly influenced by the work of Freedman (1958, 1966, and 1970). He initially raised the "corporate model," seeing clan or lineage a separate entity with an economic focus. Inspired by his work, Western and Chinese anthropologists in Taiwan made great efforts to explore the late imperial pattern. They searched for evidence of the corporate model through fieldwork in Taiwan, as the alternative of Fujian, and the New Territories in Hong Kong, as the alternative of Guangdong. (Baker 1979; Skinner 1963–65; Anderson 1998; Watson 1982). During that period, Elizabeth Croll was one of few Western scholars that were allowed to conduct fieldwork in mainland China. Her work was mainly concerned with women and marriage life in rural China during the transformation era of clans between the 1950s and the 1970s (Croll 1978, 1981). The third or current stage started in the early 1980s. Following Deng's open door policy, Western and oversea Chinese scholars resumed their fieldwork in the mainland. At first they continued to concentrate their work on Fujian and Guangdong, though some studies shifted to Northern and Eastern China and to clan status in the collective era (Chan et al. 1992; Wang 1995; Dean 1993; Lamley 1990; Siu 1989; Zheng 2001; Szonyi 2002; Cohen 2005; Faure 2007; Brandtstdter and Goncaloo 2009). Then, researchers left away from the classical model and turned to contemporary, rural China. Some showed interest in exploring specific issues including: family, marriage, women status, gender relations, filial piety, reproductive norms, and private life that are embedded in accounts of the clan system (Whyte 1995; Judd 1994; Zhang 2008; Rosenlee 2006; Yan 2003; Wu 2003; Friedman et al. 2008; Yuen et al. 2004; Shi 2009; Cong and Silverstein 2008; Ikels 2004).

Clan studies have flourished in China since the 1980s. At first, this subject was mainly treated as a branch of history and the initial focus was placed on archival research and the imperial pattern between the Zhou and Qing Dynasties (Feng 2009; Xu 1992; Li 2008). Entering the 1990s, economists and sociologists began to join in. Like many Western scholars, their emphases were placed on interactions between modernization and clan culture, aiming at the role traditional values play in economic development and ignoring changes as brought by modernization (Qian 1999; Wang 1991; Chang 2007). Chinese scholars noticed that clan power enjoyed a revival time in many rural areas between the 1980s and 1990s as the contracted responsibility system was carried out and class power was withdrawing (Wang 1991, 1995; Ren 2004; Huang 2003; Song and Zhang 2009).

However, few of these studies made differentiations between clan society, clan culture (including ethics, customs, etc.), and clan organization. Few of them were involved in analyses of commonalities and discrepancies between the general and particular clan cultures. As these researchers were mainly concerned with the positive or negative roles played by traditional values in economic development, they ignored the impact on rural clans and clan culture brought about by the process of modernization, especially urbanization.

In addition, many studies consist of only concepts and ideas—lacking empirical and quantitative analyses. In these scarce empirical and quantitative studies, data mostly comes from surveys conducted by official agencies. In our experience, data collected in this way is less reliable because some respondents are not willing to be honest or they do not know how to answer the questions. Consequently, the real situation of clan culture and local clan communities has not been adequately reflected in the data provided by these surveys. Furthermore, since researchers do not participate in these investigations, they do not know the stories behind respondents' replies.

This research attempts to overcome the above shortcomings. Using data collected in Anhui rural areas, we intend to explore the impact on clan culture and people's sense of rural clan communities as brought by urbanization and industrialization. Starting with the late 1990s, a large movement from rural areas to urban regions has rapidly changed China. Now more than 270 million peasants live and work in cities and towns and the size is growing day by day.[1] The largest migration or urbanization in human history would probably lead to an end of the clan system since the geographic mobility undermines the common residence—a structural foundation of the clan (Braudel 1992). Under the circumstances, what changes have already taken place or will come to China's clan system and clan culture? Will the system and the culture continue to revitalize or die out? So far, studies have focused on issues like the socioeconomic status of migrant workers and the impact on local economy, so these questions are still waiting to be answered (Guang and Zheng 2005; Biao 2004; Jacka 2005; Chen 2006).

Between the 1960s and 1970s, some Western and overseas Chinese scholars detected certain changes in the New Territories, Hong Kong, during the process of urbanization. In his research on the Deng clan, Potter (1968) reported a changing value orientation. Traditional values, loyalties, and sentiments were not as important as before. On the contrary, according to Chan's observation with the Peng clan, traditional clan values continued to flourish in the 1990s. Their commonwealth also grew up, though it transformed into a trust funding from land (Ching-Chan 2001). Of the few valuable researches in mainland China, Gao (2005) discovered capitalist factors in influencing ritual activities in a village near Guangzhou.

As we know, clan power was completely destroyed in Mao's time. When a rapid urbanization arrived, clans in the mainland situated differently from Hong Kong and would manifest distinctive features in the course of modernization. Being a complex system, clans in China are exceptionally rich in regional flavor. The New Territories, as a part of southern China, does not represent the whole country. Besides, all the studies mentioned above focused on changes in clan culture when villages were merged into a metropolitan area. This geographical extension of a city is merely part of urbanization. The internal urbanization, or a large number of peasant workers moving to cities and settling down there, would be more

[1]See China's National Bureau of Statistics. *Statistical Bulletin of National Socioeconomic Development in 2014*. http://www.stats.gov.cn/tjgb/ndtjgb/qgndtjgb/t20140222_402786440.htm.

meaningful. This study will examine the internal migration and its cultural impact, emphasizing normative changes with regard to clan sentiment, family values, filial piety, ancestor worship, decent relations, patriarchal power, and rituals, which have been long neglected by pioneer studies.

There was an intense debate on the role that economic development plays in the process of cultural changes. Some argued that economic development or modernization brought pervasive cultural or ideological changes, and that traditional values and religions would fade away gradually (Marx [1859] 1973; Nietzsche and Lerner 1958; Bell 1973). Others, including Weber ([1904] 1958) and Huntington (1993), questioned this statement by claiming that traditional values and religions could possess an enduring and autonomous impact on people's behavior. This impact would not diminish with time. Using data from the World Values Surveys covering 75% of the world population, Inglehart and Baker (2000) discovered evidence of both massive cultural changes and the persistence of distinctive tradition values. In this research, we will review whether China's modernization is accompanied with this type of duality.

Clan culture, a foundation of traditional Chinese ideology, covers a wide range of subjects, including: clan norms, ethics, traditions, customs, rituals, and practices that are based on principles in dealing with blood relationships in a patriarchal society. On the one hand, Confucianism, the Song-Ming Rationalist School in particular, was built upon clan culture and practices. On the other hand, clan culture exhibits detailed applications of general Confucian doctrines. From this perspective, discussions of clan culture would inevitably involve traditional ideology in general.

10.2 Research Methods and Investigated Areas

Fieldwork and ethnographic techniques are valuable tools to sociologists and anthropologists. In fieldwork, researchers are able to explore in-depth historical changes, process, and things inherent in a small region through their observations. However, traditional "fieldwork" provides a particular focus on a certain village or a small community, and it is unlikely to obtain a large area of observations and data. Using data collected in this way, researches are hardly of universal significance. To overcome these drawbacks and obtain certain geographical span for horizontal comparisons, we extended fieldwork to seven administrative villages in four counties in Anhui, including: Yatanzhen in Wangjiang county, Shecun in Fanchang county, Fengcun in Jingxian or Jin county, and Xiongcun, Censhandu, Changxi, and Xitou in Shexian or She county. The author and assistants visited these villages in 2009 and 2014 respectively, and conducted a nine-month investigation.

The research strategy is a combination of sociological survey and ethnographic methodology. Direct data was collected first by observing villagers' daily lives and behaviors. During the time of fieldwork, there were a series of traditional festivals with great importance to clan culture, including the Spring Festival (or the Chinese New Year) and the Qing-Ming Festival (or the Festival of Pure Brightness), giving us a great chance to observe clan ceremonies, rituals, religious activities, traditions, and customs. To collect information on clan ethics, norms, history, organization, descent structure, and other socioeconomic variables, we managed deep conversations and group interviews with key and senior figures in these clans as well as government officials at various levels such as village, township, and county. Meanwhile, a sample survey was implemented. We visited and had face-to-face interviews with 528 households. Based on the population size for each clan and administrative village, households were selected randomly using a stratified proportional sampling method. In 2009, we randomly selected 226 households. Some of them were not willing to take interviews, and some did not want to answer certain questions or did not provide complete answers to those specific questions. Finally, we completed 213 successful household interviews. In 2014, the sample consisted of 302 households, and 279 valid interviews were completed. Since the survey inquires all family members and their married children in that household, the actual coverage is much larger than 528 households.

Interviewees are household heads aged 18 or older. Using the composite design mentioned above, we were able to collect a number of variables in a broader region and conduct quantitative analyses. Meanwhile, the face-to-face interview and ethnographical approaches allowed us to carry out a nuanced and deep exploration of how villagers think of themselves contextually, therefore, detecting socioeconomic factors behind villagers' responses to survey questions. In this way, we could take advantages and simultaneously avoid disadvantages of ethnographic approaches and sociologist survey.

The survey-questionnaire contains questions regarding (1) socioeconomic characteristics and descent links of the family and family members, (2) socioeconomic characteristics of *nongmingong* or migrant workers in that household, and (3) participants' attitudes toward clan traditions and ethics. Analyses in this research are primarily based on responses to questions in the third section.

Table 10.1 shows the socioeconomic characteristics of respondents in 2009 and 2014 surveys. Among them, "occupation," a key variable for this study, retains two categories: farming and non-farming. "Farming" refers to respondents who engage in traditional farming work and others including forestry, tea and vegetables, sericulture, poultry, and other sidelines. "Non-farming" refers to respondents who make more than 60% of their income from work or business in cities and towns. In 2009, those who fully engaged in farming accounted for 55% of the total respondents, and 45% the non-farming. In 2014, the farming population dropped to 28%, and the non-farming increased to 72%, showing that more and more peasant workers moved to cities and towns during the period of five years.

The four counties under investigation can be classified into three types: (1) the plain region along the Yangtze River, including Yatanzhen (the farming community) in Wangjiang and Shecun in Fanchang; (2) the hilly region in southern Anhui, including Fengcun in Jingxian; and (3) the mountain region in southern Anhui, including Changxi, Xiongcun, Censhandu, and Xitou in Shexian. These regions represent three levels in historical clan development. Shexian was the political and cultural center of ancient Huizhou, where clan culture and local clan communities

Table 10.1 Socioeconomic Characteristics of Respondents, 2009/2014

Age	Age (%)		Schooling years		Occupation (%)				Sex (%)			
					Farm		Non-farm		Male		Female	
	2009	2014	2009	2014	2009	2014	2009	2014	2009	2014	2009	2014
19–39	44	38	9	11.1	27	21	73	79	67	68	33	32
40–60	39	44	7.2	7.4	49	24	51	76	68	69	32	31
61+	17	18	5.6	4.8	84	73	16	27	65	66	35	34
Average/Total	43	47	7.0	8.1	55	28	45	72	67	68	33	32

grew first among the three regions. Huizhou is well known for its solid Confucian traditions and groundings. Zhu Xi, the most important initiator of the Song-Ming Rationalist School, was born and discoursed on his teachings there. Clans for two contemporary presidents, Jian Zemin and Hu Jintao, are all located in that region. Being a mountainous inland area, Huizhou was less affected by wars and Western culture during the late Qing and the Republic era in comparison with Guangdong and Fujian, containing a best-preserved clan system and clan culture in China.[2] Jingxian, its southern part in particular, is a region between Huizhou and the plains along the Yangtze River. In modern times, Southern Jingxian, as a part of Huizhou cultural zone, appeared more traditional than coastal areas and plain regions. At the same time, it contained a certain degree of Jiangnan or Jiang-Zhe culture.[3] In the beginning of the last century, Western culture and commodities first reached the coastal and plain regions, and then spread to inland areas via the Yangtze River. Due to the geographical characteristics, Southern Jingxian as a whole received Western influences, commercial economy, and new ideas earlier than Huizhou. Fanchang and Wangjiang are all located in plain regions along the Yangtze River. Similar to Guangdong and Fujian, this region was disturbed greatly by wars and Western culture in modern times.

When conducting fieldwork in Shexian, we took a consideration of both the overall situation and the specific cases. The county government recommended a number of villages to us. Among them, some villages such as Tangyue have become tourist attractions. Other villages such as Xucun have developed into prosperous towns. We finally chose four administrative villages that still retain rural characteristics, including: Censhandu (also known as Hanbucun), Changxi, Xiongcun, and Xitou. Because of geographic conditions, there is no sufficient land for farming in Huizhou. To survive, residents had to leave home for cities and towns and engage in commerce. Having become wealthy, they invested money in education, giving their children a better chance to study at schools and to be officials in the government. The selected four villages reflect this prominent feature characterized by the integration of being officials, merchants, and Confucian scholars.

Of the four villages, Changxi, a mountainous area, is located in southern Shexian, thirty kilometers from the county-town and seven kilometers from the Xinan River. In the Tang Dynasty, five clans including Yao, Ye, Zhu, Fang, and Wang lived there. The village was called Cangxi because of the Cang Mountain and the Changyuan River in the territory. During the time of Chunxi in the Southern Song Dynasty (1174), the Wu clan moved in, and renamed the village as Changxi. In the Yuan Dynasty, the Zhou clan moved in the south of the village. After

[2]Since the mid-1980s, clans in southern Anhui have taken notice from Chinese scholars. With the tremendous amount of historical documents (including genealogical records, business contracts, travel notes, and literary works) discovered in that region, those scholars have principally engaged in archival research and the imperial model of the Song, Ming, and Qing Dynasties (Bian 2006; Tang 2005; Ye 1995; Zhao 2004; Zhu 2006; Zheng 2008).

[3]Jiangnan culture is the culture in southern Anhui, southern Jiangsu, and Zhejiang.

becoming the largest clan, they renamed the south as Zhoubangtou. Since the Ming Dynasty, until today, Wu and Zhou have become the two largest clans. Changxi is an administrative village with 973 households and 2979 residents (in 2009), including three natural villages, namely, Hongqi, Hongxin, and Changyuan. The Wu clan mainly lives in Hongqi and Hongxing, or the Upper Changxi, while the Zhou clan lives in Changyuan, or the Lower Changxi.

Xiongcun, located in the lower areas of Jianjiang or the Jian River, is only 7.5 km from the county town. With elegant and graceful scenery, its natural environment is extremely beautiful. With 628 households and 2485 residents (in 2009), Xiongcun administers four natural villages. From the Tang Dynasty to the Yuan Dynasty, a few surnames including Mei, Xia, Hong Li, and Shi, resided in Xiongcun. In the 13th year of Hongwu, the Ming dynasty (1381), Cao Yongqing moved in with his uncle, and then married a woman from the Hong clan. Afterwards, the Hong clan declined, and the Cao family developed into the largest clan, renaming the village as Xiongcun. The Cao clan had 284 households and 1042 members (in 2009). In the Ming and Qing Dynasties, this clan was well known in Huizhou because a few clan members held very high-ranking positions in the government. During the two dynasties, clan members obtained 52 *juren* and 29 *jinshi*.[4]

Walking along the Jian River to the north, one can see a small island called Censhan with beautiful scenery surrounded by water. That is why the village is named Censhandu, where Cheng, one of the most popular surnames in Huizhou, is the largest clan. The Cheng people in Huizhou have compiled a few genealogical books during various periods, making their branch descent links quite clear. However, the Cheng Genealogy in Censhandu does not tell us when the first Cheng person migrated there. We estimated that it would be between years of Daizong (the 7th emperor of the Ming Dynasty) and Yingzong (the 8th emperor of the Ming Dynasty), or between 1450 and 1465. This clan enjoyed a great reputation in Shexian as the slang says, "Censhandu's Cheng people, being merchants and Confucian scholars, are extremely talented." As early as the late Ming, this clan began to engage in salt trade in Jiangsu, and reached a great success in that business.

Xitou, surrounded by mountains, is located in northeastern Shexian, 21 km from the county town. Xitou consists of two natural villages: Xitou and Lantian. We conducted fieldwork in Lantian, which contains 270 households and 760 residents. Lantian was formerly known as Chantian, after the Ye clan moved in, the village was renamed Lantian in commemoration of their ancestor, Ye Fuze, the county magistrate in Lantian, Shanxi. Ye is the largest clan in Lantain today and also one of distinguished surnames in Shexian. It is difficult to calculate how many generations the clan has handed down. But one fact is indisputable, that this clan has lived in this village for more than one thousand years. There have appeared many

---

[4]*Juren* was the successful candidate in the imperial examinations at the provincial level. *Jinshi* was the successful candidate in the imperial examinations at the national level.

talented people, business leaders, and senior officials in the Ye clan. Their most glorious period was between the Tang and Song Dynasties. In the Qing Dynasty, no one was successful in the imperial examination at the provincial level, not to mention the national level.

Fengcun, with 675 households and 2166 residents (in 2014) is under the township of Maolin and located in southern Jingxian (or Jing county). Feng is the largest clan in this village. Feng Shijie, the progenitor of the Feng clan, passed an imperial examination for local officials during the years of Chun Xi, the Southern Song Dynasty (1174–1190), and was appointed as the Education Instructor for Jingxian district in the first year of Jiading (1208). After he retired from that position, he settled down in Fengcun. Since then, the Feng clan has lived there for more than 800 years.

Shecun, an administrative village with 3462 residents (in 2014), is located in the south bank of the Zhang River, and was under the administration of Fanchang for long time.[5] This village was selected mainly because of the location, only 25 km from the center area of Wuhu, a big city beside the Yangtze River. In modern times, Wuhu was well known as one of "Four Big Rice Markets." Due to the Treaty of Yantai, signed in 1876 by the Chinese and British governments, Wuhu turned into a trading port, becoming a pioneer opening to the outside world. The She people have settled in that area for about 660 years since their first ancestor moved in during the late years of the Yuan Dynasty.

Yatanzhen, located in the northwest of Wangjiang County, consists of an urban area and a rural community, which is equivalent to an administrative village with 13 natural villages and 5760 residents. For most natural villages, there is only one surname. All the surnames have built their branch ancestral halls, or branch *citing* (支祠). We investigated three surnames including Dong, Ho, and Peng. Each surname has about 300 residents. Their ancestors all moved in during the years of the late Ming Dynasty. The local communities did not develop into clans until the Republic era. Their migration history is the shortest and clan traditions are the weakest among the investigated areas.

Anhui is a large province for exporting peasant labors to flourishing urban areas. In the villages we visited, peasants who were living and working in cities and towns made up about 60–70% of the local labor forces. Therefore, these villages are ideal windows to observe cultural changes as brought by the internal urbanization.

---

[5]In 2009 it was put under the direct administration of Wuhu.

10.3 Impact on the General Clan Culture as Brought by Urbanization

The urban effect on clan culture can be examined in two ways: (1) impact on the general clan culture, and (2) impact on the local clan culture. This section focuses on the first part. The general clan culture, as a distillation from local clan cultures, can be considered ethics applicable to all clans, such as ancestor worship, filial piety, loyalty to the state, and so on. We designed a series of questions to ask villagers in survey (see Table 10.2). Their answers are classified into five categories: strongly agree, agree, neutral, disagree, and strongly disagree. For simplicity, Table 10.3 (and other tables) list only three categories: agree (= strongly agree + agree), neutral, disagree (= disagree + strongly disagree). Since certain items measured in percentages are difficult to make an accurate judgment, we calculated the weighted index (WI). The higher the WI value, the higher the closer the confirmation to the chosen issue by the interviewees, and vice versa.[6]

10.3.1 Ancestor Worship

Ancestor worship, a religious presence of clan culture, was viewed as the spiritual pillar of the Chinese patriarchal society. In the survey we asked the villagers if they agree with the statement that ancestors should be worshiped (see Table 10.3, Qn. 1). (The questions and question numbers are listed in Table 10.2). 77% of the respondents said they agreed with it, 13% were neutral, 10% disagreed. For villagers, ancestors could be specific or general, and could be ancestors of a family, a clan, or a nation. Villagers' responses indicate clearly that ancestor worship is still the cornerstone of Chinese culture. However, urban effect can be felt.

In Table 10.3, villagers are divided into two groups: farming and non-farming. They are also grouped into two periods based on the survey time: 2009 and 2014. In the farming group, 80% agreed with the statement, while in the non-farming group, 74% agreed. In 2009, 91% agreed, while in 2014 the proportion dropped to 67% (see Table 10.3). The weighted index reflects the same situation. It should be noted that the variable of time is an important indicator of urbanization as migrant workers are growing over time. However, since this variable affects all the population, including both migrant workers and villagers who still engage in traditional farming work, the weakened value over time is not only a result of urbanization, but also a product of modernization in the whole society.

[6]WI (for each issue) = total value/ the number of respondents in that issue. Total value = $\sum$ (specific categorical value x the number of respondents in that category). Categorical value: strong agree = 5, agree = 4, neutral = 3, disagree = 2, strong disagree = 1.

Table 10.2 Survey questions

No.	Questions or statements
1	We should worship ancestors
2	Filial piety is still the most important family value
3	We should unconditionally obey parents
4	We should obey parents as much as possible
5	Of the three unfilial conducts, the greatest is to have no male descendants
6	National interests should be above personal and family interests
7	The father or male is the decision-maker in a family
8	Looking after children is mainly the responsibility of women
9	Even if both men and women have jobs, women should still take more housework
10	Women depend more on men
11	Sexual relationships are much more open than before
12	Go out to work would lead to marital problems
13	The relationship between husband and wife is better than before
14	Even if there is a problem with the couple, they should not get divorced
15	It is easier to get a partner than before
16	People are worth more trust than before
17	Clan interests are above family and individual interests
18	Family interests are above personal interests
19	Clan rituals should be restored
20	Genealogical books should be rebuilt
21	I am willing to participate in clan fights against others
22	The clan role in village public affairs is declining
23	The clan role in private lives is declining
24	I am willing to participate in activities related to the clan
25	I am willing to participate in other activities organized by the clan
26	Relations with the relatives are better than before
27	In-clan cadres are more trustworthy than out-clan ones

10.3.2 Filial Piety

Confucians treated filial piety as the most important ethics, which links family members from generation to generation, and determines the ethical order of the family and clan, so that family and clan members could maintain a stable and orderly state. Since the Qin and Han Dynasties, all the rulers without exception emphasized the importance of *xiao* or filial piety and ruled the country in the name of *xiao*.

In survey, we asked, "Do you agree that filial piety is still the top family value?" 99% of the respondents agreed, 0.5% were neutral, and only 0.5% disagreed (see Table 10.3, Qn. 2). Has the urbanization brought any impact on this value? We use the weighted index for explanation. For the farming group, the WI value is 4.70. For the non-faming, this value is 4.68. The difference is so small that it can be

Table 10.3 Villagers' attitude to clan culture

No.	Total			Occupation								Time							
				Farming				Non-Farming				2009				2014			
	Agree (%)	Neutral (%)	Disagree (%)	Agree (%)	Neutral (%)	Disagree (%)	*WI*	Agree (%)	Neutral (%)	Disagree (%)	*WI*	Agree (%)	Neutral (%)	Disagree (%)	*WI*	Agree (%)	Neutral (%)	Disagree (%)	*WI*
1	77	13	10	80	11	9	*4.29*	74	16	10	*4.11*	91	5	4	*4.53*	67	19	14	*3.89*
2	99	0.5	0.5	99	0	1	*4.7*	99	1	0	*4.68*	99	0	1	*4.8*	99	0	1	*4.6*
3	30	7	63	32	7	61	*2.73*	29	7	64	*2.69*	30	3	67	*2.98*	32	18	50	*3.16*
4	97	2	1	98	1	1	*4.38*	97	2	1	*4.4*	97	1	2	*4.32*	97	2	1	*4.44*
5	51	23	26	63	18	19	*3.62*	38	31	31	*3.11*	72	10	18	*3.7*	34	35	31	*3.04*
6	77	16	7	79	16	5	*4.37*	77	16	7	*4.25*					77	16	7	
7	43	27	30	50	24	26	*3.37*	37	29	34	*3.04*	54	17	29	*3.33*	33	35	32	*3.08*
8	35	13	52	52	14	34	*3.3*	21	13	66	*2.45*	50	10	40	*3.12*	24	16	60	*2.62*
9	37	16	47	47	16	37	*3.19*	28	16	56	*2.64*	54	10	36	*3.22*	23	22	55	*2.6*
10	44	25	31	52	24	24	*3.61*	39	24	37	*3.08*	59	19	22	*3.52*	34	29	37	*3.04*
11	80	18	2	81	19	0	*4.38*	78	19	3	*4.15*					80	18	2	
12	49	36	15	47	38	15	*3.7*	50	35	15	*3.68*					49	36	15	
13	34	44	22	35	50	15	*3.43*	34	39	27	*3.19*					34	44	22	
14	71	24	5	72	21	7	*4.14*	71	24	5	*4.05*					71	24	5	
15	36	32	32	44	34	22	*3.49*	32	30	38	*3.05*					36	32	32	
16	15	22	63	13	21	66	*2.11*	17	22	61	2.29					15	22	63	

negligible. In the 2009 survey, the WI is 4.8, and it is 4.6 in the 2014 survey. It can be seen that urban effect on this value is extremely limited.

Zengzi (曾子) suggested that the first goal for filial piety is to respect parents (see *The Book of Rites* or 礼记·祭义). The so-called "respecting" in the traditional clan society meant not contrary to wishes of their parents, or in other words, to obey parents without conditions. To explore whether the villagers still agree with this traditional duty, we designed two questions: First, "Do you agree with unconditional obedience to parents?" Second, "Do you agree to obey parents as much as possible?" (see Table 10.3, Qns. 3 and 4). Unconditional obedience shows an absolute patriarchal power in the family, the clan, and the country. Based on this, a patriarchal social order and an authoritarian political system were established. Members of families and clans all prostrated at the foot of this authority, and lost their individuality and subjectivity. "As much as possible" refers to a conditional obedience. Respect and obey their parents, but not blindly, not beyond their capacity and conditions. Although the difference between the first and the second is only one word, it reflects a progress with time, embodying not only an adhering to traditional inheritance and the essence of traditional culture, but also a rising of personal values and individual freedom. It shows a resistance to the authority and an awakening of the democratic consciousness as well.

As shown in Table 10.3, 30% of the respondents agreed with the "unconditional obedience," while 97% of them agreed with "conditional obedience." Most villagers demonstrated a denial of the past patriarchal system, indicating that a new type of filial piety or a new family value has been established in rural areas. As it would probably affect villagers' political and economic behavior, any recovery of the pyramid system built on the absolute patriarchal authority would hardly take place in the future.

Of farming-villagers, 32% agreed with the "old" duty. For non-farming-villagers, the proportion is 29%. In the 2014 survey, 32% of the respondents accepted the "old" duty, higher than hat portion (30%) in 2009, contrary to our expectation, though the margin is small. The WI shows the same situation. It tells us that urban development might play a role in weakening this tradition, but the effect was not significant—especially in recent years. Abandoning the old and adopting the new would be a long process and could not simply be attributed to the recent urbanization. Historically, this change started in the "May 4th Movement, and developed in the Land Reform Campaign and the Great Proletarian Cultural Revolution. It has witnessed a struggle by the Chinese in many generations, and absorbed the essence of both Eastern and Western cultures.

Attitudes may affect a person's behavior. However, one's deeds do not always match one's words. In fieldwork, we learned that many seniors did not have sufficient maintenance from their children. It has become a serious issue today. "Conditions" are usually used to justify their unfilial conduct.

We asked the elderly (aged 61 and over) whether they preferred to live by themselves or whether they preferred to live with their married children. 81% of them chose to live by themselves. Living with married children made them feel like to live under other's roof. This situation, to some degree, reflects a rising sense of independence accompanied by an increasing economic independence resulting from the contract responsibility system and the social security system. Meanwhile, it reveals a declining parent authority. We found that the elderly, especially those who largely depend on their children's financial support, completely lost their decision-making power in an extended family, further explaining why they are unwilling to live with their children. We had a conversation with a senior who lived with his married son. He told us that the elderly status between the present and the past was like something between the earth and the heavens. He said, "It is totally two different worlds." The ideological modernization seems to not bring much benefit to the old villagers.

Even that, the situation has recently improved due to better living. We asked villagers, "Compared with 10 years ago, do you agree that people now show more filial obedience to parents?" Of the respondents, 40% agreed, 25% disagreed, and 35% were not sure. According to the local officials, villagers are still willing to show filial obedience to parents "as much as possible" when they are in a good financial position. Some respondents said, "Without money, how can we show filial piety?"

From the Han to Qing Dynasties, *xiao,* or filial piety, was treated as a moral principle and also a law compelled by the governments at various levels and by the clans as well. Any unfilial conduct would be convicted of felony. Under the circumstances, no one dared to challenge this principle. This kind of legal and political environment is no longer present today, though some improvements have been made.[7] Without enforcement, practicing *xiao* would largely depend on individual consciousness. A villager's devotion to his parents today, as some said, to some degree depends on his relations with his wife and his wife's kindness.

Confucianism does not provide an ultimate destination to the Chinese. The continuation of life only lies in the endless family line. So Mencius said, "There are three unfilial conducts, the greatest is to have no male descendants." Thus, filial piety went beyond the obedience to parents, and became a religious consolation. In survey, we asked villagers if they still agreed with Mencius' teachings (see Table 10.3, Qn. 5). Of the farming-respondents, 63% agreed. Of the non-farming, 38% agreed. In the 2009 survey, 72% of the respondents agreed, and this proportion significantly dropped to 34% in the 2014 survey. Obviously, a rapid development of urbanization and modernization has weakened this traditional influence. More and more migrant workers began receiving the urban idea of having fewer children. Some of them no longer adopt this norm because of the increasing cost of raising children and the pressures and hardships on them while working in urban areas.

[7]One example is the 2013 "Law of the Security of the Elderly" (老年人权益保障法). According to this law, parents cannot fall into neglect. Family member must visit their parents a few times a year if they do not live with parents. Besides, in the 1985 "Law of Succession" (中华人民共和国继承法), how much property family members could inherit mainly depends on how much maintenance they offered to peasants.

10.3.3 Zhong (Loyalty)

Confucians extended the principle of filial piety to the whole society, turning it into filial loyalty. In ancient times, the object of loyalty was the emperor, the head of the big family or the country. Thereby, *zhong* can be also understood as loyalty to the country. In that way, the country's needs take precedence over personal and family interests. Sun Yat-sen said: "In ancient times, *zhong* is loyal to the emperor… Now it is the Republic, we still need to follow the principle of loyalty, not loyal to the emperor, but loyal to the country, to the people, to the four hundred millions of people."[8] Mao inherited this thought, and advocated the people's interests and the revolutionary interests over personal requirements. His opinion was in the same strain as Confucian ethics on loyalty.[9]

In survey, 77% of the respondents agreed with the statement that the national interests are above the family and the individuals. 16% were neutral, and 7% disagreed (Table 10.3, Qn. 6). The WI value for the non-farming villagers is 4.25, slightly lower than 4.37 for the farming. Thus, the urban effect is not significant.[10]

10.3.4 Jie (Moral Integrity and Chastity)

Jie refers to the performance of moral constraints or moral integrity. For women, *jie* refers to chastity, or loyalty to marriage and to her husband. Confucian ethics put an emphasis on *jie*, to some degree, illustrating gender inequality in the patriarchal society. Although women's status was notably improved after the communists took over China, due to the long-history of self-sufficiency in the small production and the presence of labor division between men and women, men's dominant socioeconomic status did not change much in many rural areas. To examine such a situation, we designed four questions in survey.

First, we asked them, "Do you agree that the decision-maker in a family should be the father or a man?" 43% of respondents agreed, 27% were neutral, and 30% opposed (see Table 10.3, Qn. 7). Second, "Do you agree that taking care of children is mainly the responsibility of women?" 35% of respondents agreed, 13% were neutral, 52% objected (see Table 10.3, Qn. 8). Third, "Do you agree that even if both men and women have jobs, women should still take more chores?" 37% of the respondents agreed, 16% were neutral, 47% opposed (see Table 10.3, Qn. 9). Fourth, "Do you agree that women's dependence on men is greater than men's dependence on women?" 44% of the respondents expressed agreement, 25% were neutral, 31% opposed (see Table 10.3, Qn. 10)

---

[8]http://baike.baidu.com/view/122715.htm.

[9]Mao expressed this opinion in many of his articles.

[10]This question was asked only in the 2014 survey.

Responses to the four questions indicate two interesting social phenomena. First, for the first and fourth questions, proportions of villagers who expressed agreement with the statements are significantly higher than those who disagreed, demonstrating that male villagers are still dominant in social and family life. Second, for the second and third questions, endorsing ratios are substantially lower than opposing ratios, illustrating that even in rural areas, more and more people began to advocate sharing housework between wife and husband, and that women's status in a family has been improved to some degree.

Looking at WI values, for the four questions, the farming-respondents hold higher WI values than the non-farming. Respondents in the 2009 survey hold higher values than those in the 2014 survey, showing that urban experience and the socioeconomic development in recent years helped to reduce the influence of traditional patriarchal ideology.

10.3.5 Sexual Relations and Marriage

"Jie," on the other hand, is to require both men and women, especially women, to follow the rule that close contacts outside of marriage are not allowed. Premarital and extramarital sexual relations are considered a violation of ethics as well as unlawful conducts. The goal is to preserve the stability for marriage and family, which is considered the precondition for the stability in the whole society. Since the Han Dynasty, all the governments, including the ruling communists, have remained conservativeness to the issue of sexual relations. Anyone with premarital and/or extramarital sex would receive certain disciplinary or administrative penalties.

Contacts between men and women in rural areas were particularly limited. Because of geographic inconvenience, young men and women could see each other only within the village or neighboring villages, mostly among clan members. In the investigated regions, marriages with clan members were strictly prohibited even beyond five generations. Parents and matchmakers arranged most marriages before the 1980s. Even in 2014, according to our survey, parents determined 10% of marriage partners, 42% were arranged by matchmakers, and only 42% were free choices. In the group aged 61 years and older, 30% were determined by parents, 51% were arranged by matchmakers, and only 19% were free choices. In the group aged 40–60, 11% were determined by parents, 50% were arranged by matchmakers, 39% were free choices (see Table 10.4). That is to say, until 20 years ago, arranged marriages were the mainstream in rural areas.

Although rural residents were conservative in sexual relations before the 1980s, it varied with regions. Historically, more controls on women and more official-recognized widows who kept their chastity were found in Huizhou than in other regions. Sexual relations between unmarried clan members were very rare, however, stories about a married woman having sex with a man in her husband's clan or other clans were heard of from time to time.

Table 10.4 Types of Marriage (%)

Types	19–39	40–60	61+	Subtotal
By parents	0	11	30	10
By matchmakers	25	50	51	42
Free choice	75	39	19	48
Total (%)	100	100	100	100

When more and more villagers left for cities, contacts between men and women began to go beyond clan members. In the 2014 survey, we found that no young couples (aged 19–39) were arranged by parents. Of them, marriages introduced by matchmakers dropped to 25%, and free choices increased to 75% (see Table 10.4). Attitudes towards sexuality, especially among the youths, became more open. We asked in survey, "Do you believe that sexual relations have become more open now?" Of villagers with farming careers, 81% believed so. Of those with non-farming careers, 78% believed so (See Table 10.3, Qn. 11). Basically, the two groups hold the same viewpoints.

According to the *2015 Anhui Family Development Report* published by Anhui Provincial Health and Family Planning Commission, the marital status of rural residents was not as stable as urban ones mostly due to a large number of peasants working outside, making many couples live separately.[11] Based on our 2009 survey, couples that consisted of one working in cities and another being left behind to take care of children accounted 17% of the total. Couples that did not work in the same city accounted 26% of the total. Generally, these couples could see each other only a few times a year, generating a lot of family problems and raising divorce rate sharply. In Shexian, the divorce rate that was 11% in 2006, increased to 14% in 2009, jumped to 22% in 2012, and further jumped to 33% in 2015. In Fanchang, the rate was near 40% in 2014, higher than that in Shexian.[12]

In the 2014 survey, we asked if they agreed that working outside would lead to marital problems. 49% of the respondents agreed, 36% were not sure, and 15% disagreed (see Table 10.3, Qn. 12). Of the non-farming respondents, 50% agreed. Of the farming respondents, 47% agreed. Villagers' viewpoints on this issue are very similar.

We asked them, "Whether or not the relationships between husband and wife are better than before?" 34% said "better" and 22% said "worse" (see Table 10.3, Qn. 13). Of the non-farming, 27% said "worse," while of the farming, 15% said "worse." That is to say, those who were working in urban areas were more likely to feel that the marital relationship was worse than before.

Despite the sharp rise in the divorce rate, the vast majority of villagers were still in favor of family harmony— a traditional value. We asked them, "If there appeared problems with a couple, do you think the couple should get divorce?" 71% of them

---

[11]Source: http://www.ahnw.gov.cn/2006nwkx/html/201601/%7BA95CDFB4-9790-4122-9288-142D59618BE2%7D.shtml.

[12]Source: http://tjj.wh.cn/tjnj/2015/2015/_397.htm. The regional difference in divorce rate to some degree reflects regional traditions in history as mentioned.

did not support a divorce. Both farming and non-farming groups hold almost the same attitude towards this issue (see Table 10.3, Qn. 14).

According to the *2015 Anhui Family Development Report* mentioned above, the proportion for single males in rural areas was higher than that in cities. Many female peasant workers were married to urban men because of economic considerations. This leaves a narrowed space for young male villagers. Of the surveyed villagers aged 24–45, the proportion for singles was 13% among men, and 8% among women. We asked them, "Do you think that it is easier now to find a partner?" 36% of the respondents believed that it was easier now, and 32% said that it was actually more difficult. For the non-farming group, 38% said that it was more difficult now, while for the farming group, 22% said that it was more difficult (see Table 10.3, Qn. 15). From the perspective of getting married, villagers, especially young male villagers, did not win in cities.

10.3.6 Yi (Righteousness)

Yi, or righteousness in Confucianism, covers a series of moral categories. Confucius said, "A gentleman remains righteousness, and a villain values profits" (See *The Analects·Liren* or 论语·里仁). In the past, merchants in Huizhou advocated *yi* in doing business, believing that *yi* could generate profits. *Yi* contains two important aspects: *xin,* or integrity/trust, and *you,* or friendship/brotherhood. The two are related to each other because integrity is the key to maintaining friend ties. In the 2014 survey, we asked villagers, "Do you think that the people are the same honest as in the past?" (see Table 10.3, Qn. 16). 63% said "No." For the non-farming group, 61% said "no" as compared with 66% of the farming. Villagers working in cities often need help from others. This perhaps explains why they were less likely to feel the deterioration of integrity.

While human integrity declined, the role of friends in social relations was rising. In the survey, four questions regarding the importance of friends were asked. Table 10.5 lists the questions and the first choice respondents selected. As for the question, "When faced with economic difficulties, who would be the first choice looking for help?" 77% chose family members, 11% chose friends, and 10% chose relatives. For the second question, "When faced with emotional difficulties, who would be the first choice looking for help?" 53% of them chose family members, and 34% chose friends. For the third question, "Who is the primary source for migrant-job information?" 39% chose friends, and 24% chose family members. For the fourth question, "Who would be the most helpful when working outside?" 48% chose friends, and 44% chose family members. It can be seen that the importance of friends exceeded relatives and clan members. As for migrant workers, the role of friends turned to be the first. With convenient transportation and communication, especially the popularity of cell phones among peasants, their social circles have surmounted the blood and geographical constraints.

Table 10.5 Villagers' views on the role of relatives and friends (%)

First choice	Qn. 1	Qn. 2	Qn. 3	Qn. 4
Family members	77	53	24	44
Relatives	10	8	22	7
Friends	11	34	39	48
Village cadres	2	5	1	1
Media	0	0	14	0
Total (%)	100	100	100	100

Questions:
1. When faced with economic difficulties, who would be the first choice looking for help?
2. When faced with emotional difficulties, who would be the first choice looking for help?
3. Who is the primary source for migrant-job information?
4. When working outside, who would be most helpful?

10.4 Impact on Local Clan Culture and Local Clan Community

Local clan culture refers to norms and ethics connected to a local clan community, such as rules and provisions on the handling of personal relationships with the local clan organization and the like. In fieldwork, we asked villagers if they knew any clan rules made in the past. Most of them did not know of any and only a few elders remembered some, but limited to "filial piety," "no stealing," and so on. Then, how to figure out the remnants of the local clan culture? We determined to make this as (1) how villagers treat their personal interests and clan interests, which can also be applied to testing their understandings of clan identity and (2) local rituals of ancestor worship. Issues related to clan identity, clan power, clan influence, and descent relations will also be examined in this section.

10.4.1 Qun (Group) and Geren (Individuals)

As mentioned above, traditional ethics applicable to all the Chinese people were established on specific clan culture. Discussing the relationship between a man and his clan involves general principles in dealing with the relationship between the individual and the collective, or *qun*. The term "collective" in Chinese traditional culture and Western culture conveys different connotations. In Western culture it involves a group with some common social, cultural, or economic characteristics (such as occupation, sex, religion, class, etc.). The group members may share common interests and loyalty. In traditional Chinese culture, the collective or *qun* was mainly understood as *jia*, a combination of a small *jia*, or family, and a big *jia*, or clan (Tang and Zuo 1997). According to Liang, an important difference between Chinese and Western cultures is that, in the former, *jia* is the basic unit of a society, while in the latter the individual is the starting point. In traditional Chinese ethics, first, the small family must be obedient to the interests of the big family. Secondly, individuals must be obedient to the interests of both the small family and the big family. This moral code is actually an extension of filial piety. Through this arrangement, individual interests are replaced by family interests and, finally, by clan interests.

There was no room for *geren* or individuals in the traditional clan society. Clan members were always taught that they should sacrifice themselves to clan interests. To examine villagers' clan identities and attitudes towards clan interests, we asked them, "Do you support that the needs of the clan take precedence over individual requirements?" (see Table 10.6, Qn. 17). Since there are no common economic interests for clan members today, clan needs are mostly recognized as clan reputations, loyalties, and others when clan members are required to undertake. 36% of the respondents expressed support to that statement, 34% opposed, and 30% remained neutral. For the farming group, 39% supported, and for the non-farming group, 33% supported. In the 2009 survey, 52% of the respondents supported. And in the 2014 survey, this ratio significantly decreased to 22% (see Table 10.6, Qn. 17).

Next, we asked them, "Do you agree that the needs of the family take precedence over individual requirements?" (see Table 10.6, Qn. 18). 87% of the respondents agreed, only 4% disagreed. For the farming group, 92% agreed. For the non-farming group, it dropped to 81%. In the 2009 survey, 97% of the respondents agreed. In the 2014 survey, it dropped to 79%.

Responses to the two questions demonstrate two interesting facts. First, *qun,* or group as represented by the clan and the family, is still of importance to villagers. Second, they are more likely in favor of family interests than clan's, and clan influence is giving way to family. This would be perceived as a progress toward ideological modernization. Different from the West, however, this modernization does not shift villagers to individualism but to the family, or the small *jia.* The content of *jia* alters but the importance of *jia* does not change much. Villagers are emigrating from the big *jia* (or clan) and retaining at the small *jia* (or family). Thus, we can see that this kind of modernization is accompanied with strong Chinese traits. Nevertheless, from their responses, we discovered that villagers' sentiment of clan and family has been greatly attacked by the wave of urbanization and modernization. Western individualism is rising.

10.4.2 Rituals of Ancestor Worship

In the villages investigated, *jiaji* (or family rituals of ancestor worship) and *zuji* (or clan rituals of ancestor worship), which were all prohibited during the Great Proletarian Cultural Revolution (GPCR), have come back since the early 1980s. *Jiaji* is usually held three times a year, including sweeping graves during the periods of *Qingming* (the Festival of Pure Brightness) and *Dongzhi* (the Festival of

Table 10.6 Villagers' attitude to local clan culture & local clan communities

No.	Total			Occupation								Time							
				Farming				Non-Farming				2009				2014			
	Agree (%)	Neutral (%)	Disagree (%)	Agree (%)	Neutral (%)	Disagree (%)	*WI*	Agree (%)	Neutral (%)	Disagree (%)	*WI*	Agree (%)	Neutral (%)	Disagree (%)	*WI*	Agree (%)	Neutral (%)	Disagree (%)	*WI*
17	36	30	34	39	28	33	*3.2*	33	31	36	*2.99*	52	15	33	*3.28*	22	43	35	*2.4*
18	87	9	4	92	7	1	*4.5*	81	11	8	*4.18*	97	3	0	*4.62*	79	14	7	*4.08*
19	42	39	19	47	36	17	*3.68*	37	40	23	*3.41*	80	12	8	*4.25*	45	30	25	*3.19*
20	61	33	6	61	34	5	*4.28*	61	32	7	*4.02*	77	15	8	*4.15*	56	39	5	*4.05*
21	15	15	70	14	10	76	*2.23*	16	15	69	*1.79*				*3.7*	15	15	70	
22	71	16	13	77	13	10	*3.9*	67	19	14	*3.73*	85	7	8	*4.01*	79	7	14	*3.92*
23	74	14	12	82	8	10	*3.93*	67	18	15	*3.7*	85	5	10	*3.99*	81	4	15	*3.93*
24	64	22	14	64	22	14	*3.9*	65	22	13	*4.04*					64	22	14	
25	64	24	12	60	26	14	*3.85*	66	23	11	*4.03*					64	24	12	
26	30	32	38	29	30	41	*2.8*	30	33	37	*2.9*	32	17	51	*2.68*	29	40	31	*2.99*
27	22	25	53	21	18	61	*2.48*	22	30	48	*2.59*	34	14	52	*2.78*	11	34	55	*2.28*

Solstice) and offering sacrifices to ancestors in the Chinese New Year's Eve. As we observed, when the time came out, families were all bogged down with activities.

We asked villagers what they mostly expected from *jiaji*. They said that it was to cherish memories and express gratitude to ancestors for life-giving. Those who were respected in *jiaji* were largely limited to three generations in descent links. Few families offered sacrifices to ancestors up to five generations. No attention was paid to remote ancestors, not to mention the common ancestor of a clan.

Jiaji is thriving everywhere, but *zuji* is still hardly seen. Of the investigated areas, the three clans in Yatanzhen are the only ones engaged in *zuji* yearly. The Feng clan was held once in 2007 and since then it has never been seen. In survey, we asked villagers whether they supported *zuji* (see Table 10.6, Qn. 19). 42% of them supported, 39% expressed neutrality, and 19% opposed. Of the farming people, 47% supported, and of the non-farming, 37% supported. In the 2009 survey, 80% of the respondents supported. In the 2014 survey, this proportion dramatically dropped to 45%.

During the five years of period, *zuji* lost significant support. A number of factors contributed to this situation. First, since most *citing,* or ancestral halls, were completely destroyed or seriously damaged between the 1950s and 1970s, there are no buildings for holding clan rituals in most villages.

Second, clans are deficient in financial resources. Before 1949, clan's commonwealth yielded stable and sustainable income in supporting *zuji*. During the campaign of land reform in the early 1950s, all the common wealth and property were confiscated and redistributed to poor villagers. Because of the removal of economic base, ceremonial life could not be sustained, and clans almost immediately collapsed (Baker 1979). Without an established funding, clans would be difficult to carry out *zuji* normally. A possible solution is to ask for donations from households one by one, like the Feng clan did in 2007. This might be done occasionally, but is hardly to run sustainably.

Third, few villagers are willing to organize or coordinate clan rituals. In rural areas, it is not arduous to find organizers and volunteers for many activities, including local religious ceremonies, folk custom celebrations, and so on. However, it is not easy to find organizers for clan rituals. Why? The key lies in governmental attitudes. Concerned with possibilities in generating factionalism and instability in their administrative regions, officials at local governments keep vigilant eyes on collective activities based on blood ties. Having no permissions from the government, few people want to take the political risk.

Fourth, ancestor worship conveys two things to the Chinese. First, ancestors are the origins of life. In the classic book *Li Chi* (*Ritual Texts*), Confucius and his disciples stated, "As everything originates from the heaven and earth, so the people are reproduced by their ancestors. The contribution made by ancestors is parallel to the heaven and earth." From there, it generated the second meaning: Similar to deities, ancestors possess supernatural powers. Accordingly, clans attempt to achieve two goals in rituals: expressing gratitude to ancestors for life-giving and imploring ancestors to bless their descendants. The latter delivers religious and utilitarian orientations. With the sacred code of ancestors fading out, an increasing number of villagers no longer perceive their ancestors as superpowers, making *zuji* less prominence to the second goal. Lacking religious and utilitarian initiatives, villagers would feel no enthusiasm for taking part in.

Finally, as mentioned, people's sense of clan identity is declining and may have lost their interests in such an activity. We will further discuss this later.

By contrast, *jiaji* does not need great efforts to carry out, nor does it depend much on money, space, or organization skills, which partly explains why *jiaji* is thriving everywhere. The situational difference between *jiaji* and *zuji* may further provide evidence of a trend breaking away from the clan and turning toward the family as discussed previously. Villagers are increasingly tending to treat rituals of ancestor worship as a part of domestic life rather than public affairs.

10.4.3 Updating Genealogical Records and Villagers' Sentiment of Clan Identity

In history, when a population grew up, clan branches appeared more and more complex, and descent relations became blurred day by day. Consequently, the solidarity in that community was weakened. Being the state, clans were required to update or re-compile genealogical records in order to clear off descent links in hierarchy and rebuild cohesive forces. However, from the Republic era to Deng's time, few clans in Anhui were able to accomplish this work due to various reasons. In the past, as the saying goes, it would be considered unfilial conduct if the updating work was not done over three generations. In that case, the clan tree became disordered, and a clan member could not identify his position in a genealogical rank.

In fieldwork, we asked villagers, "Do you support updating genealogical records?" 61% of them expressed support, 33% were neutral, and only 6% opposed (see Table 10.6, Qn. 20). Many senior villagers were actually enthusiastic about engaging in this work. There was not much attitudinal difference between the farming and non-farming groups. In the 2009 survey, 77% of the respondents expressed support. In the 2014 survey, this proportion dropped to 56%. During the past five years, some clans completed this work already, and some were working on it. This perhaps explains why the supporting percentage dropped so much in 2014. Another possible reason could be that some villagers lost interest as their sense of clan identity declined in the process of urbanization and modernization.

In the investigated area, a few clans including the Wu, the Cao, and the Ye have not started this work so far. A shortage of funding is probably an answer, but the truth is more complicated. Like many others, the three clans have not updated their genealogical records in over a century. Descent disorders have already emerged and have become a serious problem. When we visited, nobody was able to tell us how they were related to each other genealogically beyond five generations. Few of them could clarify what *fangzhi* (or clan branches) they belonged to. Under the circumstances, it is extremely difficult to make up the missing links. Moreover, a number of villagers have moved out over the last century, and many of them have lost contact with native clans. Without them, a clan tree is hardly in a full shape. As we know, many clans with a long history in Huizhou wanted to update their genealogical records and print out a new pedigree. After initial trying, most of them had to give up.

Exclusive defense, which probably leads to a battle against others, was considered an important role by a local clan in the past. In the 2014 survey, we asked if they were willing to participate in this kind of fight (see Table 10.6, Qn.21). 15% of the respondents expressed willingness, 15% were neutral, and 70% opposed. Those who expressed willingness stated that they were willing to come only when the clan owned right reasons. It can be also seen that the farming group holds a higher WI value than the non-farming group (2.23 vs. 1.79) though both are very low—showing that the latter would be less likely to participate in such fights.

In the survey we asked villagers, "Do you think that the local clan influence on public affairs is declining?" (Table 10.6, Qn. 22). 71% of the respondents thought that it was declining, 16% were neutral, and 13% did not think so. Of the farming group, 77% believed in that way. For the non-farming, it dropped to 67%. A possible explanation is, as compared with the non-farming, the farming people stay longer in villages and have seen more declining. In the 2009 survey, 85% of the respondents believed that it was declining, while less people held the same opinion in the 2014 survey. As mentioned, during the five-year period, a number of clans completed their work on pedigree. This would probably lead some to believe that clans still played a role in public affairs.

Another question is, "Do you think that the local clan influence on personal life is declining?" (Table 10.6, Qn. 23). 74% of the respondents believed that it was declining, 14% were neutral, and 12% did not believe so. Of the farming population, 82% believed so as compared with 67% of the non-farming. In other words, villagers working outside would be less likely to feel such declining. When they were working in cities, their strong homesickness, to some extent, would turn to their home villages and clans. Some might feel distinguished from others and attributed it to their unique clan culture. All of these possibly made them experience more clan influence on their personal life. In the 2009 survey, 85% of the respondents believed that it was declining, compared with 81% in the 2014 survey. The margin is not evident and can be neglected. At least, clan influence did not further decline during the five years.

Qn. 24 in Table 10.6 is to ask if they are willing to participate in clan activities such as relocating ancestral graves and so on. 64% of them said "yes," 22% were undecided, and only 14% said "no." Of the farming people, 64% said "yes," and 65% of the non-farming said "yes." The margin is very small. We further asked them if they are willing to come to other activities organized by the clan (Table 10.6, Qn. 25). 64% of them said "yes." Of the farming people, 60% said "yes," compared with 66% of the non-farming. The non-farming people expressed more interest in joining such activities as they did not come back very often, and therefore these activities would be more attractive to them. However, as observed, perhaps also owing to the short stay at home, their actual participation was not as active as expected.

10.4.4 Descent Relations

Descent and kinship relations can be viewed as an indicator of clan cohesiveness among members. In survey, we asked them, "Do you agree that your relations with relatives are better than before?" (see Table 10.6, Qn. 26) Of the farming people, 29% agreed and 41% disagreed. Of the non-farming, 30% agreed and 37% disagreed. That is to say, the non-farming people showed less negative attitude. As mentioned, these villagers returned home only a few times or even only once a year. When they stayed at home, they visited friends and relatives.

In the 2009 survey, 32% of the respondents believed that it was better, and 51% said "it was worse." In the 2014 survey, 29% believed "better," and 31% believed "worse." The "worse" percentage dropped significantly in 2014. Why? Deng's reform has generated income gaps between peasants. In the 1980s, this gap was not evident as all the villagers still worked agriculturally. From the mid-1990s, when more and more peasants were leaving for cities and working there, the gap began to be widened— hurting the descent relations since they were not equal any more. This situation turned out to be worse as more technologies and machineries were put to agriculture and dramatically reduced the burden of farming work. Mutual assistance decreased and less help was needed from relatives and clan members, even in busy seasons. Meanwhile, salary was required once help was needed. Blood relationships were therefore replaced by money. It explains why more than half of the respondents in the 2009 survey felt pessimistic about their descent relations. Five years since then, changes continued, but the situation mostly remained unruffled. Consequently, respondents in the 2014 survey appeared less negative to their kin relations.

Stated by those optimistic respondents, money was required for visiting relatives and participating in weddings and funerals. In the last two decades, peasant income grew quickly due to the booming economy— offering them a great chance to improve kinship relations. In our investigation, the average amount spent on such activities (i.e., *renqing kaizhi* as called by them) was about 1350 *yuan* at least for a family in 2011. To a certain degree, money kept kinship active. The more money spent, the closer the relationship was. Thereby, economic development and urbanization have imposed positive and also negative changes in descent relations.

To further understand descent relations, in the 2014 survey, we classified the kinship into four categories: (1) five generations and beyond including clan members, (2) between three and five generations, (3) within three generations, and (4) family members. This time, WI values are used in illustration. It is 2.99 for the first and the second groups, 3.47 for the third group, and 3.65 for the fourth group or family members. It reveals two facts. First, the socioeconomic development has alienated villagers from their distant kin and clan members. Second, at the same time, it has improved relationships with their close kin and family members, reflecting a trend of shifting from the big family to the small family.

To explore the impact of descent relations on public affairs, we asked them, "Do you agree that in-clan-cadres are more trustworthy than out-clan-cadres?" (see Table 10.6, Qn. 27). The WI for the farming group is 2.48, and 2.59 for the non-farming, showing that although the two groups were all inclined to oppose this statement, the non-farming group would be less likely to be opponents. The WI is 2.78 in the 2009 survey and 2.28 in the 2014 survey, indicating that, as time goes on, more people tended to oppose this statement. Occupation and time, the two variables representing urbanization, seemed to play contradictory roles. First, we should say, working and life experience in urban areas did not particularly dilute their feelings of descent relations. Second, increasing awareness of citizenship and decreasing sense of kinship with time can be mainly attributed to ideological modernization in the whole society. As mentioned, the variable "time" acts on all categories of the people.

For villagers, the primary task for cadres was to lead them to a better life. Logically, the first concern for them in electing cadres was candidates' capacity and morality. Even for those who were in favor of in-clan cadres, "in-clan" referred to their kin within five generations. "Clansmen beyond five generations are not worth the same trusting as friends," they said. In the investigated areas, cardinal officials in these villages, including the village heads and the party secretaries, all came from *xiaoxing* (or the small surnames or clans) rather than *daxing* (or the dominant surnames or clans) except for Censhandu. Stated in a different way, most of them were out-clan cadres.

10.5 Regression Analysis

In the previous sections, using two variables of occupation and time, we analyzed villagers' views on a range of issues, examining the impact of urbanization as well as modernization on clan culture and local clan communities. Villagers' views and attitudes are affected not only by socioeconomic development at the macro level, but also by individual socioeconomic characteristics at the micro-level. Their views and attitudes are also affected by macro historical features. Socio-economic development can be understood as urbanization or the process of urbanization, while historical features can be treated as regional clan history and cultural traditions. In order to discuss these macro and micro effects and examine the impact of urbanization in the case of these factors under control, we established 11 regression models. In these models, four independent variables represent individual characteristics: Age (X_1), Gender (X_2), Education (X_3), and Occupation (X_4). Since villagers engaging in non-farming work are mostly migrant workers in cities, the variable "occupation" can be regarded as a measure of urbanization at the macro level. The other two macro variables are: Region (X_5) as the representative of regional historical environment and cultural traditions, and Time (X_6) as the index of the process of urbanization. As mentioned previously, in a broad range of space and time, the variable "time" can be considered a measure of the process of modernization, and urbanization is part of that process.

Mentioned at the beginning, the investigated regions consist of three types of areas, including the mountain area, the hilly area, and the plain area. A comparison among the three areas would be useful to examine (1) regional historical traditions, and (2) regional divergence in cultural evolutions during the process of urbanization. A regional mainstream culture was established on the basis of local clan cultures in that region, and in turn affected all clans there.

Eleven questions, selected from Table 10.6, will be dependent variables for 11 regression models, namely: (1) attitude towards "filial piety," or Y_1 in Model 1; (2) attitude towards "ancestor worship," or Y_2 in Model 2; (3) attitude towards "without male descendants," or Y_3 in Model 3; (4) attitude towards "father or husband being decision-maker at home," or Y_4 in Model 4; (5) attitude towards "housework mainly taken by women," or Y_5 in Model 5; (6) attitude towards "family above the individual," or Y_6 in Model 6; (7) attitude towards "local clan influence on public affairs," or Y_7 in Model 7; (8) attitude towards "local clan interests above family and individuals," or Y_8 in Model 8; (9) attitude towards "in-clan cadres being more trustworthy," or Y_9 in Model 9; (10) attitude towards "resuming clan ritual of ancestor worship," or Y_{10} in Model 10; and (11) attitude towards "updating pedigree," or Y_{11} in Model 11.

Of independent variables, age and education (measured by schooling years) are ratio measurements. Three normative variables including sex, occupation, and time need to be converted into quantized values. For sex, male is coded as 0, and female as 1. For occupation, engaging in farming work is coded as 0, and non-farming as 1. For time, the 2009 survey is coded as 0, and the 2014 survey as 1. Region is an ordinal variable according to the geographical features as well as clan history and traditions. Group 1 or clans in Shexian is coded as 1, Group 2 or clans in Jingxian as 2, Group 3 or clans in Fangchan as 3, and Group 4 or clans in Wangjiang as 4. Fanchang and Wangjiang counties are all located in the Yangtze River Plains. They are separated into two groups because the latter's history is shorter and the clan size is smaller. Historically, clan cultural traditions weakened in order from Shexian or the Huizhou region to the Yangtze River Plains. Jingxian was between the two.

Dependent variables or Y's in all models are ordinal. "Strongly Agree" is coded as 1, "Agree" as 2, "Neutral" as 3, "Disagree" as 4, "Strongly Disagree" as 5. Table 10.7 shows the results.[13] All models are statistically significant as indicated by the F test. To facilitate understandings for readers, we simplified the following statistical analyses. The discussion will be limited to variables showing statistical significance ($p \leq 10\%$) in each model.

In Model 1, three variables including sex, age, and region show significance at a 5% level. The B value for sex is positive, indicating that, as compared with women, men would be more likely to follow the moral principle of filial piety. In a

[13]SPSS is the statistical software.

Table 10.7 Regression Models

X	Models										
	1	2	3	4	5	6	7	8	9	10	11
Age	−0.01**	−0.009**	−0.005	−0.007	−0.003	−0.011**	0.006**	0.000	0.006	0.000	−0.007*
Sex	0.970*	0.246**	0.272**	0.363**	−0.188	−0.127	0.124	0.255**	−0.150	0.264**	0.196**
Education	0.020	0.016	0.018	0.059**	0.041**	0.016	−0.025	0.002	−0.002	0.002	−0.022
Occupation	−0.074	0.141*	0.249**	−0.081	0.087	−0.050	0.109	0.106	−0.119	0.028	−0.008
Region	0.118**	0.316**	0.107**	0.226**	0.424**	0.016**	−0.021	−0.218**	−0.148**	0.458**	0.310**
Time	−0.007	0.388**	0.724**	−0.014	−0.197	0.230**	0.204	0.300**	0.628**	0.222	−0.477**
F	16.473	16.735	19.095	18.745	18.745	21.818	18.816	13.869	18.521	10.539	14.119

Note $*P < 0.1$; $**\ P < 0.05$; others > 0.1

patriarchal society, this traditional value is passed on from generation to generation mostly by men. The B value for age is negative, showing an enhanced recognition of this value with increasing age. The elderly would be more traditional. The B value for region is positive, confirming our observations in fieldwork that the influence of this value declined sequentially from Huizhou to the Yangtze River Plains. It also shows regional variations on people's attitude to filial piety. Other variables did not reach the level of significance, however, it by no means says that these variables do not generate any difference. In the previous sections, we discussed attitudinal differences caused by variables of occupation and time though these differences were not impressive.

In Model 2, the variable "occupation" is statistically significant at the 10% level, and variables including age, sex, region, and time show significance at the 5% level. The B value for occupation is positive, indicating that villagers who engaged in farming work would be more likely to stand with "ancestor worship" as compared with the non-farming population, which is consistent with the analysis made in the previous sections. In this model, age appears negative, and sex is positive, showing that the old and male villagers would be more likely to accept this traditional value. Once again, the B for region appears positive, indicating that this traditional influence is diminishing from Huizhou to other areas. Time is also positive, showing that the recognition of this value in the 2014 survey is lower than that in 2009.

In Model 3, three variables including sex, occupation, and time are significant at the 5% level. Same as in Models 1 and 2, the B value for sex is positive, illustrating that men would be more likely to approve the statement that the greatest unfilial act is not to have a son to carry on the family line. The B value for occupation is positive, indicating that the farming population would be more likely in favor of this value. The B value for time is also positive, showing a lower acceptance in the 2014 survey.

In Model 4, three variables including sex, education, and region are significant at the 5% level. The positive B for sex indicates that males would be more likely to support the statement that men should be the decision-makers at home. At the same time, women are eager to share the family power with men, reflecting their pursuit of social equality as well as confidence in their abilities. The B value for education is positive, telling us that villagers with more education would be more likely to support gender equality. The positive B for region affirms our finding that the patriarchal influence declines from Huizhou to other regions.

In Model 5, two variables including education and region are significant at the 5% level. The positive B for education shows that education would weaken the value that women should take more housework. Shown by the positive B for region, this patriarchal influence declines successively from Huizhou to other regions. The variable sex does not show significance this time. In fact, as we found in fieldwork, women were willing to take more housework and tended to believe that it was still their responsibility for caring for children and the family. Meanwhile, men were more willing to share the burden of housework with their wives, reflecting a progress in family relations.

In Model 6, three variables are significant at the 5% level. Indicated by the negative B for age, with the increasing age, villagers would be more likely to accept the value that family interests are over individuals. The B values for both region and time are positive, showing that this value is decreasing from Huizhou to other regions, and that this influence has diminished since 2009.

In Model 7, the only variable showing significance (at the 5% level) is age. This time, the B value turns to be positive. The increasing age would more likely lead people to perceive that local clan influence on public affairs is declining. As illustrated previously, this situation emerges possibly because of their experience in making judgment. Compared with the youths, the old and mid-aged villagers have more knowledge to determine that clan power is greatly undermined.

In Model 8, three variables including sex, region, and time are significant at the 5% level. The B value for sex remains positive. As compared with women, men would be more willing to accept the value that clan interests are over families and individuals. Different from previous models, the B for region exhibits a negative value, demonstrating that people's sense of clan identity or cohesion in Huizhou is not the same strong as that in other regions. The positive B for time shows a less acceptance of this value in the 2014 survey.

In Model 9, the only variable with significance (at the 5% level) is time, and its B is positive, indicating that acceptance of the statement that in-clan cadres are worth more trust has run down since 2009.

In Model 10, two variables including sex and region are significant at the 5% level. The B value for sex is positive. Men expressed more enthusiasm in resuming clan rituals of ancestor worship than women. As shown by the B value for region, the willingness to resume clan rituals was descending from Huizhou to other regions. It must be noted that resuming clan rituals to a large extent is an appeal for restoring clan culture rather than clan interests. Attitudinal variations with this issue manifest historical divergence in these regions. A strong aspiration for clan rituals in Huizhou is consistent with a solid Confucian foundation in that area. As observed, many clans in the Yangzi River plains were practicing clan rituals and did not need to resume it, explaining from another perspective why people in these regions presented less interest.

In Model 11, four variables including age, sex, region, and time are significant statistically. From the B values, we can see that the interest in updating pedigrees went up with increasing age. Meanwhile, men demonstrated more interest than women. Since most clans in the Yangzi River Plains have completed this work, villagers in that region showed a lower will. In addition, respondents in the 2014 survey expressed less interest, which confirms our analysis in the previous sections.

10.6 Discussions and Conclusions

This chapter examines the impact of urbanization on clan culture, local clan communities, and kinship relations. As shown by descriptive analyses and regression models, in general, the socio-economic development represented by education and occupation (as the index of urbanization) is a force weakening traditional influence. Young and middle-aged villagers who have working experience in urban areas are more likely to embrace the new world. Male villagers are more traditional than females in supporting patriarchal values. Meanwhile, individualism is rising, villagers are making great strides from big families to small families, and they give less prominence to relations with clansmen.

However, the role in weakening traditions played by the above variables, urbanization in particular, should be carefully analyzed. Villagers with good educations are more inclined to the idea of gender equality, but in other issues, especially core values, education does not generate much difference. Young people are always the most receptive to new ideas. However, when they get older and come back from the city to the countryside, whether or not they will return to traditions, is still something that needs to be explored.

It can be seen from the descriptive analyses that the experience in cities would generally weaken traditional influence. In the regression analyses, the variable "occupation" as the representative of urbanization only showed statistical significance in two models, demonstrating that the urban role, as generated by changes in working and living environment for peasants, cannot be exaggerated. Its impact is limited in scope and intensity. Migrant workers are still in their rural roots. The current development is not sufficient to completely separate them physically and mentally from their native villages and clan communities. China's urbanization is distinguished from European model because of a changed technological environment today. New technical conditions in transportation and information make the distance between migrant workers and their villages relatively shorter. Their spiritual communication with their family members, relatives, and local clans is not loosened. Their various links with home-villages do not cut off, but continue to be close and smooth. The native clan culture remains not only in their memory but also in their daily life. Thereby, the urban effect moves slowly on them. It would be considered an important feature of cultural changes in the process of China's urbanization.

The variable "time," an important indicator of urbanization, shows statistical significance in a number of regression models. Its role in weakening traditions is obvious and comprehensive. However, since this variable works on all categories of people, including those staying home and engaging in farming, the weakening role is both a result of urbanization and a product of modernization in the whole society.

The variable "region" appears statistically significant in most regression models, reflecting historical characteristics as well as regional variations in cultural changes during the process of urbanization. In Huizhou the local clan people still maintain more traditional values compared with other regions. However, due to the long history, most clans have become numerous and jumbled in branches, and descent lines have appeared increasingly blurred and estranged. The solidarity and the identity in these communities have run down. In contrast, in the plain region along the Yangtze River, clan cultural influence in general is not as strong as in Huizhou, but their consanguineous relationship is clear. Clan organization at the branch level has mostly set up and clan identity and cohesion are not lost. Therefore, these local clans still exert influence on village public affairs.

Revealed by this research, the duality of cultural change exists with the rapid urban development. Although urbanization challenges patriarchal traditions, the majority of respondents take a firm stand on a series of traditional core values including ancestors worship, filial piety, and loyalty, illustrating persistence and historical continuity of culture.

In our observation, clan subculture or the culture related to a specific clan, for instance, ethics and rules in regulating the relationships between individual members and their particular clan, is disappearing. Few villagers, including the elders, are able to tell us these specific rules made by their clans. Local clan culture that still retains influence mainly means ethical and customary traditions applicable to all clans in that area, which, to a large degree, have become a local or regional culture and are replacing the local clan subculture. It indicates a trend to a cultural convergence, a result of urbanization and a product of ideological modernization in the long run. It should be pointed out that a cultural convergence cannot be achieved overnight. The key element or the religious composition of the local clan culture still influences the behavior of clan members. In rituals of ancestor worship, regardless of clan or family, strong local clan characteristics are always present.

It must be emphasized that Chinese characteristics are deeply engraved upon cultural changes in the investigated areas. Although the sentiment of patriarchal authority is declining among the young and mid-aged villagers, the general principle of filial piety is still respected by all age groups. *Jia,* the foundation of the Chinese society and Chinese culture, continues to be of more importance than individuals. We admit that Western influence is growing up quickly. It has changed many aspects of peasant life. As the appearance goes, a trend of Westernization seems irresistible. Nevertheless, even if peasants divested themselves of some clan traditions, they held firmly to core values. Changes in their dressing style, which can be seen handily, do not necessarily mean changes in their inside. As we all know, Chinese traditional culture suffered heavy blows during the 1949 revolution and the Great Proletariat Cultural Revolution. It is the people rather than the government that started to rebuild it in the 1980s. The core values and traditions rooted in the hearts of ordinary people provide them with a kind of religious comfort and happiness. Being full of vital power, these values and traditions that grew out of China's clan society for thousands of years and transmitted generation after generation would not easily alter with time. With economic success, the Chinese people will have more confidence in their culture and history.

References in English

Anderson, B. 1998. *The spectra of comparisons: Nationalism, Southeast Asia, and the world*. New York: Verso.

Baker, H. 1966. The five great clans of the New Territories. *Journal of the Hong Kong Branch of Royal Asiatic Society* 6: 25–48.

Baker, H. 1979. *Chinese family and kinship*. New York: Columbia University Press.

Bell, D. 1973. *The Coming of post-industrial society*. New York: Basic Books.

Biao, X. 2004. *Transcending boundaries: Zhejiangcun: The story of a migrant village in Beijing*. Leiden: Brill.

Bird, D.N. 1992. Beyond the original affluent society: A culturalist reformation. *Current Anthropology* 33 (1): 25–47.

Bossen, L. 2002. *Chinese women and rural development*. Lanham: Rowman & Little Field Publishers Inc.

Brandtstdter, S., and S. Goncaloo. 2009. *Chinese kinship: Contemporary anthropological perspectives*. London: Routledge.

Braudel, F. 1992. *Civilization and capitalism, 15th–18th century*, vol. III. Berkeley, CA: University of California Press.

Buchler, I.R., and H.A. Selby. 1968. *Kinship and social organization: An introduction to theory and methods*. New York: Macmillan.

Campbell, B.G. 1998. *Human evolution: An introduction to man's adaptations*, 4th ed. New York: Aldie de Gruyter.

Chan, A., R. Madsen, and J. UNGER. 1992. *Chen village under Mao and Deng*. Berkeley: University of California Press.

Chen, A. 2006. Urbanization in China and the case of Fujian province. *Modern China* 32: 99–130.

Ching-Chan, S. 2001. Selling the ancestors' land: A Hong Kong lineage adapts. *Modern China* 27: 262–284.

Cohen, M.L. 2005. *Kinship, contract, community, and state*. Stanford: Stanford University Press.

Cohen, R., and E.R. Service. 1978. *Origins of the state: The anthropology of political evolution*. Philadelphia: Institute for the Study of Human Issues.

Cong, Z., and M. Silverstein. 2008. Intergenerational support and depression among elders in rural China: Do daughters-in-law matter? *Journal of Marriage and Family* 70: 599–612.

Croll, E. 1978. *Feminism and socialism in China*. London: Routledge.

Croll, E. 1981. *Politics of marriage in contemporary China*. Cambridge: Cambridge University Press.

Davin, D. 1999. *Internal migration in contemporary China*. New York: St. Martin's Press.

Dean, K. 1993. *Taoist ritual and popular cults of Southeast China*. Princeton: Princeton University Press.

Dura, P. 1988. *Culture, power and the state*. Stanford: Stanford University Press.

Du, Y. 1998. Rural labor migration in contemporary China: Analysis of its features and the macro context. In *Rural labor flows in China*, ed. W. Zhao, 37–51. New York: Columbia University Press.

Dubois, T.D. 2005. *The sacred village*. Honolulu: University of Hawai'i Press.

Fan, C. 2004. Out to the city and back to the village: The experiences and contributions of rural women migrating from Sichuan and Anhui. In *On the move: Women and rural to urban migration in contemporary China*, ed. A. Gaetano, and T. Jacka. New York: Columbia University Press.

Faure, D. 1986. *The structure of Chinese rural society: Lineage and village in the Eastern New Territories*. New York: Oxford University Press.

Faure, D. 2007. *Emperor and ancestor: State and lineage in South China*. Stanford: Stanford University Press.

Fei, X. 1939. *Peasant life in China: A field study of country life in the Yangtze Valley*. London: Routledge & Kegan Paul.

Feuchwang, S. 1992. *The Imperial metaphor: Popular religion in China*. London: Routledge.
Freedman, M. 1958. *Lineage organization in Southern China*. London: Athlone Press.
Freedman, M. 1966. *Chinese lineage and society: Fukien and Kwangtung*. London: Athlone Press.
Freedman, M. 1970. Ritual aspects of Chinese kinship and marriage. In *Family and kinship in Chinese society*, ed. M. Freedman, 76–101. Stanford: Stanford University Press.
Fried, M.H. 1970. Clans and lineages: How to tell human apart and why - with special reference to Chinese society. *Bulletin of the Institute of Ethnology* 29: 11–36.
Friedman, E., P.G. Pickowicz, and M. Selden. 2008. *Revolution, resistance and reform in village China*. New Haven and London: Yale University Press.
Giddens, A. 1985. *The nation state and violence*. Cambridge: Polity.
Gellner, E. 1997. *Nationalism*. New York: New York University Press.
Geertz, C. 1980. Blurred genres: The refrigeration of social thought. *American Scholar* 29: 165–179.
Guang, L., and L. Zheng. 2005. Migration as the second-best option: Local power and off-farm employment. *The China Quarterly* 181: 22–45.
Hastings, A. 1997. *The construction of nationhood: Ethnicity, religion, and nationalism*. New York: Cambridge University Press.
Hobsbawn, E.J. 1992. *Nations and nationalism since 1780*. New York: Cambridge University Press.
Hsu, F. 1948. *Under the Ancestors' shadow: Chinese culture and personality*. New York: Columbia University Press.
Huang, P.C.C. 2011. The modern Chinese family: In light of economic and legal history. *Modern China* 37: 459–497.
Huntington, S. 1993. The clash of civilizations? *Foreign Affairs* 72 (3): 22–49.
Ikels, C. (ed.). 2004. *Filial piety: practice and discourse in contemporary East Asia*. Stanford: Stanford University Press.
Inglehart, R., and W. Baker. 2000. Modernization, cultural changes, and the persistence of traditional values. *American Sociological Review* 65 (February): 19–51.
Jacka, T. 1997. *Women's work in rural China*. New York: Cambridge University Press.
Jacka, T. 2005. *Rural women in urban China: Gender, migration, and social change*. Armonk: Sharpe.
Jiang, L. 2008. Migration, urbanization and special dispersion in China. Presented at the 2008 annual meeting of Population Association of America (PAA).
Judd, E. 1994. *Gender and power in rural North China*. Stanford: Stanford University Press.
Kottak, C.P. 2010. *Cultural anthropology*. Boston: McGraw Hill.
Kutsche, R. 1998. *Field ethnography: A manual for doing cultural anthropology*. Upper Saddle River, NJ: Prentice Hall.
Lamley, H. 1990. Lineage feuding in Southern Fujian and Eastern Guangdong under qung rule. In *Violence in China*, ed. S. Harrell, and J. Lipman, 27–64. New York: State University of New York Press.
Lang, O. 1946. *Chinese family and society*. New Haven: Yale University Press.
Lerner, D. 1958. *The passing of traditional society: Modernizing the Middle East*. New York: Free Press.
Lin, Y.H. 1947. *The golden wing: A sociological study of Chinese feminism*. New York: Oxford University Press.
Macionis, J.J. 2013. *Society: The basics*. Upper Saddle River: Pearson Prentice Hall.
Marcus, G., and M. Fischer. 1986. *Anthropology as cultural critique*. Chicago: Chicago University Press.
Marx, K. 1973. *Foundations of the critique of political economy*. New York: Vintage Books.
Myerson, R., Y. Hou, H. Tang, Y. Cheng, Y. Wang, and X. Zhe. 2010. Home and away: Chinese migrant workers between two worlds. *The Sociological Review* 58 (1): 26–44.
Murphy, R. 2002. *How migrant labor is changing rural China?*. Cambridge: Cambridge University Press.

Oaks, T., and L. Schein (eds.). 2006. *Translocal China: Linkages, identities, and the reimagining of space*. London: Routledge.

Osgoog, C. 1963. *Village life in old China: A community study of Kao Yao, Yuennan*. New York: Roland Press.

Parkin, R. 1997. *Kinship: An introduction to basic concepts*. Cambridge, MA: Blackwell.

Perkins, T. 2002. *Village, market and well-being in a rural Chinese township*. New York: Routledge.

Potter, J. 1968. *Capitalism and the Chinese peasant: Social and economic change in a Hong Kong village*. Berkeley: University of California Press.

Qian, M. 1993. *An introduction to the history of Chinese culture*. Taipei: The Commercial Publishing Company.

Roberts, K., R. Connelly, Z.M. Xie, and Z.Z. Zheng. 2004. Patterns of temporary labor migration of rural women from Anhui and Sichuan. *China Journal* 52 (July): 49–69.

Roserberry, W. 1988. Political economy. *Annual Review of Anthropology* 17: 161–185.

Rosenlee, L.L. 2006. *Confucianism and women: A philosophical interpretation*. New York: State University of New York Press.

Sangren, P.S. 1987. *History and magic power in a Chinese community*. Stanford: Stanford University Press.

Saso, M. 1999. *Velvet bonds: The Chinese family*. Carmel: New Life Center.

Schwartz, B. 1985. *The world of thought in ancient China*. Cambridge: Harvard University Press.

Shi, L.H. 2009. Little quilted vests to warm parents' hearts: Redefining the gendered practice of filial piety in rural-eastern China. *The China Quarterly* 198: 348–363.

Siu, H. 1989. *Agents and victims in South China*. Yale: Yale University Press.

Skinner, G.W. 1963–65. Marketing and social structure in rural China, parts I, II, III. *Journal of Asia Studies* 24(1–3): 3–43, 195–228, 363–399.

Su, F.B., T. Ran, X. Sun, and M.X. Liu. 2011. Clans, electoral procedures and voter turnout: evidence from villagers' committee elections in transitional China. *Political Studies* 59: 432–457.

Szonyi, M. 2002. *Practicing kinship*. Stanford: Stanford University Press.

Tang, Z.L., and B. Zuo. 1997. *Maoism and Chinese culture*. New York: Nova Science.

Wallerstein, I. 1974. *The Modern world system*. New York: Academic Press.

Wang, F.L. 2004. Reformed migration control and new target people: China's hukou system in the 2000s. *The China Quarterly* 179: 115–132.

Watson, J. 1975. *Emigration and the Chinese lineage*. Berkeley: University of California Press.

Watson, J. 1982. Chinese kinship reconsidered: Anthropological perspectives on historical research. *China Quarterly* 92: 589–622.

Weber, M. (1958, orig. 1904). *The Protestant ethic and the spirit of capitalism*. Translated by T. Parsons. New York: Charles Scribner's Sons.

Whyte, M. 1995. The social roots of China's economic development. *China Quarterly* 144: 999–1019.

Wilk, R.R. 1996. *Economies and cultures: An introduction to economic anthropology*. Boulder Co: Westview.

Wolf, E. 1982. *Europe and the people without history*. Berkeley: California University Press.

Wu, B. 2003. *Sustainable development in rural China*. London: Routledge.

Yan, Y.X. 2003. *Private life under socialism*. Stanford: Stanford University Press.

Yuen, S.P., P.L. Law, and Y.Y. Ho. 2004. *Marriage, gender, and sex in a contemporary Chinese village*. Armonk: M.E. Sharpe.

Zhang, H. 2007. From resisting to 'embracing?' The one-child rule: understanding new fertility trends in a central China village. *The China Quarterly* 192: 855–875.

Zhang, W.G. 2008. State, gender and uxorilocal marriage in contemporary rural north China. *The China Journal* 60: 213–234.

Zhao, Z.W., and F. Guo (eds.). 2007. *Transition and challenge, China's population at the beginning of the 21st Century*. Oxford: Oxford University Press.

Zheng, Z.M. 2001. *Family lineage organization and social change in the Ming and Qing Fujia.* Translated by Szonyi, M. Honolulu: University of Hawai'i Press.

References in Chinese

Bian, L. 2006. Ming qing huizhou de zongzu guangli, jingjijichu ji qi jishi yishi [Clan management, economic basis, and rituals in Huizhou, the Ming and Qing Dynasties]. *Shehui kexue* 6: 13–21.

Chang, J.H. 2007. Song ming yi lai zongzuzhi xincheng lilun biangxi [On the theory of clan system since the Song and Ming Dynasties]. *Ahnhui shixue* 1: 11–21.

Feng, E.K. 2009. *Zhongguo zongzu shehui [China's clan society].* Hangzhou: Zhejiang renming chubanshe.

Gao, C. 2005. Dushihua jincheng zhong huanan zongzu de yanbian dongtai, yi nanjingcun wei li [Changes in clans in Southern China during urbanization, a case study in Nanjingcun]. *Zhejiang daxue xuebao (shehui kexue ban)* 35 (3): 137–144.

Huang, S.M. 2003. Cunluo zongzu wenhua de fumeng ji qi jiejue duiche [Reinvigoration in rural clan culture and solutions]. *Yangbei shifan xueyuan xuebao* 2: 47–49.

Ke, D.W., and Z.W. Liu. 2000. Zongzu yu defang shehui de guijia renting [State recognition of clans and local communities]. *Lishi yanjiu* 3: 23–38.

Li, W.Z. 2008. Song yuan ming Qing jicheng shehui chixu de xing jiegou [The new structure of local communities during the Song, Yuan, Ming, and Qing Dynasties]. *Nankei xuebao (zexue shehui kexue ban)* 3: 42–50.

Liu, S.H. 2008. Zongzu wenhua he shehui hexie [Clan culture and social harmony]. *Changjiang daxue xuebao* 31(1): 23–27.

Qian, H. 1999. *Jiating jiegou biandong yu zongzu zhuanxing [Changes in family structure and clans].* Hefei: Huangshan shushe.

Ren, Y.H. 2004. Chayi yu qiehe: cunluo jiazu wenhua yu xiandaihua [Difference and integration: Modernization and village clan culture]. *Qiusuo* 8: 89–92.

Song, Y.Q., and J.H. Zhang. 2009. Jin 30 nian lai wanzhong cunluo de fuxing yu yianbian [Reinvigoration and changes in villages in the Central Anhui during the last thirty years]. *Dandai zhongguoshi yanjiu* 16: 78–86.

Tang, L.X. 2005. 20 shiji shang ban ye zhongguo zongzu zuzhi taishi [China's clan organization during the first half of twenty century]. *Shanghai shifan saxue xuebao (zexue shehui kexue ban)* 34: 103–111.

Wang, H.L. 1991. *Dangdai zhongguo cunluo jiazu wenhua: dui zhongguo shehui xiandaihua de yixian kaocha [Village clan culture in contemporary China: An observation on modernization of Chinese society].* Shanghai: Shanghai renmin chubanshe.

Wang, M.M. 1995. Yige minnan cunluo de jiazu: shehui yu guojia [Clans in a village of Southern Fujiang: Society and state]. *Zhongyang yanjiuyuan minzuxue yanjiusuo jikan* 83: 51–120.

Wu, W.Z. 2010. *Lun shehuixue zhongguohua [On sociology in China].* Beijing: Shangwu yinshuguan.

Xu, Y.J. 1992. *Zhongguo jiazu zhidushi [History of China's clan system].* Beijing: Renmin chubanshe.

Ye, X.E. 1995. Huizhou yu zhujiang sanjiaozhou zongfazhi bijiao yanjiu [Comparative studies of clan system between Huizhou and Zhujiang Delta]. Presented at the international conference of Huizhou Studies, 1995.

Zhao, H.F. 2004. *Huizhou zongzu yanjiu [Studies on Huizhou clans].* Hefei: Anhui daxue chubanshe.

Zheng, X.C. 2008. Ming qing huizhou zongzu yu xiancun zhili: yi qimen kanshi wei zhongxin [Huizhou clans and rural management during the Ming and Qing Dynasties: A case study in the Kan clan, Qimen]. *Zhongguo nonshi* 3: 27–39.

Zhu, K.L. 2006. *Keju shehui diyu chixu yu zongzu fazhang: song ming jian de huizhou, 1100–1644 [Imperial civil examination society, regional orders, and clan development in Huizhou during the Song and Ming Dynasties, 1100–1644]*. Taibei: Taiwan daxue chuban weiyuanhui.

Chapter 11
Local Clan Societies and Migrants to Cities in the Qin and Han Dynasties

Shijing Qiu

Abstract The autocratic monarchy system of ancient China was established on the basis of patriarchal clans. In the Qin and Han Dynasties, as cities expanded and business flourished, the clan system developed from the ancient pattern into a feudal one, by experiencing three major changes. At the same time, the noble descent of the system began to weaken. The further development of cities and business made the local clan societies stable, and under certain conditions it also became an unrest factor. In the Han Dynasty, Confucianism achieved ideological supremacy. The rituals of ancestor worship were more regulated and rigorous, which gave more power to local clan societies. The great unity in the Qin and Han Dynasties promoted the formation of a cultural melting pot. A new clan culture as well as a unified clan society was born.

Keywords Local clan society · Migration · Qin and Han Dynasties

11.1 Introduction

Today hundreds of millions of young farmers have left their villages and become or will become new urban citizens. These changes will inevitably bring a number of contradictions and conflicts between traditions and realities, and between an urbanizing society and a patriarchal clan system. Urbanization is the trend of historical development we must face, for it cannot be avoided. As a modern concept, it was still very preliminary in the Qin and Han Dynasties, largely different from the current transition from a traditional agricultural society to a modern urban society. This chapter, by tracing urban development through history, tries to explore the relationship between urbanization and local patriarchal clan society in an attempt to seek a way for solving issues that have appeared in today's urbanization.

S. Qiu (✉)
Anhui Normal University, Wuhu, China
e-mail: qiuwang@ahnu.edu.cn

Z. Tang (ed.), *China's Urbanization and Socioeconomic Impact*,
DOI 10.1007/978-981-10-4831-9_11

It is stated in *Baihu Tongyi* (or 《白虎通义》) that *zong* refers to the honorable person. He is the ancestor in a descendant line and respected by all the people in that clan. Among all members of a clan, that person is respected as the most honorable one and holds relatively centralized power. *Zu* refers to a group of people with blood lineages. Thus, *zongzu* is a patriarchal clan formed by people with close and distant blood relationships and headed by the patriarch (or *zongzu*). The autocratic monarchy system in ancient China was established on the basis of the patriarchal clan system, and the two supported each other. It was a system in which the family and the nation shared the same structure. The ancient society in China was a class society, maintained by patriarchal clans.

11.2 Integration of Centralization and the Patriarchal Clan Society

In the long course of the Chinese history, dynasties changed frequently. Some lasted for two to three hundred years, while others only lasted for tens of years. Dynasty changes were accompanied by changes in social structures, but the patriarchal clan system linked by the consanguineous bond remained unchanged. In the Qin and Han Dynasties, the autocratic centralization system that existed for about two thousand years in history was established, from which a series of relevant systems were derived. Meanwhile, the patriarchal clan system was developed into the feudal pattern from the classic form. Three major changes took place, integrating the imperial power with the patriarchal clan system more solidly, and making the system popular in folk.

The first change was an establishment and improvement of the autocratic centralization system in the country and an implementation of the system of prefectures and counties in regions. During the period of abolishment of the enfeoffment system by the First Emperor of Qin and the awarding of feudal lordships and kingships in the Han Dynasty, customs of living together with clan members were preserved and strengthened. It played a positive role in promoting urban development.

After the Spring and Autumn Period, the King of Zhou Dynasty gradually lost his authority, and ritual collapse became a common phenomenon. The patriarchal clan system, in a strict sense, began to decline. With states being in a great disorder during the Warring States Period, there appeared a few things, including the system of prefectures and counties, the system of military exploit, the system of bureaucracy, and the system of salary, especially appearance of "statute laws" and political reforms in some states, which had a great impact on the old patriarchal order. Except for throne succession, which was still in accordance the rule of inheritance to the eldest son, officials at all levels were appointed by a selection procedure rather than their relationships to the royal blood. The system of enfeoffment as the basis of the patriarchal clan system changed also. The Qin Dynasty vanished partly due to abolishing the enfeoffment. It generated chaos when Xiang Yu implemented enfeoffment. In the Early Han Dynasty, chaos took place as a result of the government abandoning state kings with non-Liu surnames and awarding those with Liu surnames. A conflict between enfeoffment and anti-enfeoffment and between unity and division was prominent. On the one hand, the central government wanted to expand imperial power infinitely. On the other, it extended the patriarchal clan pattern to local regions, even to remote and backward areas. Under Emperor Wu of the Han Dynasty, Confucianism, which was determined as the ruling thought at that time, was applied to laws. Confucian ethics such as ruler guiding subjects, father guiding sons, and husband guiding his wife, became the cornerstone of laws. In other words, patriarchal clan values became the spirit of official laws.

Even though the system of enfeoffment was almost abolished, the conflict between the imperial power and the separatist forces was long standing. In the Qin and Han Dynasties, clan power expanded continuously everywhere. Consequently, powerful landlords and clans emerged and generated conflicts with the central and local governments. Conflicts and struggles intensified gradually. The closely linked clan forces had positive effects on local economies, and at the same time became local evil forces that mutually reinforced and neutralized each other. A kind of urbanization and problems with local clans appeared therewith in the Qin and Han Dynasties. The potential division factors and forces represented by the system of enfeoffment continued to weaken. The basic feature of powerful landlords and local clans was that they lived together as a group. When wealth and power were accumulated, a relatively centralized residence was required, which was a benefit not only for management and clan development, but also for needed protection and maintenance. If the time spent living together was long enough, such as tens of years and even hundreds of years, this clan would grow quickly and attract other populations with different surnames to join, forming affiliated groups and resulting in complex social relations.

11.3 Integration of Urbanization and the Patriarchal Clan Society

The second change was the further integration of urbanization and clan development in the Qin and Han Dynasties. It was helpful to social stability and order, but could also be a factor of social unrest under certain conditions.

The common people in the Qin and Han Dynasties were confined to small spaces by the household registration system, which restricted their migration and movement. At the same time, due to low productive forces and economic interdependence, it was hard for people to flow, and the scale of movement was limited unless there was turmoil. Even then, towns and cities emerged in pre-Qin period. Towns can be traced back to the prehistoric stage, and most of them were military defensive fortresses with relatively centralized people (Qiu and Yao 2003). Cities, as political, military and economic centers, along with population aggregation, were often chosen as state capitals. Because of their position in transportation, cities played important roles in the annexation territory wars. When society became stable, a city's social functions were further developed. Linzi (the capital of Qi), Xianyang (the capital of Qin), and Jinan City (the capital of Chu) were all developed very well. Cities in the Han Dynasty developed further. In addition to the two large-scale imperial capitals in the east and west, a number of cities with concentrated population and political and military importance appeared in various regions. All cities held mixed functions of economy and defensive, equipped with walls, civil houses, and commercial facilities.

It was an important measure of control in the Western Han Dynasty to consolidate power by moving five large clans in Qi and Chu states, including Zhao, Qu, Jing, Huai, and Tian to the capital city. Ostensibly, the reason for moving them was that there was a shortage of population in the capital area. But more importantly, "in peace, they could guard against the northern ethnic minorities; and when vassal states revolt, they could be used to put down the revolt." (*Hou Han Shu: Biography of Diwu Lun*) These clans were the basis of the conquered states, lived in these regions from generation to generation, and had become powerful forces. Moving them to the capital city was actually a measure for better control. This measure became a constant national policy for later dynasties.

In the Qin and Han Dynasties, there appeared more clan organizations, and the clan relationships became a common phenomenon. In *Han Shu: Biography of Xiao He*, Liu Bang once told his ministers, "You individually followed me, some took two to three people to follow me, but Xiao He led tens of his clansmen, so I would not forget his contribution." Clan members lived together from generation to generation. Meanwhile, clans expanded and diversified. They lived in capitals, cities, and small towns. In the Eastern Han Dynasty, the manorial economy grew quickly. Lord manors were the epitomes of medium and small towns. The small ones were called castles or manors, the larger ones were called county towns, and the largest ones were called prefecture cities, vassal state capitals, and capitals.

In the Early Han Dynasty, the government adopted the policy of governing by doing nothing, and then the economy was recovered and local clans started expanding, which turned out to be a big social issue in the periods of Emperor Jing and Emperor Wu. Emperor Wu treated the local despotic clans poorly by appointing cruel officials, and made certain achievements. According to *Han Shu: List of Official*, at that time, it was stipulated that there were six tasks for feudal provincials. The first one was to investigate and deal with the despotic clans that occupied excessive lands and houses, bullied the weak, and maltreated the minorities. In *Shi Ji—Cruel Official: Biography of Zhi Du*, it is recorded, "Clan Jian in Ji'nan, with over three hundred households, was despotic, and officials under the level of prefecture chief could not handle." Again in *Han Shu: Biography of Zhao Guanghan*, at the end of the period of Emperor Zhao, Zhao Guanghan served as the mayor of the capital, and was then promoted to be the chief of Yingchuan. "The Clan Yuan and Clan Chu were arbitrary in Yingchuan, people there were suffering, and the former chief failed in treating them. Zhao Guanghan, a few months after his arriving, killed the chief criminals of those two clans, shocking the entire prefecture." There were a large number of cruel officials like Zhao Guanghan in the Western Han Dynasty, who effectively governed the local despotic clans.

At the end of the period ruled by Wang Mang, local clans became more unbridled. Actually, they were the rulers in their regions, coming from self-preservation to occupation in a region, and finally becoming rivaling warlords and establishing numerous separated kingdoms. In *Hou Han Shu: Biography of Feng Yi*, it is recorded, "Chi Mei and Yan Cen revolted, and large clans in these prefectures owned their own forces. Yan Cen settled in Lan Tian. They called themselves the generals, some owned soldiers of more than ten thousand, and some owned soldiers of several thousand." These of big and powerful clans in various regions constituted local forces with various sizes of arms. In order to obtain the support from clans, local officials had to accept the existing relationships and influences, which was necessary for their survivals. Xue Ying recorded in his *Praise of Emperor Guangwu*, "During the period ruled by Wang Mang, the entire state was in chaos, and many clans occupied lands and acted against the royalty." In dealing with the constantly changing chaos, it was not surprising that these clans established their own armed forces to protect themselves.

At that time, these large local powerful groups were all formed on the basis of clans. For instance, Wei Xiao's group in Hexi Prefecture was a typical alliance of powerful clans. It was recorded in *Houhansshu* that "Wei Xiao took the power … formed an alliance and stated: The alliance consisted of generals and lots of people, we would follow the rule of heaven and assist Clan Liu." These powerful clans, with a large population and land, were financially independent and self-sufficient, owning their own armed forces. Leaders and trusted followers usually lived in cities or central zones with defense structures. Between cities and rural areas, there were great walls and moats.

When the Eastern Han Dynasty reached social stability, the forces of powerful clans declined. Within a clan, families were all economically independent, but unequal. In some situation, there would be guests and writers serving the large clans. Guests in the Warring States and the Western Han period had subject-object relations with their hosts, so they could come and leave at their will. In the Eastern Han Dynasty, the relations gradually became adherent, and the same was true in relationships between clans. With increasing adherent relationships, the degree of freedom declined. Though the rich families did not have responsibilities and obligations to support the poor families, in order to strengthen internal cohesion and maintain the unity in a clan, the rich and powerful formed a kind of common practice in peacetime: supporting the poor clan members financially. In the Eastern Han Dynasty, the manor economy developed very well. Lord manors were the miniatures of the medium and small towns. The smaller ones were called the fortified manor houses or manors, the large ones were county towns, and the largest could be capital cities for a province, a kingdom, or even a country.

11.4 Unity of Thought and Clan Worship Ceremony

The third change was to respect Confucianism as the supreme religion. The ancestor worship rituals were strengthened and became stricter, extending the power of patriarchal system. The great unity in the Qin and Han Dynasties merged diverse cultures that existed in the pre-Qin period into one. With the system getting constructed and improved, a brand new and unified cultural community was formed.

Emperor Wu of the Han Dynasty established the superb status of Confucianism through setting the hall of enlightened rules, advocating rites and music, respecting education, and selecting officials based on their knowledge of Confucianism. Dong Zhongshu, on the basis of the relations between heaven and man and the thought of "noble and humble," established a branch of ethics of "three principles and five virtues." He standardized the relations between emperors and subjects, fathers and sons, and husbands and wives to the principle of yin and yang, stating that "subjects shall submit to their emperors," "sons shall submit to their fathers," and "wives shall submit to their husbands." These Confucian principles and ethics became the cornerstone of the law, and the patriarchal spirit was recognized and continued in law (Zhou and Qiu 2014). The powerful clans in the Eastern Han Dynasty were notable for their knowledge of Confucianism, or more precisely, confucianization. As a result, the notable families, powerful clans, and Confucianism were combined as a whole (Yu 1980).

Through the development in the Wei, Jin, Sui and Tang Dynasties, the patriarchal system entered into a new era in the Song Dynasty, updating genealogy, constructing ancestral halls, selecting clan heads, and setting clan disciplines became popular. Clan customs were expressed in the written form. Four rights (state power, clan power, divine power, and husband power) were combined. Its influence did not come to an end along with the ending of the feudal system. It has inextricable link with the Chinese worldly wisdom and has become an obstacle in current modernization. In the Ming and Qing Dynasties, the state gradually abolished restrictions on building ancestral halls and worshipping ancestors. Then ordinary clans rapidly grew up, being the basic organizations in civil society, and developing into a civilian and popular system.

As we all know, it is regarded as a general trend for human civilization for social organizations to shift from blood relationships to geographical relationships. The Greeks, who engaged in business activities in early times, gradually got rid of the consanguineous bond of clans, and replaced the patriarchal clan organizations based on blood relationship by the polis organizations based on geographical relationships and property relationships. Toynbee once pointed out that the consanguineous bond of ancient Greeks rapidly disintegrated due to frequent migration and the blood relationship being replaced by the contractual relationship (Gu 1982). China, a country based on agriculture, maintained the custom and tradition of living by clans for long time. Its disintegration of consanguineous bond was insufficient, making the clan system last for several thousands of years. In the Qin and Han Dynasties, the clan system was consolidated and developed. The impact on Chinese traditional society was not only on throne hereditary in the political system, resulting in the forming of the "Family-Governed Monarchic Country" in the feudal society, but also as an institution and concept it permeated into all fields of the society, forming an ethical culture characterized by distinctive oriental features.

Clan culture is a kind of conventional folk culture experience that spans thousands of years. It is inherited among clansmen and recorded by words, and some is engraved on people's minds. This is a unique aspect of Chinese traditional cultures, Confucianism and the feudal ethical culture, which complement each other. With the development of urbanization, the rural population continuously migrated to cities. Ancestral halls gradually got out of people's sight. Some were shabby and some collapsed from years of lack of repair. In ancient China, clans were connected by blood relationships, people living together with their clan, and building ancestral halls and family temples. Clan activities were the concrete reflection of the clan culture.

Very often, clan members came together to participate in activities aiming to strengthen their sense of identity and belonging to the clan, deepening the relationships among clansman. One of the most important clan activities is the worship ceremony. Worshiping ancestors has been an activity for the Chinese throughout the ages, and it is sacred and solemn. For people in the same clan, it is not only an activity with a significance linked to traditional education, but also a kind of means to maintain the clan and strengthen connections among clansmen.

One of the original functions of the clan is the use of clan property to support poor families and fund their children's education. But this function was not carried out well due to many reasons. In a modern society, the state power expands to rural areas, breaking the closed natural society and replacing most functions run by the clan. When the state tries to replace traditional clan organizations with regional administrative organizations to manage the society, the power and status of a clan is weakened. Not all of the vestiges left by the clan system have vanished, including living patterns, ideological forms, and clan culture. Urbanization generated a great challenge to the tradition of living together with a clan. People gradually changed their custom of living together in the past thousands of years, disaffiliated from rural villages and native clans linked by blood relationships, and integrated into a modern community linked by geographical relationships.

Influences of the patriarchal system on Chinese laws are various, both positive and negative. The positive influences include the state attaching importance to the role of the law enforcement and obedience in the social primary-level organizations of families and clans; focusing on playing the role of intermediation functions, which embodies the combination of principle and flexibility and the combination of rationality and legality and through which a large number of disputes are settled by the intermediation of relatives, friends, acquaintances and primary-level organizations, reducing the pressure of judiciary authorities and saving the litigation cost; focusing on displaying the exemplary function of the person in power and the elder in obeying laws, which is good for the formation of an atmosphere of law. The negative influences include that the patriarchal social class combines with the privilege, which makes the law have class distinctions and violate the principle that all people are equal before the law. The clan has power that surpasses the law to its members and even has the power to resist the law, influencing the law enforcement processes and procedures. For handling internal affairs within a clan, people depend on the judgment of the clan, not the official courts and laws, influencing the justice, prestige and dignity of the law. In the patriarchal society, rights and obligations are just on one side. The young and the inferior people have to obey the elder and the superior ones and have no rights. It generated servile personalities among officials and the public. Under the circumstances, the spirit of civil rights was hard to develop.

For more than a hundred years, during the modernization process in China, clans have been obstinately defiant in the remote and backward areas. Expansion of the state power in rural villages has broken the closed society, and replaced most functions of clan organizations. Under the impact of urbanization, traditions have experienced severe challenge.

11.5 Conclusions

Ancient Chinese society was a clan society. Urban development and local clan society growth were linked to each other. In the Qin and Han Dynasties, the patriarchal system experienced a transition from a classical form to a feudal form and experienced three major changes. The autocratic monarchy system in ancient China was established on the basis of the clan system, and both supported each other. In that society, family and country shared the same structure. Although ancient China was a class society, it was mainly maintained by patriarchal clans.

References in Chinese

Gu, Z. 1982. *Xila chengbang zhidu [Greek polis regime].* Beijing: Zhongguo Shehui Kexue Chubanshe.

Qiu, S.J., and Y.B. Yao. 2003. *Zhongguo shiqian chengzhi de fenbu jiqi gongneng fenxi* [Analysis on the Distribution and the Function about the Site of Prehistoric City in China]. *Zhongguo Lishi Dili Luncong* 18(1): 100–106.

Yu, Y.S. 1980. *Zhoongguo zhishi jieceng shilun* [*History of Chinese intellectuals*]. Taibei:Taiwan Lian Jing Chuban Shiye Gongsi.

Zhou, X.G., & Qiu, S.J. (2014). *Zhongguo chuantong wenhuashi* [*History of Chinese traditional culture*]. Hefei: Anhui Daxue Chubanshe.

Chapter 12
Farewell to Villages: Forced Urbanization in Rural China

Youqin Huang

Abstract With rapid urbanization in China, settlement patterns are changing dramatically. While there is a large body of research on changes in Chinese cities, we know relatively little about the countryside despite the profound transformation that is taking place in rural China. At the turn of the 21st century, the traditional rural Chinese settlement—natural villages—are being systematically demolished, and villagers are being resettled into apartments and urban communities at an astonishing scale and speed. Unprecedented forced urbanization with profound socioeconomic and spatial transformation is taking place in much of rural China. This chapter aims to understand the dynamics and impact of the rapid urbanization of rural China by taking rural Jiangsu Province as a case study. The author argues that local governments' thirst for more construction land for economic development under the strict land use management system and land-based revenue system is the root cause for this forced urbanization in rural China, which is further driven by the central government's call for developing the socialist new countryside. While villagers may benefit from the improved housing conditions, they suffer serious social and economic consequences. This forced urbanization is especially detrimental to the elderly and the poor, which overshadows the campaign for a modern countryside and a harmonious society.

Keywords Land development · Urbanization · Resettlement housing · Displacement · China

12.1 Introduction

Leading the "second wave" of urbanization in developing countries, China is in the midst of an urban revolution of unprecedented speed and scale. In 2011, for the first time in history, more than 50% of the Chinese people live in cities (NBS 2011).

Y. Huang (✉)
University at Albany, State University of New York, Albany, USA
e-mail: yhuang@albany.edu

Z. Tang (ed.), *China's Urbanization and Socioeconomic Impact*,
DOI 10.1007/978-981-10-4831-9_12

In its New Urbanization Plan unvailed in 2014, China aims to move 250 million villagers to cities by 2025, with 70% of the population living in cities (Johnson 2013). While driving the dazzling economic growth, urbanization in China has also resulted in profound changes in settlement patterns and caused many social problems, such as displacement and discontent. There has been a large body of literature on urbanization, migration, and their impact on people and places in China (e.g. Chan 1994; Ma 2002; Wu and Ma 2006; Zhu 2007; Fan 2008; Hsing 2010). However, most existing studies focus on cities and (sub)urban population (including voluntary rural-to-urban migrants), while we know little about the impact of forced urbanization on the rural population and the countryside. This chapter aims to study forced urbanization in the countryside and its impact on villagers and the rural settlement.

Thirty years after the implementation of the Household Responsibility System (HRS), a second wave of rural reform is taking place in China with much more profound social, economic and spatial impact. The most visible change is the profound transformation in rural settlement patterns: the thousand-year old settlement of natural villages is disappearing rapidly. In 2000, there were 3.7 million villages in China. By 2010, there were only 2.6 million villages, a loss of about 300 villages a day (Johnson 2014). Traditional villages with one- or two-story farmhouses are being demolished systematically and replaced with planned communities with multi-story apartment buildings and high-rises—the so-called "villager apartments" (*nong ming gong yu*) (see Photo 12.1). Zhuchen city (Shangdong Province) became the first city in China that has fully gotten rid of villages, with 208 planned communities replacing 1249 villages (Deng 2010). By 2011, there are 27 provinces and regions that are experimenting different versions of moving villagers into planned communities (CBLR 2010; Wang et al. 2010; MLR 2011). This campaign is conventionally called "Villagers Concentrated Living" (hereafter VCL). A wave of forced urbanization and massive displacement is taking place in the Chinese countryside. Despite its astonishing scale and speed and significant impact on the settlement and lifestyle in the countryside, we know very little about VCL.

Photo 12.1 Villagers' traditional homes (*left*) in Jiangsu Province are being demolished to be replaced with "villager apartments" (*right*) (Photo by the author)

Displacement, resettlement and consequent conflicts between households and developers/local governments have been seen all over China in the last three decades. Yet, existing literature focuses mainly on displacement in cities and suburbs where households are affected by urban renewal and urban expansion (For example, Guo 2001; Hsing 2006a; Ho and Lin 2003). The massive scale of resettlement and land loss in the countryside has not really gained much attention. This paper focuses on displacement in the countryside during forced urbanization, and aims to understand its socioeconomic and political drives and impact.

The world has witnessed the dazzling economic growth in China in recent decades. One of the consequences is the massive loss of arable land. The amount of farmland declined steadily at a rate of 8.5 million *mu* per year during 1982–1986, and reduced from 130 million ha in 1996 to 122 million ha in 2005 (Wang et al. 2009).[1] Concerned about food security, the Chinese government set up the "red-line" target of maintaining at least 1.8 billion *mu* of arable land, and established a centralized land management system (Wang et al. 2009). As a result, local governments are severely constrained in converting arable land into construction land for non-agricultural use. Yet the Ministry of Land and Resources (MLR) allows a "dynamic linkage" between the increase of construction land in urban areas and the decline of construction land in the countryside (MLR 1999, 2005). In other words, if local governments can reduce the use of construction land or increase the amount of arable in the countryside, they can increase the quotas for construction land in urban areas. Thus the land development rights in the countryside can be transferred to urban and suburban regions.

Facing the development bottleneck due to the lack of available land, local governments have adopted various strategies to increase the quota for construction land. For example, in Jiangsu Province and Chengdu City, Sichuan Province, the principle of "three concentrations" (*sange jizhong*) has been promoted, which refers to the concentration of industries in industrial parks, the concentration of agriculture in large scale farms, and the concentration of villagers in towns and rural new communities. Among the "three concentrations," "the concentration of villagers" is the focus of many local governments due to the potential of saving massive amounts of construction land. Nationwide, rural residential land accounts for 51% of all construction land in China, and the per capita construction land in rural areas is 229 m^2, much higher than that in urban areas (MLR 2011). Thus by moving villagers into farmer apartments, a massive amount of construction land can be saved for other purposes. In cities such as Tianjin, Beijing and Jiaxin, local governments are experimenting with the practice of "*zhai ji di huan fang*," which means villagers can use their residential land—"*zhai ji di*" to exchange for apartments in towns. As a result of these initiatives, a massive number of villages in China have been demolished, and villagers are being systematically resettled into farmer apartments. Thus, in much of the countryside in China, the traditional rural village settlement has become history.

[1]"Mu" is a measure commonly used in China. 1 mu is 1/15 ha.

To better understand dynamics and the impact of this profound transformation in rural China, this chapter will conduct a case study of Southern Jiangsu province, focusing on Wuxi municipality, which includes Wuxi city, Jiangyin city and Yixing city. The per capita arable land in this region is only 0.55 *mu*, the lowest among 13 prefectural level cities in Jiangsu. Yet, it is one of the most developed regions in the nation, and is known for its prosperous Township Village Enterprises (TVEs) and rapid urbanization. With 0.05% of the national land, Wuxi produces 1.7% of national GDP and 1.3% of national revenue (Editorial Committee 2007). As a result, the already very limited arable land in this densely populated region has been decreasing at an alarming rate, with an annual rate of 11,405 ha during 1990–2006 (Liu et al. 2010). Thus preserving arable land on the one hand and providing more land for economic development on the other hand have becoming the topmost concerns of local governments. As a solution, the principle of "three concentrations" was originated in this region, and it has been implemented throughout this region. It has been so "successful" that "three concentrations" is being implemented in the rest of Jiangsu Province and in many other provinces, which justifies a close examination of the Southern Jiangsu Province.

Information for this chapter was collected through both archival research and fieldwork conducted on multiple trips during 2006–2015 with field observations and interviews of both villagers and local government officials. In the following sections, I will first trace the origin of "three concentrations" in Jiangsu Province. While the concentrations of industries and agriculture deserve the attention of another paper, this paper focuses on VCL, aiming to understand its political-economic dynamics, the compensation policy, and its impact. The chapter concludes with some reflections.

12.2 The Xinqiao Model and the Campaign of "Three Concentrations"

Xinqiao Town is located in the southeast of Jiangyin municipality with less than 45,000 people living in 10 village committees and 4 residents' committees (XTG 2007a). It is known for textile industries, hosting two of the top-ten textile corporations in the world. With the rapid industrial development and limited land resources, the town government has always tried hard to increase the intensity of land use. In 2001, with the help of professional planners, the town territory was divided into three functional zones: industrial park, ecological agriculture district, and residential and commercial district. For the first time, the Xinqiao town government raised the concept of "three concentrations," aiming to move all factories into the industrial park, agriculture into the ecological district for large scale farming, and villagers into the residential and commercial district (a.k.a. VCL). By 2006, more than 99% of its industrial output came out of the industrial park, 82% of agricultural land was for large scale horticulture, and 70% of the town population lived in urban communities in the town buildup area (XTG 2007a). Since factories were relatively concentrated to begin with, VCL became the most important way to save land. The land for villagers' housing decreased from 0.72 to 0.25 *mu* per household (XTG 2007b). By the end of 2008, the village committee system was abolished and all villagers have been resettled to towns, which saved 3000 *mu* land for housing. This is considered by Xinqiao town government an enormous achievement, and Xinqiao has since made great economic achievements.

The "Xinqiao Model" offers a welcomed solution to desperate local governments in Jiangsu province, and "Three Concentrations" has been adopted everywhere including Wuxi municipality. First of all, factories are encouraged to move into or set up in industrial parks (WMGO 2005). By the end of 2006, there were 64 industrial parks in Wuxi municipality with 16,240 enterprises, which accounted for more than 75% of total industrial output (WBTVEM 2007). At the same time, multi-story factory buildings have been encouraged by giving out various financial incentives (Editorial Committee 2007).

Secondly, small plots of farm land that are collectively owned but managed by individual families under the Household Responsibility System (HRS) are "circulated" (*liu zhuan*) to specialized households and companies for large scale farming, while landless villagers are provided a basic social security system (JPG 2005). With rapid industrialization and expensive farming inputs, many households in this region have moved away from farming, and a large amount of land often lies fallow. Thus concentrating small plots of land from individual households into the hands of specialized households and companies for large-scale farming becomes the obvious solution. By the end of 2006, 53% of the farm land in Wuxi municipality was operated with "descent scale," and the goal was to reach 80% by 2010 (WMGO 2005).

Thirdly, with VCL, villages with detached or semi-detached houses are being demolished, and villagers are being resettled into apartment buildings. At the beginning, only five types of natural villages were to be demolished: villages affected by construction projects, villages within industrial parks, villages with a small number of households, villages with poor infrastructure, and villages with high degrees of urbanization (WVCLO 2005). Later, more villages became subject to demolishment, and many local governments aim to demolish all villages with 3000 or fewer people. In addition, farmer apartment buildings are being built in increasingly higher density. In general, they are 6-story walk-up buildings. In 2005, the district government in Wuxi New District required that all farmer apartment buildings have to be 12+ story high. In Wuxi, more than 35 million km^2 of farmer apartments have been built within five years, which saved more than 100,000 *mu* land (EC 2007). In Jiangsu province, VCL can potentially save 4 million *mu* of land (Chang 2006).

Acknowledging the intertwinement of the "three concentrations," this paper focuses on VCL as it is the most important method to "save" land, and its implementation has met the most resistance from villagers. After starting with a relatively small scale and mostly related to development projects, VCL has entered a new stage with unprecedented speed and scale since 2005. For example, in Wuxi municipality, 721 natural villages were demolished and more than 14,000 households were displaced and resettled in 2006 alone (WVCLO 2006a). The astonishing scale and speed of VCL also makes it deserve a scrutiny.

12.3 Villagers Concentrated Living (VCL): A Government-Led Land-Based Political Campaign

Despite its economic rational, I argue that VCL is mainly a government-led land-based political campaign. The massive scale, the unprecedented speed, and the revolutionary zeal associated with the VCL all point to a Great Leap Forward style political campaign by the government. While different levels of governments have played different roles and have different rationales, they have all helped to drive VCL.

12.3.1 The Central Government: Policy Encouragement

The central government has played a very important role by setting up the policy environment that guides and encourages VCL. First of all, starting from the late 1990s, the central government has issued policies that set up strict land use quotas. For example, to control the loss of farmland for urban development, the central government strengthened its regulatory authority in land management through the 1998 Land Administrative Law and consequent instruments including the Land Use Master Plan and Annual Land Use Plan (Wang et al. 2010). These two plans set long-term and annual regulations, respectively, on the quantity and distribution of farmland in a locality that is allowed to be converted to construction land. All levels of local governments have to follow these plans, and the conversion of farmland into construction land is strictly regulated through various quantitative targets (Wang et al. 2010). Meanwhile, the central government allows the transfer of land development rights. It initiated the concept of a "dynamic linkage between the increase of urban construction land and the decrease of rural construction land," which was formalized in 2004 by the State Council (No. 28), and further formalized and detailed by MLR in 2005 and the State Council in 2008 (No. 138). While the central government aims to improve the efficiency of land use, this concept of "dynamic linkage" has been mistakenly understood by local governments as a permission to massively demolish villages and grab the land in rural areas for urban development. Thus, it has been utilized by local governments as a fundamental strategy to solve the dilemma of the lack of construction land for rapid urban development, and consequently a direct cause for VCL.

Secondly, the central government initiated the campaign of "developing socialist new countryside" in 2005, which indirectly encouraged VCL. In its 11th Five-year Plan, "developing socialist new countryside" was considered the major historic task in the nation's modernization. One of the principles for "developing socialist new countryside" is "neat villages" (*cunrong zhengjie*), which encourages local governments to significantly improve the physical conditions of villages and upgrade rural infrastructure.[2] While there was no call for demolition and reconstruction of entire villages from the central government, local governments have recently considered VCL a legitimate shortcut to "develop the socialist new countryside" with brand new housing and planned neighborhoods replacing entire villages.

Thirdly, in recent years, as China experiences an economic slowdown—so-called "new normal," the central government aims to accelerate urbanization to drive economic growth and eventually achieve modernization. Prime Minister Li Keqiang argued in 2012 that urbanization has the greatest potential for boosting domestic demand, with rural residents increasing their consumption as they become urban dwellers, thus a "huge engine" of China's future economic growth. This would also facilitate China's economic restructuring from an export oriented economy to a domestic consumption based economy. Despite massive rural-to-urban migration every year, the natural process of urbanization is apparently not fast enough to the government. In 2014, the central government unveiled a National New-type Urbanization Plan (2014–2020), the first of its kind, to accelerate urbanization, aiming to have 60% of its population living in cities/towns by 2020 (Xinhuanet 2014).

Finally, the central government has directly encouraged VCL to achieve economic and intensive land use. In 2004, MLR required local governments to guide villagers' housing construction with plans, and gradually but systematically move villagers to small towns and central villages (MLR 2004). It also suggested local governments to build farmer apartment complexes. This document clearly laid-out the blueprint for VCL, and has resulted in massive demolishment of natural villages and construction of urban-like communities in the countryside. Together with the formalization of the dynamic linkage between urban and rural construction land in 2004/2005, this document contributed to the fact that the year of 2005 is a major turning point toward massive demolishment and resettlement. In 2008, State Council issued another document promoting economic and intensive land use, which further encouraged VCL (State Council 2008a, b).[3]

12.3.2 Local Governments: Economic and Political Drives

While the central government is interested in macro-goals such as preserving arable land and developing the socialist new countryside, local governments have more direct political and economic interests at stake, which motivates them to actively

[2]This was also included in National Committee of Development and Reform (NCDR), 2006.

[3]According to State Council, land unused within 2 years will be taken back with no compensation, land unused within 1 year will be charged 20% of the land transaction fee as land fallow fee.

promote VCL. Due to fiscal reform in 1994, local governments are entitled to an increasingly small share of tax income while they shoulder an increasingly larger fiscal responsibility for public services (Tsui and Wang 2004; Lin and Yi 2011; Huang 2012). Thus, most local governments face severe fiscal pressure. As the *de factor* owner of urban land and the only expropriator to convert rural land to urban land, local governments have depended on land-related revenue such as land conveyance fees to meet their budgetary needs (Xu et al. 2009; Lin 2009, 2010; Hsing 2010). Thus local governments have strong financial incentives to promote VCL, which can save massive amount of construction land and potentially can bring massive land conveyance fees. In addition, the construction land saved through VCL would fuel economic growth, which further leads to higher revenues for local governments through various taxes. Furthermore, the performance evaluation system for government officials encourages local governments to focus on the short-term goals that are easy to see and measure (Huang 2012). VCL completely revamps the countryside with brand new housing and orderly neighborhoods, which is considered an obvious achievement towards a "socialist new countryside." Thus both economically and politically, local governments are motivated to promote VCL.

Not surprisingly, once given the green light by the central government, local governments acted swiftly to implement VCL. In November 2005, one month after the central government raised the concept of "developing socialist new countryside," Jiangsu Provincial Government demanded lower level governments to promote "three concentrations" actively and steadily, and listed VCL as the important direction for village development (Chang 2006). Three months later, the Jiangsu Province Town and Village Distribution Plan was completed, which aimed to replace about 250,000 natural villages in Jiangsu with 40,000 planned communities in the next 20–25 years (Chang 2006). In addition, the provincial government designated 10 towns as "experiment towns" to further study and promote "three concentrations," and offered specific guidance for VCL housing, such as its development and pricing (JBC 2006; JBP 2007).[4]

Compared to the provincial government, municipal and town governments are more instrumental in VCL, with the former as the architect, setting up policies and goals, and the latter as the operator engaging in actual demolishment and resettlement.

First of all, specific government agencies are set up to work on VCL. For example, in Wuxi, the Villagers Concentrated Living Office (WVCLO) was set up in 2005 and headed by directors and vice-directors of various departments in the Wuxi municipal government (WVCLO 2005).[5] Its main responsibility is to draft

[4]If VCL housing is built by the local government, no profit should be made; if it is built by developers, profit should not be more than 3%.

[5]WVCLO is headed by the director of Wuxi Bureau of Construction (WBC), together with vice-directors of WBC, Municipal Development and Reform Committee, Bureau of Financial Affair, Bureau of Civil Affair, Planning Bureau, and Land Bureau in Wuxi.

policies, direct and coordinate, organize and promote, evaluate and monitor work related to VCL. Corresponding organizations are established in subunits under its jurisdiction, such as Jiangyin City, Yixin City and four suburban districts in Wuxi.[6] At the town level, Office of Demolishment and Resettlement (*chai qian ban*) is established to carry out the actual demolishment and resettlement. Thus a three-level administrative organization (municipality, city/district, and town) specifically for VCL was established in Wuxi, which makes it possible to implement VCL effectively and efficiently.

Secondly, municipal governments set up clear annual goals and tasks related to VCL for lower level governments. For example, in its 2005 work plan, WVCLO aimed to move 1/6 of villagers into new communities during 2005–2007, and another 1/3 during 2008–2010 (WVCLO 2005). Lower level governments further establish their own goals. At the end of each year, local governments have to report their performance of annual goals and tasks, and it gives them a great sense of achievement when they accomplished more than 100% of the annual task for that year (JMG 2006).[7]

Third, a comprehensive evaluation system is established to evaluate and monitor local governments' performance in VCL. For example, in Wuxi municipality, WVCLO conducts a comprehensive evaluation of each city twice a year, and inspects lower-level VCL offices' work at least once per quarter (WVCLO 2006b). WVCLO also requires lower level VCL offices have a meeting every month, and report monthly statistics and summaries which will be publicized to foster peer pressure and a sense of urgency (WVCLO 2005). In addition, every quarter, a work plan meeting is called by the Vice-Mayor who is in charge of VCL, which provides a summary and analysis of the work done by then, and lays out the work for the next phase. "Rate of concentration," measured by the percentage of villagers who live in farmer apartments, is used as an overall indicator for the performance of local governments in VCL.

Since village leaders are appointed by the town government, not surprisingly they are more likely to carry out policies from town governments than representing villagers' interests. In general they do very little on behalf of villagers except distribute compensations and allocate new housing among villagers. They also act as a middleman between villagers and the Office of Demolishment and Resettlement especially when there are "nail households" (*ding zi hu*) who are not happy with the resettlement scheme and refuse to move.

In contrast to the official slogan that VCL is "driven by the market" (WVCLO 2006b), most local governments suffer huge deficits due to VCL. In addition to compensating villagers, local governments need to pay for the development of farmer apartments, the land for farmer apartment development and related

[6]They are Binhu District, Wuxi New District, Xishan District and Huishan District.

[7]For example, in the annual work summary for 2006 by JMG, it claimed Jiangyin has accomplished 133% of the goal by demolishing 120 villages, resettling 6650 households, completing farmer apartments 1,615,000 m^2, and saving land 4320.38 mu.

infrastructure. Yet, villager apartments are heavily subsidized, and local governments are not allowed to make profits (Jiangsu Bureau of Price 2007, No. 265). For example, in Shenggang Town, the local government has to pay on average a net payment of 800,000 yuan for each displaced household,[8] which has imposed huge financial burden on the local government. In theory, the local government would profit from leasing the construction land saved through VCL, and land conveyance fees should have increased significantly over time.[9] Yet, there may not be investors available right away, and the profit from land leasing has to be shared between different levels of the government (Zhu and Qu 2006; Interview).[10] Furthermore, the saved construction land is often used for public infrastructures, which won't result in direct financial gains for the local government. Not surprising, most local governments, especially town governments, are in huge fiscal deficit due to VCL. They often ask different government agencies and even local entrepreneurs to share the bill.[11] Households in the same village are often resettled in batches, and many of them have to live in temporary housing for years because their new apartments have not been built yet due to local governments' fiscal deficit. In some cases, developers have completed apartments but refuse to turn the keys over to the government as the latter has not paid them yet.

So given the huge financial burden, why are local governments still so enthusiastic about VCL? One representative of the People's Congress in Jiangyin city summarized in two words: "*zheng ji*" (political achievement).[12] In addition to the thirst for construction land, VCL has been implemented as a measure for political achievement of local governments. Not surprisingly, VCL has been promoted with zeal in Jiangsu province to pursue impressive scale and speed, regardless local conditions and villagers' objections. Started as a land use strategy, VCL has evolved into a government-led campaign that is more political than economic.

---

[8]Interview. Shenggang is a typical town in Southern Jiangsu province with about two thirds of its economy in industry and about one third in service. More than a quarter of all local households were resettled during 2005–2006, and about 50% of all population lived in villager apartments. According to its town planning completed in 2007, only 3 out of 10 administrative villages will be kept, and the rest will be demolished (JPI 2007).

[9]Interview. For example, in Shenggang town, the land conveyance fee increased from less than 200,000 yuan/mu in 2006 to 1–2 million yuan/mu in 2010.

[10]According to my interview, 60% of the profit belongs to the town government, 20% to the municipal government, and another 20% to the provincial government. According to a study in another city in Jiangsu Province, more than 56% of gains from development goes to municipal government, 14% goes to village collective, 26% for villagers, and 1.55% for central government, 1.2% for provincial government (Zhu and Qu 2006).

[11]For example, in one village, half of the village has already been resettled, while households living along the river have not. Villagers have been told about the plan of widening the river for more than three years, yet, the project has not started. It appears there is a disagreement between the town government and the Municipal Bureau of Water and Irrigation regarding who should pay for the resettlement.

[12]Interview.

12.4 Displacement, Discontent and Differentiated Responses

With VCL heavily promoted by both the central and local governments (although for different reasons), millions of villagers have been displaced nationwide, although the actual number is hard to come by. It was estimated that up to 88 million villagers have become landless (Sargeson 2013). While there is a national push for this forced urbanization, it may be more appropriate for more developed rural areas than less developed areas (Rosenberg 2013). Discontents have been widespread in rural China, with numerous protests and even suicides and self-immolations (Johnson 2013). Meanwhile, villagers are active agents, often trying to maximize their interests within the framework set up by the government. "Rightful resistance," a term coined by O'Brien and Li (2006), is used to refer to villagers' resistance to defend rights they had already been granted, or rights they believed could be derived from the regime's policies, laws, principles, and legitimate ideology. Yet, this forced urbanization and displacement has had different impacts on villagers.

12.4.1 The Compensation: A Sunshine Policy?

Unfair compensation for displaced households has been a main reason for conflicts between displaced households and developers/local governments (Hsing 2010). In rural areas, land expropriation has become the top source of state-society conflict, accounting for about 65% of "mass incidents" in the countryside each year (Sargeson 2013; Yu 2010). Despite massive displacement in rural areas, we know relatively little about the compensation plan and how villagers respond to it.

Officials in Jiangsu Province consider their compensation scheme a "sunshine policy," which offers generous compensations to displaced villagers. While the compensation scheme in rural Jiangsu has been improved over time, it is still far from fair compensation.

Before 2005, the compensation scheme was based on household size. For example, in Wuxi, displaced households could purchase 35 m^2 of subsidized housing for every person in the household.[13] Households could buy larger apartments but had to pay market prices for additional floor space. This was a simple but very crude compensation method as it did not consider the conditions of villagers' existing housing. In this region, most villagers had large and decent houses that could not be fully compensated with this method; thus the demolishment had met much resistance from villagers. "Nail households" and protests were common.

---

[13]Interview. The price was 350 yuan/m^2 in Wuxi.

The year of 2005 marks a major dividing point in compensation, as the compensation method was changed to the so-called "house for apartment" that year. This means in principle that the compensation allows villagers to purchase apartments similar to the size of their original houses. For villagers who live in houses of 250 m^2 or smaller, they can buy apartments of the same size at the subsidized price (JMBC 2005a).[14] For those with larger houses, they can buy an apartment of 250 m^2 at subsidized price, and they will receive monetary compensation for their floor space exceeding 250 m^2 with a price of the difference between the market and subsidized price.

Households are also compensated for their housing conditions. A "Convenience Booklet" is distributed to villagers, with detailed compensation fees for every possible item in and around the house (JMBC 2005a).[15] A third-party assessment company is hired by the local government to give independent assessment for villagers' houses, and villagers have to sign on the assessment report before their houses can be demolished (JMG 2005). In addition, villagers receive subsidies for moving and renting temporary housing while waiting for resettlement housing (JMBC 2005b).[16] Thus compared to the pre-2005 compensation method, the post-2005 compensation scheme is much more sensitive to the existing housing conditions and related costs during relocation. My interview with villagers shows that most of them are quite happy with this method.

While labeled as "sunshine policy" by officials and welcomed by most villagers, this compensation method is still far from being fair, with two central issues remaining unmentioned. First of all, the existing compensation focuses on houses while villagers' land ownership and rights are not compensated. There are mainly two kinds of land that are affected in this process: (1) the residential land that villagers' houses are built upon (*zhai ji di*) and (2) small plots of family land in the village that is often used to grow vegetables (*zi liu di*). Started as private land, "*zhai ji di*" was converted into collectively owned land in 1962, and each household is entitled to a plot for housing construction (Luo 2007). In 1990, a "use right deed for rural collective construction land" was issued to villagers, which legally acknowledged their property rights for "*zhai ji di.*" Yet, "*zhai ji di*" was not compensated at all in this campaign. The official position is "*zhai ji di* exchange," meaning town governments use land for farmer apartments to exchange for "*zhai ji*

[14]For example, in Jiangyin, the subsidized price for resettlement housing was 550 yuan/ m^2 in 2005, which was about one third of the market price (JMBC 2005C).

[15]For example, floors, ceilings, walls, doors, windows, built-in furniture, bathroom and kitchen facilities, lights and faucets, flower bed, fence, wells, and trees/bushes. There are also different prices for the same item that is made of different materials.

[16]Each household receives 600 yuan as moving subsidies. If the resettlement housing has not been completed, each household receives 3 yuan/m^2 per month for the qualified amount of floor space of its demolished housing for up to 12 months. If the waiting period exceeds 12 months, the compensation rate is 6 yuan/m^2 per month. Households may also receive 200 yuan per day for up to 60 days if they sign the resettlement contract before the deadline, or 15–50 yuan/m^2 if they complete their move before the deadline.

di" in villages; thus there is no need to pay. Yet, with high density apartment buildings in resettlement communities, the residential land for farmer apartments is much smaller than "*zhai ji di*" in villages. While in some places the land for farmer apartments is still collectively owned, although smaller, in other places such as Jiangyin city, the land under farmer apartments is urban land, which means villagers no longer have collective ownership of it.[17] The same is true for "*zi liu di.*" During the resettlement, villagers receive compensations only for large plants such as trees/bushes on "*zi liu di*" while receive nothing for the land itself. Thus, through VCL, town governments are able to access "*zhai ji di*" and "*zi liu di*" in villages without compensating villagers for their land.

Secondly, villagers' life style has forever changed because of VCL, and their future livelihood is not considered in this compensation method. When living in villages, many households can maintain a somewhat self-sufficient lifestyle by growing grains on their farm land, growing vegetables on "*zi liu di,*" raising pigs/chickens for meat or cash, and using rivers/wells for water. After resettlement, they need to pay for not only things they did not need to pay for before, such as vegetables and water, but also new services such as property management and gas for fuel. While farm land is taken away for large scale farming, alternative employment for villagers is not provided, causing high unemployment rate among villagers and lower income for many households. For households without stable non-farming income, even supporting daily living can be difficult. This is especially the case for older villagers who can no longer find employment in industries and services.

In addition to financial losses, psychological consequences due to dramatic changes in life style and possible lower standard of living are not considered in this compensation scheme. Many households have to live in temporary housing with poor conditions for years while waiting for resettlement housing. It is also common that extended families that used to live next door have to split as they are often resettled into different housing projects. The displacement is especially difficult for the elderly, as most rural landlords refuse to lease housing to them for fear of possible death in their houses.[18] Living in apartment buildings without elevators imposes another challenge to the elderly. Thus the displacement has created tremendous stress on the elderly, who often have to live alone, away from their adult children, and live in very poor and unstable housing conditions.

Despite improvement, the existing compensation is far from a fair one, which focuses on housing only while ignores villagers' land rights and other costs due to this forced urbanization.

---

[17]In places where the land is still collectively owned, households are constrained to sell their apartments, while in places where the land is urban land, villagers receive the deed for both housing and land such that they can sell their farmer apartments on the market with no constraints.

[18]Having someone die in the house is often considered a bad luck, due to superstition.

12.4.2 Villagers' Differentiated Responses: Passive and Active Agents

Public participation in decision-making is rare in rural China, and Chinese villagers have been conventionally considered to be passive, docile and to accept their fate no matter how unfavorable it is. There is no exception in VCL. Most villagers tend to obey the local government's decisions and passively accept their compensation and resettlement. Yet, within this generally passive framework, they also act as active and calculative agents, adopting various strategies to maximize their compensation.

Village XHT in Shenggang Town is located about two miles south of the town center, with one third of the village demolished and the rest to be demolished. A widow in her 50s lives with her four adult sons. When I asked whether her family wished to be resettled, she responded with an ironic smile.

> Wish to be resettled or not? It does not matter at all. I cannot act against (the country). If the country wants you to resettle, you have to move. There is no other way. What good can there be if you act against the country?… I do not see any benefit from living in apartments.

This shows villagers tend to be passive followers of the government, with blind patriotism, despite their objection to the resettlement. The town government represents the state and the central government in villages. Thus for villagers, the town government has unchallenged authority over their lives and properties such that they do not even question the legitimacy of its policies and actions. At the same time, they are fully aware of their vulnerable status in relation to the state machinery and potential consequences if they act against the government.

Yet, villagers also act as active agents to maximize their compensation by adopting various strategies. For example, after learning about the new compensation scheme that is mainly based on the size and condition of their existing houses, they rushed to build additional houses and remodel existing houses with cheap materials to increase compensation. For example, while the mother claimed "I cannot act against [the country]" (see above), her adult sons added an addition to their existing two-story house, and divided the addition into 3-story instead of two-story (with the same building height) to maximize the floor space. In addition, they planted hundreds of small trees in high density on their "*zi liu di*" in front of their house which is used to grow vegetables, as compensation is paid for trees but not vegetables. These strategies—building new houses, upgrading housing conditions, and planting trees—were so popular among villagers such that later the government forbade villagers to do so.

Protest, either collectively or individually, is a more radical strategy to gain better compensation. The post-2005 house-based compensation is much higher than before, which made those who were resettled before 2005 very unhappy. They protested collectively in front of the town hall, demanding additional compensation (Interview). Individually, some households refused to move and demand higher compensations than they were offered (so-called "nail households"), which happened both before and after 2005. The town government is usually willing to negotiate with "nail households," as conflicts resulted from resettlement can damage the reputation and rating of local governments with the central government's emphasis on harmonious society (JMG 2007). Yet, there are cases that "nail households" ask so much more than what the local government is willing to offer that the latter is unwilling to compromise. The government would go ahead with the demolition and resettlement of the village without the particular nail households.[19] Among those who are yet to be resettled, many would consider delaying moving if the compensation is too low. This shows villagers are becoming more aware of their rights, and are more willing to act radically to protect their interests. Yet, they tend to enact "rightful resistance" (O'Brien and Li 2006), protesting near the boundary of authorized channels and employing government policies and laws.

12.4.3 Age and Class Stratification

In the face of profound changes in life style, villagers respond differently to the resettlement process. In general, there is an age and class stratification, and the young and better-off tend to fair better as they usually have more resources to cope with the demolishment and resettlement. The elderly tend to suffer the most as they are more fearful of losing their traditional lifestyle and are anxious toward their new lifestyle. An old lady expressed her concerns for the resettlement.

> I cried, could not sleep after hearing the news… I can no longer play cards with my neighbors…where can I store my old furniture and farming tools? …I do not like the apartments. The ceiling is so low, suffocating. … At least here in the village, we can grow all sorts of vegetables during the summer.[20]

Her reactions are very common among villagers, especially the older generations. She is afraid that the resettlement will destroy her social network and change her daily routines, and she will have to give up many things in her life including her recreation and belongings. At the same time, she is concerned about the new life in farmer apartments with a different housing environment and high cost of living, which cause much anxiety and fear.

On the contrary, many households, especially those who are younger and have stable non-farming income are more interested in and even actively pursue the demolishment and resettlement. One couple with two adult children working in the city wish the demolishment could happen as soon as possible. They have a large house in good condition, and they believe they can pocket a large amount of cash in

[19]In XHT, all houses have been demolished except one, which stands at the end of a road between two new resettlement buildings.

[20]Interview.

Photo 12.2 Jiangnan Garden (Jiangyin City), featured with basketball courts (*left*), a kindergarten (*right*), a clinic, a farmers' market, and a large open public space in the middle of the complex (Photo by the author)

addition to purchasing an apartment with the subsidized price.[21] The husband has a small family business, thus the potential higher cost of living is not a major concern for them.

This age/class difference is also evident among those who have moved into resettlement housing. The younger and better-off households tend to be more satisfied with their new housing than the older generations and those who do not have stable cash income. The former usually are happy with high quality of housing, the cleanness of the neighborhood, beautiful environment, and convenience to various services, while the latter often complain about the high cost of living, the lack of elevators, and the low ceiling of the apartments. Similar to elsewhere (Johnson 2013), they also complained about the poor quality of the building.

In addition, the design and planning of a farmer apartment development does make a difference in villagers' satisfaction. Displaced villagers tend to be happier in farmer apartments that can preserve some of the features of natural villages and offer space for them to maintain their social life. For example, Jiangnan Garden is a large resettlement project with 70 buildings, sheltering more than 7000 people (see Photo 12.2). It is divided into several "villages," each with the buildings arranged in such a way to create a large open public space in the middle of the complex, which has become the main place for residents to socialize and exercise. In addition to a farmer's market, a clinic, and a kindergarten in the complex, there is a public hall for villagers to use when they need a large space such as for holding wedding banquets and organizing recreational activities. Resettled villagers in this project are mostly happy with their new housing. On the contrary, another resettlement complex in the same town is poorly designed with densely packed apartment buildings in rows and with no public space for people to socialize. Residents there feel more

[21]They are qualified to purchase an apartment of 250 m^2 with subsidized price. But with two children away from home, they do not think they need that much space.

isolated from each other and thus experience a much more dramatic change from their old life style. Discontent is prevalent in that community.

12.5 Conclusion and Discussion

Land grabbing, unfair compensation, and massive displacement are common in countries experiencing rapid urbanization. What is unique in China is the essential role of the government and its political and economic drives in the process. This results in forced urbanization and unprecedented scale and speed of demolishment and displacement, and consequently drastic changes in settlement patterns and lifestyles in rural China (French 2007). With the ongoing campaign of VCL and "three concentrations" in general, villages and country lifestyles are disappearing. The land-based revenue system and local governments' thirst for more construction land for urban development under the strict land use management system are the root causes for these changes, which is further driven by the central government's call for developing the socialist new countryside. Starting as a land use strategy, VCL has been implemented at such an astonishing scale and speed in many regions that it is more like a political campaign than anything.

There is no doubt that VCL has brought many positive changes in the countryside. For example, housing quality and public infrastructure in rural communities have been improved significantly. While most villagers, especially the younger generations and the well-off, seem to be happy with the resettlement, there are many problems. First of all, there is no public participation, and villagers are not involved at all in the decision-making of VCL. Local governments single-handedly decide every aspect of demolishment, resettlement, and compensation, while villagers can only adopt various strategies within the government set framework for more compensation. Secondly and more importantly, while compensation for housing seems to be reasonable, especially after 2005 in southern Jiangsu province, there is no compensation for villagers' collectively owned land, which is a serious infringement of their land rights. It has been argued that the ambiguity of collective land ownership makes it harder for villagers to claim their land rights, and easier for the government to take their rights away (e.g. Ho and Lin 2004; Hsing 2006b). In addition, the dominating power of local governments, villagers' lack of awareness of their land rights, and the lack of leadership among villagers all encourage local governments' land grabbing. Thirdly, while villagers benefit from the improved public infrastructure, they do not have access to long-term profits from construction land saved through VCL. In other words, villagers are excluded from sharing capital gains from their land with local governments. Scholars have been advocating a profound reform to give rural land the same status as urban land such that villagers and village collectives can directly transfer and profit from their land on the market (Wang et al. 2010; Tao 2011). Finally, there are many problems with life in villager apartments, such as high cost of living, high unemployment rate, disrupted social networks, split extended families, and psychological stress, especially among the elderly.

To control the scale of VCL and to mitigate some of the problems, State Council issued a document in 2010, which "strictly forbad" ("*yan jin*") local governments to exceed their quota for dynamic linkage, to demolish villages in large scale and force villagers to live in high-rise apartments, and to harm villagers' legal rights (State Council 2010, No. 47). It states that the construction land saved through VCL should be converted to arable land first, followed by meeting the need for rural development and construction, and only a very limited amount of the construction land quota can be used for urban and town development, in which case, all of the capital gains have to be returned to rural areas. This document is very encouraging. Yet, this document continues to allow local governments to use the construction land quota saved through VCL. This leaves much room for local governments to continue massive demolishment and displacement. More importantly, the central government is still not ready to recognize villagers' legal land rights and give rural land the same status as urban land. Thus, local governments continue to prey on rural land and massive VCL and associated problems continue.

References in English

Fan, C. 2008. *China on the move: Migration, the state, and the household*. Oxon: Routledge.

French, H. 2007. *Homeowner Stares Down Wreckers, at Least for a While, New York Times, March 27th*. http://www.nytimes.com/2007/03/27/world/asia/27china.html?scp=1&sq=chongqing%20nail%20household&st=cse.

Guo, X. 2001. Land expropriation and rural conflicts in China. *The China Quarterly* 166: 422–439.

Ho, S., and G. Lin. 2003. Emerging land markets in rural and urban China: Policies and practices. *The China Quarterly* 175: 681–707.

Ho, S., and G. Lin. 2004. Converting land to nonagricultural use in China's coastal provinces: Evidence from Jiangsu. *Modern China* 30 (1): 81–112.

Hsing, Y. 2006a. Land and territorial politics in urban China. *The China Quarterly* 187: 1–18.

Hsing, Y. 2006b. Brokering power and property in China's townships. *Journal of Pacific Review* 19: 103–124.

Hsing, Y. 2010. *The Great urban transformation: Politics of land and property in China*. Oxford: Oxford University Press.

Huang, Y. 2012. Low-income housing policy in China: Policies and practices. *The China Quarterly* 212.

Johnson, I. 2013. New China cities: Shoddy homes, broken hopes. *The New York Times*, Nov. 13.

Johnson, I. 2014. In China, 'Once villages are gone, the culture is gone', *The New York Times*, Feb 1, A1.

Lin, G.C. 2009. *Developing China: Land, politics and social conditions*. Routledge.

Lin, G.C. 2010. Understanding land development problems in globalizing China. *Eurasian Geography and Economics* 51: 80–103.

Lin, G.C.S., and Yi, F. 2011. Urbanization of capital or capitalization on Urban land? Land development and local public finance in urbanizing China. *Urban Geography* 32(1): 50–79.

Liu, Y.S., J.Y. Wang, and H.L. Long. 2010. Analysis of arable land loss and its impact on rural sustainability in Southern Jiangsu Province of China. *Journal of Environmental Management* 91: 646–653.

Ma, L.J. 2002. Urban transformation in China, 1949–2000: A review and research agenda. *Environment and planning A* 34(9): 1545–1570.

O'Brien, K., and L. Li. 2006. *Rightful resistance in rural China*. Cambridge, New York, Cambridge University Press.

Sargeson, S. 2013. Violence as development: Land expropriation and China's urbanization. *Journal of Peasant Studies* 40 (6): 1063–1085.

Tao, R. 2011. How to achieve systematic breakthrough in land expropriation reform—Suggestions for revising land management law. Manuscript.

Tsui, K., and Y. Wang. 2004. Between separate stoves and a single menu: Fiscal decentralization in China. *The China Quarterly* 177: 71–90.

Wang, H., R. Tao, R. Wang, and F. Su. 2009. Farmland preservation and land development rights trading in Zhejing Province, China. *Habitat International* 34: 454–463.

Wang, H., R. Tao, and C. Shi. 2010. Local experiments of transferable development rights of land and villagers' concentrated living: Challenges and solutions. Manuscript.

Wu, F., and L.J. Ma. 2006. Transforming China's globalizing cities. *Habitat International* 30(2): 191–198.

Xinhuanet. 2014. (March, 16). *China Unveils Landmark Urbanization Plan*. Retrieved from http://news.xinhuanet.com/english/china/2014–03/16/c_133190495.htm.

Xu, J., A. Yeh, and F. Wu. 2009. Land commodification: new land development and politics in China since the late 1990s. *International Journal of Urban and Regional Research* 33(4): 890–913.

Zhu, Y. 2007. China's floating population and their settlement intention in the cities: Beyond the *Hukou* reform. *Habitat International* 31(1): 65–76.

References in Chinese

Chan, K.W. 1994. *Cities with invisible walls: Reinterpreting urbanization in post-1949*. China. Oxford University Press.

Chang, H. 2006. *Jiangsu nongmin jizhong juzhu deshi [The gains and losses of farmer concentrated living in rural Jiangsu]*. *Cai jing*, Nov. 26.

CBLR (Chengdu Bureau of Land and Resources). 2010. *Chengdu shi jiti jianshe yongdi shiyongquan liuzhuan guanli banfa [Management method for the transfer of use right of rural collective construction land in Chengdu]*. http://landchina.mlr.gov.cn/tdsc/zcfg/201008/t20100805_731614.htm.

Deng, J. 2010. Chen Xi Wen: xiaomie cunzhuang? – zhongguo xin chengshihua zhi you [Chen Xi Wen: Getting rid of villages?—Concerns of the new urbanization in China]. *Nanfang zhoumo*, Oct. 16th.

Editorial Committee. 2007. Jieyue jiyue yongdi, chaoyong liangxi dadi, "jingtudi" yichu huangjing xiaoyin [The economic and intensive land use has resulted in gold effect], *Wuxi xinwen*, Dec. 8. Retrieved on March 8, 2008 from http://www.wuxi.gov.cn.

JBC (Jiangsu Bureau of Construction). 2006. *Guanyu zai xiao chengzhen shiyan jiyue fazhan de tongzhi [*A notice about implementing experiment on intensive and economic development in small towns*]*. Document No. 264.

JBP (Jiangsu Bureau of Price). 2007. No. 265. *Sheng wujiaju guanyu jiaqiang nongmin jizhong juzhuqu zhufang jiage jianguan deng wenti* [A notice on strengthening price monitoring and management of villagers' concentrated living housing].

JMG (Jiangyin Municipal Government). 2004. Jiangyin shi bei chengdi nongmin jiben shenghuo baozhang zanxing banfa [A temporary method for providing landless farmers basic living protection in Jinagyin). No. 80.

JMG (Jiangyin Municipal Government). 2005. Jiangyin shi jitiyuongdi zhufang chaiqian guanli shixing banfa [An implementation regulation on demolishing and managing housing on collectively owned land in Jiangyin]. No. 50. In *Bianmin shouce [Convenience Booklet]*, pp. 1–11.

JMG (Jiangyin Municipal Government). 2006. *Jiangyin shi xiandanhua xin nongcun jianshe zhongdian gongzuo 2006 niandu zongjie* [*Annual summary about major work on constructing modern new countryside in Jiangyin*]. Retrieved from http://www.wxnb.gov.cn on Feb. 22, 2008.

JMG (Jiangyin Municipal Government). 2007. Jingyin shi guanyu jianli dui chaiqian danwei de pinggu tixi de tongzhi [A notice on establishing an evaluation system for the reputation and rating of demolishment and resettlement agencies in Jiangyin city]. In *Chaiqian xinzeng guizhe wenjian huibian* [A collection of newly added regulations on demolishment and resettlement], No. 6. pp. 13–18.

JMBC (Jiangyin Municipal Bureau of Construction). 2005a. No. 27. Jiangyin shi guanyu dui chaiqian zhufang zhuangxiu he fujian de peichang biaozhun [A notice about the compensation standard for decorations and attachments of demolished housing in Jiangyin city]. In *Bianmin shouce [Convenience Booklet]*, pp. 13–22.

JMBC (Jiangyin Municipal Bureau of Construction). 2005b. No. 28. Jiangyin shi guangyu butie biaozhun he chaiqian jiangli de tongzhi [A notice about the standard for subsidies and bonuses in housing demolishment and resettlement in Jiangyin]. In *Bianmin shouce [Convenience Booklet]*, p. 21.

JMBC (Jiangyin Municipal Bureau of Construction). 2005c. Jiangyin shi dui anzhifang jiage de erhao tongzhi [No. 2. A notice about the price for resettlement housing in Jiangyin city]. In *Bianmin shouce [Convenience Booklet]*, p. 12.

JPG (Jiangsu Provincial Government). 2005. *Jiangsu sheng zhengdi butie he dui wudi nongmin tigong jiben shehui baozhang de banfa* [Method of compensation for land expropriation and basic social security for landless farmers in Jiangsu Province]. No. 26.

JPI (Jiangyin Planning Institute). 2007. Jiangyin shenggang fazhan jihua, 2000–2020 [The master plan for Shenggang, Jiangyin city, 2000–2020.].

Luo, C. 2007. *Zhai ji di jiufen shiyong falv shouce* [A law booklet about conflicts over zhai ji di] (pp. 25–37). Beijing: Zhongguo falv chubanshe.

MLR (Ministry of Land and Resource). 1999. *Guanyu tudi kaifa zhengli gongzuo youguan wenti de tongzhi* [A notice about several issues related to land development and repair]. No. 358.

MLR (Ministry of Land and Resource). 2004. *Zhai ji di jiufen shiyong falv shouce* [A law booklet about conflicts over zhai ji di] (pp. 80–81). Beijing: Zhongguo falv chubanshe.

MLR (Ministry of Land and Resource). 2005. *Guanyu guifan chengzhen jianshe yongdi zhengjia yu nongcun jiangshe yongdi jianshao xiang guagou shidian gongzuo de yijian* [Suggestions for experiment on formalizing linking the increase in urban construction land with the decrease in rural construction land].

MLR (Ministry of Land and Resource). 2011. MLR leaders answer Questions on State Council's "Notice about strictly regulating urban and rural construction land increase and decrease linkage experiment and improving rural land consolidation." http://www.law-lib.com.

NBS (National Bureau of Statistics). 2011. *Zhongguo tongji nianjian 2011* [China Statistical Yearbook 2011], Beijing: Zhongguo tongji chubanshe.

NCDR (National Committee of Development and Reform). 2006. *Guanyu tuijin shehui zhuyi xi nongcu jianshe de yijian* [Suggestions about promoting the construction of socialist new countryside]. Retrieved from http://www.wxnb.gov.cn on Feb. 22, 2008.

Rosenberg, L. 2013. "Urbanising the Rural: Local strategies for creating" new style " rural communities in China." *China Perspectives* 3(95): 63–71.

State Council. 2004. *Guanyu shenhua gaige yange tudi guanli de jueding* [A decision about deepening reform and tightening land management], No. 28. http://www.mlr.gov.cn/zwgk/flfg/tdglflfg/200601/t20060112_642080.htm.

State Council. 2008a. *Chengxiang jianshe yongdi zengjian guagou shidian guanli banfa* [A management regulation about experimenting linking the increase of urban construction land with the decrease of rural construction land], No. 138

State Council. 2008b. *Guowuyuan guanyu cujin jieyue jiyue yongdi de tongzhi* [A notice from State Council on promoting economic and intensive land use]. Retrieved from http://www.wxnb.gov.cn, Feb. 22, 2008.

State Council. 2010. *Guowuyuan guanyu yange guifan chengxiang jianshe yongdi zengjian guagou shidian qieshi zuohao nongcun tudi zhengzhi gongzuo de tongzhi* [Notice about strictly regulating urban and rural construction land increase and decrease linkage experiment and improving rural land consolidation], No. 47. http://www.gov.cn, accessed on Oct, 10, 2011.

WMGO (Wuxi Municipal Government Office). 2005. *Zhonggong Wuxi shiwei bangongshi Wuxi shi renmin zhengfu bangongshi guanyu tuijin nongcu "sange jizhong" de yijian* [Suggestions on promoting "Three concentrations" in rural areas from Wuxi Municipal Government Office], No. 35.

WBTVEM (Wuxi Bureau of Township Village Enterprises Management). 2007. *Wo shi xiangzhen gongye jizhongqu jianshe chengxiao mingxian* [The Construction of Township Village Enterprises Concentration District in Wuxi Has Made Significant Achievement]. Retrieved on March 20, 2008 from http://www.wxjs.gov.cn.

WVCLO (Wuxi Villager Concentrated Living Office). 2005. *Guanyu tuijing nongmin jizhong juzhu de gongzuo fang'an* [A work plan for promoting villagers' concentrated living in Wuxi], Document No.3.

WVCLO. 2006a. 2006 nian gongzuo zongjie ji 2007 nian gongzuo silu [A summary of work in 2006 and a work plan for 2007]. Retrieved from http://www.wxnb.gov.cn on Feb. 2, 2008.

WVCLO. 2006b. *Guanyu zuohao 2006 niandu nongmin juzhu jizhong de yijian* [Suggestion about how to conduct work related to villagers' concentrated living in 2006], No. 1.

XTG (Xinqiao Town Government). 2007a. *San jizhong shidian kan Xinqiao* (The experiment of three concentrations in Xinqiao). Retrieved on March 28, 2008 from http://www.jyxinqiao.gov.cn.

XTG. 2007b. Xinqiao meijia keyi jiyue bai mu tudi [Every household in Xinqiao can "save" a half mu of land]. Retrieved on March 10, 2008 from http://www.jyxinqiao.gov.cn.

Yu, J. 2010. Quandi shi chengshi dui nongcun lueduo [Land enclosure is city's exploitation of the countryside]. *Xin jin bao*, Nov. 5th. A21.

Zhu, P., and F. Qu. 2006. Nongdi feinong hua peizhi zhong de tudi shouyi fenpei yanjiu – yi Jiangsu sheng N shi weili (A study on the land revenue distribution during agricultural land conversion – a case study of N city in Jiangsu Province). *Nanjing nongye daxue xuebao (Journal of Nanjing Agricultural University)* 6(3):1–6.

The manufacturer's authorised representative in the EU is Springer Nature Customer Service Centre GmbH, Europaplatz 3, 69115 Heidelberg, Germany. If you have any concerns regarding our products, please contact ProductSafety@springernature.com

Printed and bound by CPI Group (UK) Ltd, Croydon, CR0 4YY
25/09/2026
02222900-0005